Authentic Management

A Gestalt Orientation to Organizations and Their Development

Authentic Management

A Gestalt Orientation to Organizations and Their Development

STANLEY M. HERMAN

MICHAEL KORENICH

 ADDISON-WESLEY PUBLISHING COMPANY

Reading, Massachusetts • Menlo Park, California
London • Amsterdam • Don Mills, Ontario • Sydney

75613

ISBN 0-201-02886-7
EFGHIJKLM-AL-8987654321

To Georgia Herman who was a very considerable contributor to the fact that this book is here.

And to TRW Systems, of whom the same can be said, for different reasons.

Foreword

My relationship to this book and more importantly to its authors is not an impersonal one, since we have worked closely together in the past and I have therefore had the benefit of directly seeing in action the value of the orientation they are presenting here. I believe that their work is a major contribution. They have provided a very important and creative bridging for applied organizational behavioral scientists to a powerful but individual and therapeutically oriented branch of psychology—Gestalt.

The process involved in their developing this contribution is worth noting. The authors went through an in-depth, very professional exposure to Gestalt psychology, including their participation in an extensive, intensive, and comprehensive training program conducted by one of this country's leading Gestalt institutes, individual Gestalt therapy with a Gestalt-oriented psychiatrist, and cotherapist work with the psychiatrist. Then they deliberately and explicitly worked at applications in various organizational settings. Sometimes, eclectic bridging is done at too superficial a level and at too hurried a pace. This clearly is not the case with respect to the work presented in this book. Because of this, they have, in my opinion, added significantly to the eclectic reach of practitioners. (Incidentally, I believe that still more of this is needed; for example, what about a Jungian orientation to organizations and their development?)

A number of us who have had the benefit of the work done by Herman and Korenich have found many things of value in the orientation they propose: the emphasis on drawing on the capacities that are already within a person but need a coming to awareness; the importance of having individuals take responsibility for their behavior and clearly own up to their exercise of choice in what they do and don't do; the very positive view of personal power; the importance of staying focused in the here and now; the utility in having people clearly state what they want from others; the need to finish interactions; the creative use of fantasy to free people up from untested limits which can unleash energies previously not available to them; etc., etc.

The authors have usefully incorporated in a constructive context all of the emotions and behavior people engage in. A good example is their views on "positive" and "negative" emotions, which appears in Section One.

I think that the utility of this book is greatly enhanced by its very helpful, concrete descriptions of exercises, routines, and approaches that individuals can use to act out the orientation suggested. To me, an important aspect of the bridging I referred to earlier is the fact that they have been able to develop very specific techniques for implementation of this orientation. This makes it possible for the rest of us to begin the creative process of assimilating a Gestalt orientation into our way of doing things without the need for considerable basic training in Gestalt psychology.

I personally enjoyed the poetry, parables, playfulness, and clear language they have used. This book is relatively jargon free and can be read without a dictionary at one's side!

I have just reread this foreword and realize it sounds like an advertising blurb—but I'm not going to apologize for that. I think a major contribution *is* made when an important branch of psychology is thoughtfully explored and new ways to use that branch in larger settings are devised. It is one of the ways to keep the organizational behavior field vital and growing.

I guess the most significant thing I can say is that Herman and Korenich's work has directly influenced my own approach to consulting and I feel that I have benefited greatly from this.

Sheldon A. Davis
Vice President, Organization Development
TRW Inc.
November 1976

Contents

Introduction – Who Am I?

Introduction – Who Am I?

The best answers for you are within you. Principles, theories, and models can be useful only if they don't trap you.

ROLE OR REAL

A more appropriate title for this introduction might be "Who Am I, and Do I Really Want to Know?" Probably a fair number of people don't want to know who they are and spend considerable effort avoiding finding out. There is another problem with the title, too. It implies that "who I am" is a constant—that once I answer the question, I can settle back and stop looking. But for really alive people this *isn't* the case. Who I am changes almost continually and when I am able to get in touch with my own process of changing, this dynamism becomes a more and more exciting part of living.

We believe that a manager is (or rather, can be) a growing, developing, discovering human being, even at work. If you are a manager, you probably spend eight to ten or even more hours a day at work, so your experiences there are probably as important as your experiences elsewhere.

Most of us have formed some self-image of how we operate in our managerial role. For example, you may see yourself as strong in your ability to bring subordinates and colleagues together in a participative framework. You may see yourself able to draw from each of them their best ideas, their collaboration and cooperation in analyzing and solving organizational problems. Or, you may see yourself as a directive manager with the capacity to get the facts quickly, cut to the heart of the problem, provide clear directions to your subordinates, and get things done.

We believe it possible for most of you who read this book eventually to be able and willing to operate in more than one style, to use a variety of approaches, including each of the "extremes" just mentioned. This expansion will not result from a deliberate, self-imposed change program in which you study the techniques involved in the various managerial styles. Rather, it can come from increasing your appreciation of the capacities *that are already within you*—and then being able to react naturally and satisfyingly with an action that is right for you in accordance with a specific situation and organization environment.

Many things impinge on you when you're in your role of manager—other people's expectations; the rules, norms, and values of the organization; acceptable styles of behaving and talking; etc. Some of these requirements are very real and are, indeed, imposed by the organization, the boss, and so on; others, however, are frequently self-imposed. Many managers limit their power and their potential for growth by either an inability or an unwillingness to distinguish between organization-imposed and self-imposed restraints.

Self-imposed restraints often arise from "pluralistic ignorance," a fancy way of saying: "a set of things that nobody believes in, but everybody believes that everybody else believes in." For instance, in one organization we worked with, a manufacturing management group met every Wednesday morning forty-five minutes before the regular start of the workday to discuss production problems on a particular product line. They had started this series of meetings four months earlier when the line had been new. All of the major difficulties had been solved within the first month or two, but they still continued meeting, until in the course of one of their sessions a new manager, who preferred to spend the three-quarters of an hour in bed rather than rehashing old war stories, raised a question about the real use of the meetings. After a short discussion, the entire group agreed to discontinue the Wednesday morning sessions. No one had found them of much use for the last few months, but each man had been thinking that all his fellow managers wanted to continue.

MAKING CHOICES

In this book we aren't going to advocate one particular style of behavior for you as a manager. Rather what we hope to do is help increase your ability to make choices about how you live in your organization environment (and perhaps outside your organization as well). You may be surprised by the things we think you can make choices about, and some of the possible choices open to you may surprise you even more. We firmly believe that the more you are in touch with what *you personally want* and the way you can get it, the more competently you will probably operate and, at least equally important, the more stimulation and satisfaction you will get from your job.

In other words, managing can be an interesting and exciting kind of human process or a restrictive, harassing, rat race in which a lonely human being struggles against the frustrations and barriers of his or her environment and tries to survive. We want to suggest some ways in which you can approach your job in a less heavy, duty-bound, restrained fashion. We want you to free up your energy for experiencing and learning, to find the humor, adventure, and pleasure in your occupation or career. If slaying dragons is your thing, we want you to enjoy that. If being a wise old industrial statesman is more to your taste, that's fine too. We would like to see you able to boast, to feel sad, to love, to hate, to feel confident, to feel anxious—and to do all of these wholeheartedly. And, with luck, we hope you will pass some of this stuff on to your subordinates and colleagues (and maybe even your boss), so that they too can approach their task with a lighter touch and the capacity to more fully enjoy themselves.

Most business and organization life need not be grim. We know that from personal experience. It is another slice of human existence that can be suffered or enjoyed, and if you know how to be with and appreciate each part of your life, including this part, you're more likely to cope with it successfully and use your powers and capabilities more effectively and fully. There are exceptions of course—some jobs and organizations are bad no matter how you approach them. If yours is one of those, this book won't be of much use except to confirm your fears. In that case, we want to say equally strongly, if your job and/or organization are beyond redemption, you ought to get out of one, the other, or both.

AUTHENTIC-MANAGEMENT APPROACH

A considerable number of the approaches to management and organization development that have emerged over the last few decades have emphasized how to change the "system" and the people who comprise the system by determining a model of "what should be" and then developing a programmatic strategy and methodology to implement that model. The obvious assumption is that one best or right model can be determined, and that the system and its people can be made to conform to that model through some predesigned process.

Authentic-Management assumptions differ from these approaches in a number of significant ways. In Authentic Management we do not believe there is "one best way" to be or to do anything—this applies to organizations, managers, consultants, and human beings in general. What may be best for one person or system may be wrong for another, and what may be best for one person or system at one point in time may be wrong for the same person or system at another time.

Authentic Management is an approach to working with people and systems in organizations that encourages a clear focus on present and specific situations. It helps the manager and the organization consultant to set aside the distorting perceptual filters of artificial models, theories, and stereotypes and to come into more direct, vital contact with: *what is actually going on now, what needs to be done, and how to do it.* Our introduction and application of Gestalt theory and principles to organization management and consulting provides, we believe, a more complete, realistic base for understanding human behavior in and outside organizations.

Another way in which this approach differs from other current human-relations orientations is in its emphasis on managers and subordinates discovering and developing their own *individual* competence and power rather than relying on group support. In Authentic Management, each person is encouraged to become more clearly aware of what he or she wants from others and from himself or herself, and how to go about getting it. Paradoxically, this apparently "selfish" orientation does not encourage dysfunctional competition, but rather a clearer and more genuine basis for effective cooperation.

APPLICATIONS

Almost all of the concepts, approaches, and methods included in this book have been tried and have worked "in action." The action arenas have included industrial, governmental, and other organizations; the characters involved have included executives, managers, technical personnel, and non-technical personnel at a variety of levels. Problems dealt with have ranged from interorganizational conflict to interracial conflict, and from executive-level planning to planning by PTA groups and church lay groups.

We have found the Authentic-Management approach to be particularly useful in the following ways.

- Increasing both the manager's and consultant's capacity to discover, clarify, and deal with the genuinely relevant elements of organizational problems.

- Increasing the ability to identify, and help others to identify, what needs to be done in the organization, who needs to do it, and how to get it done.

- Developing the ability to distinguish, amidst the abundance of information and data available, those factors that actually make a difference versus those that are largely peripheral, verbal slogans, theories, or "academic principles."

- Developing within each person a focused sense of his or her specific strengths and capacities and his or her ability to function in more-effective ways with subordinates, clients, and co-workers.

- Increasing a person's ability to make effective contact with those he or she serves, to move quickly and easily through the obscuring obstacles of "role playing" and "game playing," and to provide direct and practical assistance to others.

- Increasing the individual's comfort and ability to work with people at all levels in the organization in ways that increase his or her self-confidence and self-respect, and the respect of others as well.

- Providing a body of knowledge, techniques, and methodology that a person may modify, adapt, and integrate to develop or enhance the management or consulting style best suited to the person and his or her organization.

- Reducing the "gaps" in communications and perspective that frequently seem to exist between organization consultants and their operations-oriented clients.

The objective of the Authentic-Management approach for organization development is to encourage awareness and increased reality in interactions between people. With increased genuineness of interaction, both individuals and their organizations benefit from a more specific and cogent concentration on what *really* matters in the processes that go on between them. Such a focus is often blurred or even entirely lost in the role playing, "tact" and "avoidance" games that frequently go on in the day-to-day work of organizations.

ORIENTATION OF THE TEXT

This book is directed to both operating managers and organization-development specialists and students. Some sections are of more specific concern to managers, while others are especially relevant to organization-development specialists and consultants. For convenience, we have appropriately titled these special segments. However, we recommend that O.D. students and specialists read the managers' segments and that managers at least skim the consultants' sections. Even though these latter sections may be somewhat more complicated reading than the general material of the book, they hopefully will contribute to a fuller understanding of the Authentic-Management orientation. While much of the organization-development work covered in this volume can be handled by managers themselves, from time to time the use of an O.D. specialist or a consultant is almost essential to accomplishing certain organization-improvement purposes. In these cases, it will be very useful for a manager to understand the consultant's basic approach.

THE FORMAT

It is our intent in the following pages to present both the "what" and the "how" of Authentic Management. We have done this by presenting Authentic-Management and Gestalt theories and methods, as well as management cases and dialogues which illustrate these concepts. A large portion of the book is also devoted to exercises and techniques for organizational applications. And, partly for instruction, but mostly for enjoyment, we have included a number of poems and parables we hope will add some pleasure to your reading.

A BIT OF ADVICE

One of the curious things about this book is that we are *not* going to suggest you do a lot of trying. Though the idea of striving is a positive value in our society and certainly an important function in all our lives, the developmental approach we are proposing here suggests you do a lot of "nontrying." We are going to ask you to get in touch with where you are at any given point in time and *allow* yourself to discover your own natural inclinations. Some of these natural inclinations can be enhanced and can help you to do your job better and perhaps to enjoy some aspects of your life more fully.

Rather than advocate a one best role or style for you as a manager, no matter how democratic and humanistic that may be, it would be better, we believe, for each of you to realize your own unique personality, wants, and problems, and to work through these to develop an authentic, unique, and internalized style of your own. Again, if this style is not consonant with a managerial role, you ought to consider changing to another specialty—probably the healthiest move for others, as well as for your own peace of mind and satisfaction.

And finally, some advice while reading. Not everything this book says will be right for you. There are at least a couple of ways of handling unfamiliar new information. One is to put up a wall in your mind and keep it all out; another is to let the new information in, chew on it for a while—even though it may have a strange taste—then spit out what you don't want and keep what feels good. We suggest the latter. Also, don't spend a lot of energy initially trying to figure out how everything fits together. Again, just let all the information come in and you will probably find that after a while it will fall together for you in its own way.

Freedom 1

No one grants you freedom
You are free if you are free

No one enthralls you
You enthrall yourself
And when you have
You may hand your tether
   to another
   to many others
   to all others, or
   to yourself

Perhaps this last is worst of all
For this slave master is hardest to see
And hardest to rebel against
But he is easiest to hate
   and to damage

I do not know how to tell you to be free
I wish I did
But I do know some signs of freedom
One is in doing what you want to do
   though someone tells you not to
Another is in doing what you want to do
   though someone tells you to

Some Basic Concepts

The Gestalt Base

At all times respect your total self. Especially pay attention to
your own contradictions and resistances.

WHAT IS GESTALT?

Before moving on to the specific and practical applications of Authentic
Management, it would be useful to review briefly a few of the theoretical
concepts from which Authentic Management has been developed. These
concepts are applicable to each of us as individuals and as members of
organizations. In fact, they are applicable to all phases of our lives. Much
of the theory of Authentic Management is derived from a branch of psychology called Gestalt therapy, an approach developed primarily by Dr.
Frederick ("Fritz") Perls within the last twenty-five years. It fits within
the general boundaries of what is called existential psychology—that is,
it deals primarily with what is going on *here and now* rather than with
the historical causes or analysis of behavior, such as those emphasized in
the more classical psychoanalytic theories of psychology.

Gestalt, a German word, is difficult to translate precisely into English.
Roughly it means "to form" or "to make into a comprehensive whole."
In the therapeutic sense, the idea is that everything in nature, including
human behavior, has a sort of built-in drive to become whole or to complete itself. Perls' view was that much of what we now typically label as
neurosis comes from cutting off our natural tendency to complete our
behavior and preventing ourselves from finishing our unfinished business.

Perls' theories grew from the findings of a group of German psychologists who observed human and animal behavior in order to get a better
understanding of how humans' perceptions of the environment influence
their learning. Based on their observations, the psychologists concluded
essentially that: first, humans do not experience the parts of their environ-

ment separately, but rather tend to organize the parts into a meaningful whole. In other words, we want things and events in our experience to make sense in terms of what we already know. A simple example of this tendency to organize parts into a meaningful whole is what you are now doing as you read this paragraph. You are organizing the individual letters to form words, words to form sentences, sentences to form paragraphs, etc. All of this is done in order to obtain meaning—in this example, the ideas or thoughts that are formed. If you stop and consider this for a moment, you will realize that we exhibit this tendency to some degree in everything we do throughout our lives.

Second, the psychologists found that a person's attention remains focused on a part of the whole only so long as his or her interest is maintained. When the person has finished "dealing with" or "attending to" this focus, interest will decline, and with that decline the "whole" becomes disorganized and atomistic until a new focus of attention develops which permits a new "whole" to emerge. The previous example about reading also demonstrates this point. Once the individual letters (parts) are organized to form a word (the whole), the reader is ready to leave that whole and form a new whole from the next letters, and so on with each word until a whole idea is grasped from the completed sentence.

FIGURE AND GROUND

Building on these two basic findings is the Gestalt concept of *figure* and *ground*. Figure is essentially a point, object, or subject on which a person focuses his or her attention. Ground is the background, or environment, or, one might say, all else that is within the individual's scope of awareness but is not the focus of attention. In the process of perception, a good Gestalt involves a sharp, clear emergence of what is figure from what is ground—the figure is well differentiated from the background or other factors and is dominant in claiming the person's attention. When this is the case, the person can respond clearly and directly and take effective action in dealing with the central focus.

For example, in playing tennis, when the ball that comes over the net is clearly figural (you have your eye on the ball), you are much more likely to hit it well and make a good return—assuming, of course, that you also have the necessary skills in handling your racket. The same principle is true for most other sports. In contrast, when your vision is distracted and the ball is not in central focus, your return is likely to be poor. These principles apply in almost all other areas as well. When a manager has a clear focus on a problem, he or she is much more likely to take effective action than when disturbed by peripheral factors or other distractions.

As noted earlier, when one gestalt[1] is completed—i.e., the person has a clear focus on the figure and finishes with it—a new figure emerges out of what has previously been ground. The old gestalt is dissolved and a new one emerges. This process of formation and completion of good gestalt goes on in each of us continually when there is good awareness, contact, and integration with the environment. When there is good gestalt formation, there is also good concentration, interest, and excitement.

INTERFERENCE TO CLEAR GESTALT

In Authentic Management we have also discovered that when these good patterns are not established (that is, the central need or problem is not in clear focus because the person is distracted by other factors), then appropriate actions and decisions are not very likely to be developed. Some signals that indicate interference with the formation of good gestalt are confusion, ambivalence, and indecision. When these are present, individuals are likely either to force themselves in one direction or another, or to restrict or hold themselves back.

Some of the interferences that affect the formation of good, clear gestalt are:

1. **Poor sensory contact with the environment and with yourself.** In situations like this you are probably not seeing, hearing, or feeling very clearly. For example, most of us have been in meetings where two or more people are engaged in a discussion ostensibly about one issue, yet they seem to be talking past one another about two different issues. They are likely not looking at one another, or hearing one another very well, or even very aware of what their own feelings are about what is going on.

2. **Holding back or blocking self-expression.** Often, a person holds back or blocks his or her self-expression either by denying the existence of certain feelings (sometimes even to himself or herself) or by inhibiting expression of those feelings because he or she anticipates negative reactions from others. In some cases, the same blocking effect may result because the person is willing to express real needs or desires only indirectly or incompletely—in other words, the expression of needs lacks wholeheartedness. In organization situations there are many examples of this condition, as when a manager is unwilling to admit even to himself that a problem

---

[1]   For convenience the word "gestalt" will be used as both singular and plural. In German the plural is "gestalten."

exists in his department. Under these circumstances, of course, managers are unable to ask for help from others.

Another familiar situation illustrating inhibited expression is when a manager feels very dissatisfied with the cooperation or support he or she is receiving from the manager of another organization, and yet is unwilling to make an explicit complaint because doing so would be "bad manners." What frequently occurs in these situations is that the suppressed complaint emerges in disguised or clouded forms anyway.

3. Repressing or holding back impulses. Frequently, this results in incongruent behavior, as when a person evidences feelings of anger or antagonism which others can sense (particularly through physical signs, such as clenched jaws or fists or other tension), and yet he or she verbally denies having such feelings.

4. Thinking, theorizing, and anticipating what is going on in someone else's mind. This is perhaps the most common interference with good gestalt formation. Most of us have been taught from childhood the value of planning and anticipating, and these processes are, of course, very valuable for some purposes. However, they can also interfere seriously with coming to grips with the here and now. When our attention is concentrated on imaginings in our own minds about what is going on in others' minds rather than on what is occurring in the environment around, we cannot be in touch with that environment and the changes that are continually taking place there.

All of us have, at some time, developed a fixed theory about some event or situation in which we are involved. During conversations, we imagine and fantasize about what the other person is thinking, what he or she is trying to do to us, or what the effects of what we say or do will be on the other person's thoughts and feelings. Very often our "mind-models" of what is going on are inaccurate or even irrelevant. Yet we may cling so tightly to our model that we are unable to really hear or see what the other person is driving at.

In the author's consulting experiences, probably one of the most common difficulties that managers have in conflict situations occurs when both parties to the conflict have theories about what the other person wants, yet neither party voices these assumptions openly. We remember particularly one long-standing feud between two members of a management team. Each attacked the other's position and staunchly defended his own, with neither apparently willing to give an inch. As we worked with the managers, they finally agreed to talk about what they imagined the other wanted. As it turned out, each believed that the other wanted to change the organization in ways that would make his job less important. When the managers learned of each other's concerns, they were both surprised, and when they had a chance to discuss more clearly what they *really* wanted of each other, it turned out to be much less threatening and relatively easy to comply with.

This clarification could only occur, however, when the managers were willing to deal with *one another* rather than with their mind-models of each other's intentions—i.e., they were able to come into real contact with their environments.

GOOD FUNCTIONING

In the framework of Gestalt theory, a well-functioning person moves through his or her life space in relatively direct and satisfying ways. The individual is in contact with the environment externally and with himself or herself internally. He or she becomes aware of a need (figure), whether it is within or without; interest, concentration, and excitement are mobilized; and the person takes action to satisfy that need. With that satisfaction, the situation (gestalt) is completed and the next need then emerges.

In reality, of course, few if any people lead so simple and straightforward an existence all the time, nor would Perls or any other Gestalt therapist suggest this simplified model represents reality. It is useful, however, as a point of contrast to the more interrupted kind of functioning many of us endure. People who are not functioning well are usually in considerably more confusion. Their needs do not stand out clearly: they frequently do not know what they want, or they are ambivalent about whether or not they want something, or their focus may be divided between two or more conflicting desires. There are many ways in which we interfere with the clear recognition and pursuit of our wants, and a number of reasons why we do so.

HOW INTERFERENCES ORIGINATE

In general, the most frequent obstacle to recognizing our needs is our cognitive or mind-model of how we believe we *should* feel, think, and be. We have in modern life placed so much emphasis on what is logical and rational that we have become preoccupied with "figuring out the right answer" in our heads rather than seeing, hearing, and feeling what is really going on inside and around us, and responding to it according to its demand and according to what we have to do to meet our needs. In this process, which Perls calls "computing," we are so busy thinking and investing energy in keeping our computer (cognitive mind) occupied that very little energy is left to experience our external and internal realities. We have learned to give eloquent explanations for *why* things happen rather than to deal with *what is* happening.

Equally important is that, in our reliance on the computing function of our minds and our rejection of our other senses, we do not allow clear gestalt to be formed and to be finished. And so we have a constant backlog of unfinished business that leaves us feeling vaguely unsatisfied; since our old business is unfinished, new needs or desires cannot emerge clearly. Thus, in order to cope with this unpleasant situation, many of us learn to deaden ourselves in an attempt to minimize our confusion. This deadening generates boredom and a general lack of interest in many aspects of life.

Modern life in general—and organizational life in particular—make it even more difficult for individuals to recognize their own uniqueness and their own specific needs and wants. Organizations contain powerfully influential norms, values, and conventions, and managers and others are so strongly conditioned by these forces that they frequently limit their perceptions of their own interests and rule out possible ways of acting. Being caught in these traps makes it extremely difficult for a person to function in a healthy way. For example, it is often assumed by managers that feelings and emotions are not appropriate for organization situations. Still, most of us cannot avoid experiencing feelings and emotions in the eight plus hours per day we spend at work.

Another condition of organization life, or at least its mythology, seems to require of the manager that he or she leave personal wants and desires at home and attend only to the needs of the organization. But in reality this cannot be, for wherever we go we carry within ourselves our wants and needs. And so, once again, we must either suppress the expression of these wants and needs or use subtle, indirect, sometimes even deceptive ways of introducing them into the system.

AWARENESS AND CHOICE

In the Authentic-Management approach, our purpose is not to prescribe new models of correct behavior, nor is it to perform extensive diagnosis and analysis of behavior in order to find the reasons *why* things happen as they do. Rather, we are concerned primarily with increasing the manager's and others' awareness of what *is* happening now. If you can be aware of what you are doing habitually and conventionally, as well as what you would like to do if you were not constrained by convention, you could then make a choice.

If you can discover what things about your job and life interest and excite you and what things bore and depress you, you can be closer to making real contact with your own internal processes.

If you can learn to allow yourself gradually, from time to time, to let go of your mind-models of what is happening in your organization and the rest of the world around you, and learn to use your eyes and ears and feelings, you may discover outside of yourself an interesting new environment with more opportunities than you had previously imagined.

If you can learn to take a step or two down the ladder of abstraction and generalities to the more specific and concrete conditions of your environment, you may develop a greater sense of power and potential for what you can do to make your life space more personally satisfying. Curiously enough, you may also be surprised to discover that, in doing so, you help improve the space of others around you as well.

Mr. A and the Stranger: A Parable

There was once a man named Mr. A who lived in Organizationville—a neat place, of course, where everything was quite orderly.

And so was he.

Orderliness, thought Mr. A, was good—or anyway, dependable, or at least, orderly. And, besides, you didn't have to spend much time thinking about it, so you had lots of time to think about other things.

Most other people in Organizationville believed that also, or anyway seemed to, or at least didn't spend much time questioning it. So they had lots of time to think about other things, too.

Mainly, the other things that Mr. A thought about were what he ought to do and what he ought to say. Sometimes he thought about what he ought to think and even feel, too.

It was one way to spend time, of course, and since Mr. A had been doing it for a long while—ever since he was a little boy, in fact—he had built up quite a large catalogue.

For instance: One thing Mr. A thought he ought to do was to smile at his secretary every morning when he arrived at work.

And another was to look efficient and confident when he met with his assistant.

And another was to act interested and alert when he met with his boss.

Mr. A also knew what he ought to say (and ought not to say). So he said, "That's a damnfine idea," to the people in the engineering department.

And he said, "Your costs are too high," to the people in the manufacturing department.

And, "Let's take it under advisement," to almost anybody who brought him a new idea.

What Mr. A usually thought about his thoughts, when he thought about them, was mostly that they ought to be positive.

He thought: I ought to think Organizationville is the best of all possible places to be.

And, I ought to become an even more important man in Organizationville than I am now.

And, I ought to treat all my employees with patience, objectivity, and politeness.

Now, as to his thoughts about his feelings, it is more difficult to say, for Mr. A didn't think about his feelings often and, in fact, he seldom noticed that he had feelings at all.

However, if one had asked him what he thought his feelings ought to be (no one ever did), Mr. A would likely have said: "My feelings ought to be self assured, constructive, helpful to others, and above all, moderate."

In fact, if anyone had ever asked Mr. A about feelings like love and hate and sadness and joy and anger and envy and lust, he would have been shocked or at least uncomfortable and certainly would have considered them immoderate indeed.

By and large, Mr. A's life style was a satisfactory arrangement, or at least not unsatisfactory. Until one night trouble and turbulence came to Mr. A. As he lay in his bed he could not sleep—instead, he felt.

It was very disturbing indeed. No matter how hard he tried to keep them away, strange and immoderate feelings kept pushing their way into his head. Instead of feeling positive, he felt negative. Instead of feeling self-assured, he felt anxious.

As nights and days went by, Mr. A's discomfort grew worse and worse. After a while, the strange and immoderate feelings troubled him by day as well as night. Not only did he feel negative and anxious, but also angry and depressed. He worked mightily to force these unwelcome visitors from him. Soon he was spending most of his time and strength in trying to push them away.

Mr. A grew tired and pale. It became difficult for him to do what he thought he ought to do, and say what he thought he ought to say, and even think what he thought he ought to think. His life grew very troubled.

Others noticed and would say (though not to Mr. A himself, of course): "Mr. A looks tired and pale"; or, "Yes, Mr. A certainly doesn't seem to be his old self. Too bad." And, then they would go about their own business which was mostly doing what they thought they ought to do.

Then one day when his life had grown so confused and difficult that he could hardly bear it any longer, a strange man came to Organizationville, a man no one had ever seen before.

He was short and stubby, and had a large nose and a wrinkled face and a bushy beard and an unruly fringe of shaggy hair that circled his head like a slipped halo.*

"Nyeh," said the strange man to Mr. A, "You look lousy" (which no one had ever said to Mr. A before).

"I guess you're right," replied Mr. A, who was too upset to remember that he thought he ought to be more reserved with strangers, especially such unusual looking strangers.

"Nyeh," said the stranger. "What's the matter with you?"

"I am very worried and upset," Mr. A murmured in a low tone, for he was embarrassed and ashamed of his condition as well as worried and upset. "I don't seem to be able to do what I think I ought to do, or say what I think I ought to say or even think what I think I ought to think. I just don't feel too well."

"Exactly!" exclaimed the stranger, then added, "Nyeh."

"What do you mean?" asked Mr. A, who somehow found himself interested.

"Just what I said," said the stranger. "I always mean what I say. There are no hidden meanings." He tugged his fuzzy beard. "And, furthermore, you meant what you said as well. You just don't *feel* too well. If you *felt* better, you'd feel better."

"I'm confused," said Mr. A, fighting his confusion.

"OK," said the stranger, "then be confused."

So Mr. A sat and allowed himself to be confused and for once didn't fight it or tell himself that he ought not be confused. And in a little while his confusion passed by itself and he felt a little better than he had for some while. When he looked back to the stranger he saw that he was writing something on the large blackboard. He read:

> *Be*
> *As you are*
> *And so see*
> *Who you are*
> *And how you are*

---

* For those unfamiliar with the world of psychotherapy, an extra hint: the stranger's description sounds a lot like Fritz Perls.

Let go
For a moment or two
Of what you ought to do
And discover what you do do

Risk a little if you can
Feel your own feelings
Say your own words
Think your own thoughts
Be your own self

Discover
Let the plan for you
Grow from within you

Mr. A read the words (which he noted were not written in a very orderly fashion) then he read them again. "I think I know what you mean," said Mr. A.

"Nyeh," said the stranger, and he turned and in a moment was gone. Mr. A never saw him again, but he thought of him frequently, and did not erase the stranger's words from his blackboard. Though he considered for a while asking his assistant to have them typed more neatly on a five-by-seven card, he decided against it and instead just drew a line around them and printed "SAVE" above it so that the janitor wouldn't erase the board.

In this way, Mr. A found himself looking at the stranger's words every day and soon began to try them out. It wasn't easy. At first it was hard to even figure out what he really did think and feel and want to say and do. But gradually those things became clearer.

Then there was the problem of being scared. Sometimes, even though he knew what he wanted to say or do, Mr. A was afraid of hurting other people's feelings and afraid that they might not like him, or afraid he would look foolish, or ignorant, or just not quite right.

What he did about that was to take risks, a little at a time. First he would say what he really meant only to people he knew very well, and only sometimes. Then, gradually, he grew more bold, until he was saying things that he really meant even to strangers. It was fun, and once he was surprised and pleased to overhear two people in the corridor saying, "One thing you can say about Mr. A is he certainly says what he means nowadays."

There was another problem, too. Every so often Mr. A would slip back into his old ways and find himself saying or thinking or doing what he thought he ought to do. Then he would tell himself he ought not to do that. But then he would realize that telling himself what he ought not to do was just the same as telling himself what he ought to do. For a while, he would be puzzled, but then he would just grin and relax and do whatever he felt like doing (including doing what he thought he ought to do). And in a while things would straighten themselves out without his worrying too much about it.

In his new style, Mr. A discovered a lot of new things.

For instance: Some mornings he felt like smiling at his secretary and some mornings he didn't. And she felt the same way.

Sometimes he was efficient and confident with his assistant and other times he was unsure. And when he was unsure, sometimes his assistant had a good idea or two that helped. Other times they were unsure together and Mr. A found it was nice to have company.

Most of the time Mr. A found he was interested in what his boss had to say and that was convenient. Every once in a while he wasn't interested and he said so. And now and again—though not too often—he wasn't interested really, but because it was a favorite project of his boss, Mr. A faked it.

Mr. A also found out that he thought and felt different ways about things at different times. Sometimes he didn't think positively. He found out that he really didn't want to be president of Organizationville—it would take too much of his time and he would rather spend that time painting pictures of seagulls near the ocean. And he found out that at times when he felt angry or impatient with his employees he could let his anger or impatience come out and his employees did not wither. In fact, some argued back—and Mr. A found he liked that too.

Maybe the best thing that Mr. A discovered was that he really liked a lot of people, and a lot of people really liked him. He also found out there were some he didn't like and some who didn't like him. And that was all right, too.

And, so, as time passed in Organizationville, Mr. A's particular place seemed slowly, almost imperceptibly, to become a little less orderly than most, and also a little more comfortable. Over the years, many Organizationville people came to visit and though he never saw the stranger again, Mr. A spoke of him in warm and mellow tones. As for his life, often Mr. A felt good and sometimes he felt bad, but one thing for sure, he always felt what he felt. And so he lived happily ever after—until something else came up.

The Contrasts

Rationality may be a useful tool for dealing with some of life's situations. It is not, however, a way to understand life.

This, as we mentioned earlier, is one of those chapters directed mostly to the management and organization-development consultants among our readers. We think it is important because it highlights the key elements that distinguish Authentic Management from conventional human relations. For our manager readers, we suggest you read it without straining. If some points aren't clear now, they may clear up later in the book—and if they don't, they probably aren't that important to you yet.

People have been thinking and theorizing about managing and organizations for a long time, and not unlike other specialties, the theories change, each theory providing its particular usefulness for that era. Back in 1895 Frederick Taylor began to tell American industry about Scientific Management. For Taylor and those who expanded his theories, what was most important for managing an effective organization was cool, dispassionate managerial efficiency—and that required planning, decision making, and control centralized in the hands of management.

In the late 1920s and early 1930s American management learned, from Dr. Elton Mayo and his associates at the Western Electric Company, that what seemed to count most among workers was their group feeling and the social environment. Most important to improving motivation was encouraging workers to believe that management *cared* about them.

More recently, beginning in the 1960s, organization behavior theory, under the general heading of "human relations," seems to have changed again. The current emphasis is on increasing participative processes, that is, getting people at all levels to participate in making business decisions. We believe this trend is a positive one for organizations and the people who work within them, and yet we also feel that the development and application of many of the specific theories and practices of what we will call today's "conventional human relations" have been too one-sided and restrictive of the most healthful development of managers and their subordinates.

For the sake of clarity and to dramatize the points we wish to make, we intend to delineate quite sharply the contrast. We do recognize that within the behavioral-science field, as in others, there is certainly a range of practice, and there has been some movement toward a broader and more-realistic approach to human dynamics on the part of a number of theoreticians and practitioners.

"POSITIVE" AND "NEGATIVE" EMOTIONS

In general, the values currently advocated in conventional human relations for organizations included:

- Participation and self-monitoring
- Logic and rationality
- Trust of, and openness toward, others
- Collaboration and participation
- Affection and responsiveness
- Group interest

While these values certainly seem important for the development of effective and humanistic organizations, we believe that many of today's human-relations theorists are neglecting values at the other end of the spectrum of human interaction. For example:

- Authority and control
- Caution and reserve
- Autonomy and separateness
- Competition and aggressiveness
- Dislike and resistance
- Self-interest

We imagine that some managers, as well as many organization consultants, will view the first list as describing healthy and constructive characteristics for people and organizations, while the second seems to represent harmful or even neurotic qualities—the qualities that the manager or consultant feels he or she ought to be trying to change.

In the Authentic-Management approach, we believe this (sometimes explicit, sometimes implicit) rejection of the "negative" aspects has weakened a good deal of organization development by barring from consideration the vigor and energy often available in these tougher qualities. What is also important is that, by avoiding and disapproving of these aspects, many managers have become less comfortable and able to cope with what might be called the tough parts of their worlds. In a sense, the "gentleness-reasonableness" bias of conventional human relations has at times fostered discomfort and guilt feelings in managers and executives. We have known several managers, for example, who, after experiencing a sensitivity-training workshop or human-relations training session, have returned to their organizations with high resolve to hold back their aggressive impulses and act more considerately toward others—with frustrating and disappointing results.

As you read further in this book, it will become increasingly clear that we do not advocate the denial or suppression of these so-called negative feelings. Authentic Management encourages the manager and those within his or her system to become fully aware of what they are *experiencing* (rather than what they, or the latest human-relations theory, think they *should* experience) and to work out viable relationships based on their own unique qualities and dynamics instead of a consultant's or anyone else's model of "best management practice." Thus, in general, we promote full exchanges that acknowledge the reality and health of the so-called negative as well as positive aspects of being a person.

Perhaps most important is that for individuals to realize their whole potential, they must be able to get in touch with their whole range of thought and feeling. The integrated individual, we think, is able to experience both love and hate; is able to exert dominance without being or perceiving himself or herself as a tyrant; and is able to experience submission without feeling crushed. It is our conviction that individuals within organizations, as well as organizations themselves, need to be in touch with these contrasting aspects of their make-up if they are to realize their potential for vitality and growth.

CONTRASTS IN CONVENTIONAL-HUMAN-RELATIONS AND AUTHENTIC-MANAGEMENT APPROACHES

In the remainder of this chapter we will comment in a more specific way on the major differences, as we see them, between the conventional-human-relations (CHR) and the Authentic-Management (AM) orientations. Again, the point we are making here is not that you ought to throw out the conventional orientation, but rather that there is a great need for more understanding and emphasis at the other end of the spectrum as well.

In talking about the principles of both approaches, we sometimes illustrate our points by examples of organization-development work utilizing organization consultants. Our main purpose at this time is to clearly illustrate the point being made rather than to provide instruction on consulting methods; later in the book we discuss in detail techniques and methods for both managers and consultants.

CHR	AM
1 Group-helping/group-building focus	Focus on recognition and mobilization of individual strength and power

In conventional human-relations theory, the emphasis is on building mutual understanding, mutual adaptation, and cooperative behavior. People are encouraged to help each other and to facilitate each other's efforts: so-called "weaker members" of the team should be supported and encouraged by stronger members; dominant members of the group are discouraged from their domination by group pressure, especially when their domination apparently inhibits the less-aggressive members. In other words, group members take responsibility for each other's welfare.

In the Authentic-Management orientation, each individual is encouraged to take responsibility for himself or herself. "Helping weaker members" is not encouraged (though functional cooperation is, of course). Each person is to take charge of his or her own action (or inaction), and to discover his or her capacity for initiating (and suppressing) behavior. In cases of relationship problems between a dominant and passive team member, we seldom discourage the dominant member by pressuring or persuading that person to hold back "domination." More often, we work with the passive member to enable that individual to interrupt the dominant member and *to get what he or she wants through self-initiated action.* In a somewhat oversimplified way, it might be said that, rather than weakening the "strong," our attempt is to strengthen the "weak" members of the group, thereby strengthening the group as a whole.

An example may serve to clarify this case further: In a typical CHR consulting intervention, a consultant observed that one member of a management group seemed to have a difficult time expressing himself, especially in an exchange with a dominant member of the group. The consultant pointed out to the dominant member that his style of expression was causing this reluctance by inhibiting the more passive member. Very frequently an intervention of this sort, especially when bolstered by other team members' "feedback," produces a feeling of guilt in the dominant member and he or she decides to try to curb a naturally strong expressive style. This effort takes a great deal of energy, and is frequently unsuccessful over any sustained period of time, since the natural forces within the strongly expressive member are still at work.

A consultant with an AM orientation would approach the situation differently. He or she would focus first on the reluctant team member and might ask whether that member would like to say something. If the answer is yes, the consultant might ask the passive person why he or she hasn't been contributing to the discussion. If the reluctant member responds that he or she is having difficulty speaking freely in the face of the strong expression of the dominant member, the reluctant member would be encouraged to become more aware of exactly how he or she stops from talking, and more specific about predicting the consequences if he or she were to be more expressive. The consultant would not, however, force the passive member to be more expressive. For example:

CONSULTANT: John, I am concerned that you haven't been saying anything even though we have been talking about the area you are responsible for.

JOHN: Yes, I know.

CONSULTANT: Is there anything that you want to say on this subject?

JOHN: I guess so, but Dick comes on so strong that I'm a little reluctant to talk up.

CONSULTANT: How do you stop yourself from saying what you want to say?

JOHN: Well, I guess I just don't want to interrupt.

CONSULTANT: What's your objection to interrupting?

JOHN: I don't know. I guess maybe it seems impolite to do that.

CONSULTANT: To whom would it be impolite?

JOHN: To Dick, I guess.

CONSULTANT: So you would rather keep yourself from saying what you want to say than be impolite, is that it?

JOHN: Well, I don't know, when I think about it that way maybe not.

BILL: (another group member) It doesn't seem to me that Dick holds himself back by being afraid of being impolite.

JOHN: No, that's true. I haven't thought about it that way.

CONSULTANT: It seems to me that you have a choice, and making that choice is your responsibility. You can decide to say what you want to say or you can continue to stop yourself from talking.

JOHN: Yes, I guess I do. And I guess I will, I do have something to say. (Turns to Dick and addresses him).

CHR	AM
2 Examination of situational elements of the interaction process: emphasis on reasons <u>why</u>	Sharpen awareness of what the individual does and <u>how</u>

In the CHR approach to organization problems, the focus most often is on an examination of the problem situation and an attempt is made to analyze the reasons for its existence. When a consultant is used, he or she helps those involved in their attempts to explain the situation, and various interpretations are examined, as well as suggestions and proposed solutions. The process proceeds in a logical, sequential way, i.e., data is gathered about the elements of the situation, a diagnosis is made, solutions proposed, etc.

In the AM orientation, the focus is on encouraging those involved to become aware of *what they are doing* and *what they are avoiding.* In the preceding dialogue, the consultant encourages John to become aware that, first, he is stopping himself from talking, and second, that *how* he does this is by imagining that he would be seen as impolite to Dick if he interrupted him. A typical organization consultant might have questioned John about organizational considerations that were inhibiting him, such as Dick being in a perceived stronger organizational position, or about his past relationships with Dick and others in the group. If the consultant were psychologically oriented, he might have explored John's past relationships with authority figures. The AM-oriented approach is seldom analytical. It emphasizes the *now* and the *how* rather than the historical and the why. The rationale for this is that, almost invariably, multiple explanations can be found for every phenomenon in behavior and, as many of us have learned, an intellectual understanding of why something happened frequently does little to help change perceptions or behavior.

CHR	AM
3 Analysis of "problem behavior" and methods for solving or correcting it	Intensification or dramatization of "problem behavior" until a change in relationship occurs

In the CHR-oriented group, behavior patterns that are seen as producing problems for an individual in the group or between two or more individuals are spotlighted and identified in explicit ways (usually through feedback). Subsequently, proposals are made for the individual to consider changing his or her behavior, e.g., to be more or less forceful, talkative, etc. Often these proposals are subtle rather than explicit—i.e., the consultant makes it clear that although the group member is in no way compelled to change his or her style, there are obvious disadvantages (sometimes in moral as well as efficiency terms) to continuing the old style. Not only is such an approach manipulative, but the consequent behavior change is frequently forced. Often the suppressed feeling comes out in other ways—through body tension, restlessness, or other signs—and produces incongruity between words and actions. In fact, as we see it, restrained irritation or affection is seldom healthy for the individual or the group. People sense either consciously or unconsciously that others in the group are playacting and a new set of "be-nice-to-everybody" principles may become the norm.

In the AM group, members are encouraged to be aware of and, when they are ready, to acknowledge their feelings and behavior. They are not, however, pressured to do so. In working with individuals, the consultant encourages them to *be where they are* rather than where they "ought to be." They are helped to recognize the polarities[1] in themselves—the forces for and against, toward and away—rather than to analyze and solve their "problem behavior."

By encouraging people to be where they are, we do *not* mean encouraging them to just spout out their feelings of aggression, dislike, sorrow, etc., no matter what the situation. What is encouraged is increased self-awareness and a gradual building of relationships that not only allow but encourage more and more straight talk. The parts and dynamics of this process will become clearer as you read on.

CHR	AM
4 Aggressiveness and conflict seen as negative forces in system. Bringing conflict to light seen as a sign of openness, but something to be resolved as soon as possible	Aggressiveness and conflict valued as vitalizing forces. Aggressiveness necessary for creativity

---

[1] More about "polarities" in Section Two, pages 79–83.

Expressions of aggression or conflict in the CHR-oriented group are generally congratulated in the early stages of the group, but primarily as indications that individuals have come to trust each other enough to open up and express negative feelings toward each other. By and large, conflicts are interrupted relatively quickly in the CHR-oriented group and efforts are made to analyze the causes of disagreement and to resolve them in a rational, problem-solving manner. Competitive behavior is not valued except when it is externally focused, that is, in competing with outside organizations. The emphasis within the organization is almost invariably on learning cooperative and collaborative behavior.

In the AM-oriented group, aggressiveness and conflict are valued as vitalizing forces, not merely as signs of openness. Conflict between individuals and groups is recognized as a natural occurrence and the manner of working with conflict tends to differ. Rather than moving very quickly into problem solving, which frequently means premature problem solving with the likelihood of later recurrence of the conflict, an effort is made in the AM group to sharpen the differences and conflict elements in the situation. Individuals may be asked to fully expound their complaints, sometimes even to the point of exaggeration. With a qualified consultant helping to highlight the issues, feelings and beliefs surface. Those involved come to recognize that full argument is less embarrassing and "damaging" than they had imagined. Equally important in this process, which is both emotionally and substantively more complete, *old issues can be finished* rather than swept under the rug, and new perspectives emerge.

In working with the conflict situation, efforts are also made to help people distinguish between the actual positions of the other person and their own inaccurate imaginings. (We will discuss methods for getting at this process in a later section.) When both parties in the situation have had an opportunity to explore where each stands in the conflict, they are in a better position to deal with each other on an interpersonal basis and to deal with the remaining *real* issues between them.

For example, in one conflict situation we worked with, the recently appointed high-level manager was black and two of his peers were white. Only after both the black manager and his white peers recognized and dealt with the awareness that some part of the manager's antagonism grew out of feelings of being patronized as a black man were he and his fellow managers really able to deal with the more-substantive issues between them.

CHR	AM
5 Emphasis on others' feedback	Emphasis on individual's own internal feedback

In the typical CHR-oriented group, the cycle of interaction generally proceeds as follows: the individual acts; he or she receives feedback from others about his or her actions and their effects; the individual then chooses whether or not to modify behavior in response to the feedback received, especially if it is negative. This approach to manager development is espoused in a number of training programs throughout the country. For example, as noted in a recent brochure advertising a sensitivity-training program:

> *The age old continuing wish of men and women to see themselves as others see them has the most practical basis for those who supervise or serve in key roles in our society. To increase the effectiveness of our relationships with others, we need to know more accurately how they see us—what we do that is useful and what we do that detracts from our usefulness.*

Thus, in the typical CHR approach, others' opinions may guide the individual in modifying his or her behavior to increase interpersonal effectiveness. As noted earlier, though, when such behavior-modification attempts are made by resolve and the individual is not ready to make them, the changes frequently prove to be forced, temporary, and ineffective, and therefore result in incongruent behavior that is sensed by others and is frequently disturbing to them.

In the AM-oriented group, the feedback of others is deemphasized. Through a variety of methods we will discuss later, the individual is encouraged to become more aware of what he or she is doing and how he or she does it; or of what he or she is avoiding, and how this is being accomplished. In this process, rather than discouraging the member from behaving in a particular way in the group, the consultant may encourage the person temporarily to behave in that way even more strongly in order to increase self-awareness.

For example, while in a CHR group, an individual might get feedback such as: "Joan, you seem very evasive and that produces a negative reaction in me. I wish you would be more direct." In the AM group, Joan could well be encouraged by the consultant to try being *more* evasive with others in the group for a while, but in a *deliberate* way.

One member of a management team we recently worked with continually spoke in halting, abstract generalizations. Even when he was asked his opinion on specific and immediate issues, he would reply hesitantly, with theoretical observations. In response to questioning from his peers, he indicated that he was not very aware of his own style of communication. In the group, we asked if he would be willing to make statements to several other members at the most abstract level he could. After a slow and awkward start, his voice, manner, and delivery gathered increasing strength and then humor as he continued from one person to the next. In increasing his awareness of his present style and *taking charge* of what he was doing, he became quite animated and energetic, much to his own pleasure and the enjoyment of his peers. After some further work, he also became aware that he used his hesitancy and abstract manner to avoid being challenged. He also discovered his own capacity to use a more direct style when he wished to do so.

In the AM-oriented group, we look on current behavior not as something to be corrected or changed, but rather as something that needs emphasis and increased awareness on the part of each individual. Once dysfunctional behavior has been fully experienced, change will usually occur naturally.

CHR	AM
6 Emphasis on interdependence	Emphasis on enhancing individual autonomy and competence: the capacity to choose independent, competitive, or collaborative behavior

Interdependence may very well be a requirement in some organizations, particularly organizations responsible for complex technological systems. If subsystems or components of a system are required to interact with each other in order for the total system to work properly, then it is of course clear that the people and organizations responsible for producing those components or subsystems must also be able to communicate and deal with one another in an integrated way. However, while interdependence may be a requirement, it is not, or ought not be, a goal in itself. Frequently, CHR-oriented consultants have translated this sometime requirement into a value for all work groups.

Often, groups have been exhorted by consultants and CHR-educated managers to work together and to find the synergy in their cooperation. Taken as an ethical or even fashionable imperative, this has sometimes contributed to considerable frustration when the actual requirements of the task to be done do not require interdependence. We have worked with a number of managers who had made repeated unsuccessful efforts to find ways of being interdependent until they finally realized that neither their functions nor their personal inclinations required this interdependence. With a sigh of relief, they were able to give up this artificially imposed demand and turn their energy to more-useful purposes.

In the AM-oriented approach, interdependence is recognized when it exists as a requirement of the situation or task to be done; under these circumstances, a competent and well-integrated individual or group is able to work collaboratively with others in order to achieve the purposes required. However, when it is not required, the group is not encouraged to strain for interdependence as a mode of operating. A person or group may operate in a solitary and separate manner when that is most appropriate, in a cooperative manner at other times, and competitively at still other times. Important here, as in other cases we have illustrated, is increasing the ability of the individual and the group to operate along a whole spectrum of styles.

CHR	AM
7 Values being "open"	Values being "up-front" (even when that means being closed)

In the CHR-oriented approach, high value is placed on trust and openness—quite frequently, in fact, group pressures are very strong, even to the point of coercion, to encourage individual team members to be open and deal with themselves and each other in intimate sharing ways. While the AM-oriented group does not discourage openness in relationships, neither does it discourage individuals from being closed when that is what they explicitly choose to do. While the group under these circumstances may also apply pressure on the individual to be more sharing, the consultant often will encourage the individual to stand up for his or her right to remain separate and to restrict sharing if he or she chooses to do so.

In the early stages of working with a group, the AM consultant places special emphasis on reinforcing the group members right to say "no" to each other. Only when they are fully in touch with their ability to decline others' requests can they experience being in charge of their own fates and really having a choice of action. Paradoxically, when people are able to say "no" fully, they become better able to say "yes" fully.

CHR	AM
8 Learning from new concepts and experiments with new behavior	Emphasis on increasing awareness of present behavior and its completion

In the CHR-oriented group, members are encouraged to learn, again primarily from others' feedback, and then to try out new methods of behaving and interacting with one another. Attention is focused on such areas as improving communication, actively listening, being nondefensive, etc. There is frequently a search for the "right way" or "most effective way" of interacting. In many cases, the consultant's approach encourages the systemization of behavior in accordance with some prescribed model such as "Theory Y" or "the manager's role," etc.

In the AM group, as pointed out earlier, clients are encouraged to become aware of their present actions. Spontaneous behavior, rather than the artificial fulfillment of prescribed role behavior, is highly valued. Thus, in allowing themselves to be authentic, individuals may well behave from time to time in ways that are less than ideal when measured against a set of guidelines for "good" human-relations practice. But an authentic exchange between human beings who allow themselves to be as they are brings about more genuine and more satisfying relationships. And these relationships do not deflect energy into "keeping up a front" or "doing the right thing." There is, we believe, room for a great deal of diversity in personality styles.

CHR	AM
9 Focus on changing organization's culture toward increased openness, democratization, etc.	Focus on increasing individual's competence in whatever the culture

Frequently, organization consultants speak of "changing the organization culture"; sending managers off to sensitivity training is not enough, say the consultants, we need to affect the norms and values back at the organization. Usually that means working with managers and their teams within the organization itself, and finding ways to encourage modes similar to those developed in the sensitivity-training group. If patterns are not changed in the "back-home culture," we are warned, then the manager returning from a positive experience at a sensitivity lab will run into an inhospitable climate and nonsupport, or perhaps even rejection, from fellow managers for his or her new, more-open style. The demise of more than one company's organization-development program has been attributed to its reliance on sending managers away to training conferences without sufficient concentration being given to changing the company's internal culture.

In the CHR framework, certain underlying assumptions are clear. First, the desired and encouraged direction of change is toward what we have been calling the positive emotions, especially group support, collaboration, and participation. Second, it is generally assumed that these values are better for the organization than what we have called the negative emotions—frequently they are assumed to be better both in terms of humanitarian and efficiency criteria. Third, it is also assumed that making these new values operable in the organization requires consensual support—i.e., it is too dangerous to be open, sharing, collaborative, etc. if others are not. So, the individual manager can only change if the system can be altered to support him or her.

The AM-oriented approach, again, is more individualistically focused and views both negative and positive emotions as available sources of human energy and vitality within the organization. While we have some admitted bias against tyranny as a management style, in our experiences we have found few business or government organizations that we could seriously categorize under that heading. (It's likely that people who run that kind of organization don't often hire organization-development consultants or read books like this one.) We have, however, worked in a number of organizations where styles of management varied significantly on the dimensions of permissiveness-control, participation, directiveness, etc., and we are far from concluding that one side of the continuum is always better than the other, either from the standpoint of effectiveness or humanitarianism.

With this set of assumptions, then, the AM-oriented consultant is less likely to focus on changing the culture[2] and more likely to help clients identify first: *what they want, how they stop themselves from getting what they want, and what alternatives are available to them.* Then, when these questions have been addressed, clients may move forward with greater clarity and vigor to deal with others in the organization, and they may do so in whatever style they find most promising, given the culture and their own personal requirements.

We believe that for the most-effective development of organization relationships, as well as for the individual's well-being, it is important for a person to first become aware of his or her own stance, including fears, projections, alienations, etc. In working these out, the individual frequently discovers that many of these worries are not real, or are far less terrifying when reduced to concrete action possibilities than when they were vague abstractions chasing around in the imagination.

One implication of this point is that effective development of team members does not always require that all meet together to deal with their concerns and conflicts. Rather, an individual team member may meet with a nonfamily group, or even in a private consultation with the consultant, and there work toward improved personal effectiveness. Under these circumstances, the individual, having recognized and mobilized his or her

---

[2]   While we acknowledge that in the O.D. context "culture" may be a useful term to describe rapidly and grossly a general impression of the way a significant number of people tend to interact in a given organization, we also find "culture" and other words like it to be lifeless abstractions that are frequently used in behavioral-science conversations as substitutes for identifying, focusing on, and doing something about specific and concrete situations. Abstracting can be a way of avoiding.

strength, is often able to transfer this mobilization back to the working environment.

	AM
CHR	
10 Consultant as neutral observer of process	Consultant as activist, director, and participant

In making our final point in this series of comparisons, we want to address our fellow organization consultants particularly, though we believe these comments have relevance for operating managers as well.

The consultant in a CHR-oriented group frequently sees his or her role as demanding detachment: the consultant is to remain somewhat outside the action and apart from the participants. This is especially true in dealing with conflict issues—the consultant is to remain objective, fair, noninvolved, and, at best, to do as little leading of the group as possible. CHR-oriented consultants frequently speak of giving attention to "the group's needs," and believe it inappropriate to pursue their own needs. Many indicate considerable concern that group members not become dependent on them.

In the AM orientation, the consultant is much more likely to take an active part, to act and react impulsively, not merely as a model to others, but also to suit his or her own needs (which is in keeping with the approach he or she is advocating). The consultant's assumption, particularly when working with organization groups comprised of people with relatively high ego strength, is that group members need not be unduly protected. They will not become dependent on the consultant if he or she is freely expressive in the group and allows them to see his or her own strengths and weaknesses. The consultant has no special image to maintain because of his or her particular professional function, and may experience and openly express a full range of emotions, including anger, affection, confusion, pride, inadequacy, and so on, just as the other members of the group may experience these feelings. There is no aura of consultant omnipotence within the group; they recognize that the consultant, like themselves, is a human being with a particular set of character traits and skills that he or she brings to a particular situation.

Another contrast worth noting is that while most CHR-oriented consultants encourage the expression of emotion in sensitivity groups and work groups, they generally treat the expressed feelings as "data" to be considered rationally—a kind of intellectualization of emotion. The AM-oriented consultant is more likely to react to the spontaneous expression of a client with a spontaneous expression of his or her own. There is less reliance on theoretical construction and more on the consultant's and others' good sense and intuition—the consultant maintains faith in the high value of authenticity, even when being authentic is difficult.

CONCLUSION

The case we are introducing in this chapter is for an active expansion of management and organization behavior to include the vitality and value of negative as well as positive emotions and attributes. We believe the values of conventional human relations today derive from liberal-democratic biases and traditions. In reaction against the mass exploitation and mechanistic outlook of the early days of industrialization, many in our society fostered, preached, and found justification for gentility, participation, and rationality. In so doing, we have often neglected or denied power, directiveness, and impulse—and these are as vitally important and legitimate aspects of being a person as their more comfortable "positive" counterparts.

I Will Do You No Favor

If I withhold my voice of anger from you
*   for your sake*
You, in listening too hard to me,
Will hear more anger than ever any
*   real voice of mine would have held*

If I curb my raucous ribald
*   pleasure voice for anticipation of your*
*   sensibilities*
You will know I have curbed and
*   pleasure will be dimmed and*
*   overlaid with grimy speculation*
*   as to why.*
(What else than pleasure was there that
*   he did not say?)*

If I damp my robust affection for you
*   and keep my arms that want to*
*   hug you bound at my sides*
(As would seem more appropriate
*   for men of our station and trade)*
Your arms, or perhaps only fingers,
*   will twitch too, stifled and pinched*
*   off meanly*
And perhaps, in spite against their
*   mind-formed shackles,*
*   will tense to fists*

All that I withhold diminishes me
*   and cheats you*
All that you withhold diminishes you
*   and cheats me*
When we hold back ourselves
*   for each other's sake*
That is no service to us either one
We only collude in the weakening
*   of us both.*

Working Concepts

In the previous section, we began with a general description of some basic Gestalt theory, as well as the significant contrasts between the Authentic-Management and conventional-human-relations approaches. In this section, we examine those concepts that are oriented more toward actual operating situations within organizations. In the chapter "Three Ways to Go: About, Should, and Is," we look at three different orientations people choose from and alternate between both in their communications with one another and in relating to the world they live in. Each of these orientations can produce profoundly different results for the person in terms of how he or she experiences and deals with events and other people, and in terms of the messages the person sends out to others and those he or she gets back.

In the chapter on "Introjection," we examine one of the main sources of many of our operating assumptions, ideas, and values. Briefly, introjection is a swallowing whole of the ideas, judgments, and styles of influential others in our lives, which then form the basis of the judgments and standards we set for our own and other people's behavior. Introjections can at times keep us locked into opinions and positions that do not serve our own or others' interest.

In "Awareness, Contact, and Withdrawal" and "Self-Boundaries and Grounding," we look at the concepts and approaches that enable us to get more fully in touch with *how* we are locking ourselves in. Also, we see alternatives we have for experiencing ourselves, others, and events in fresher and more-realistically focused ways. Each of us has the means to more clearly answer the questions: Who am I? What do I really believe? What do I want as an individual? Awareness is a requirement for good contact; contact, in turn, enables real person-to-person interaction with a minimum of the distortions generated by fixed attitudes, stereotypes, and so on. For good contact, we also require a clear sense of our boundaries and the boundaries of others.

In "Self-Boundaries and Grounding," we examine how our boundaries are defined by our physical and psychological limits, while they are also the sensing mechanisms that enable us to come into contact with other people and with things outside ourselves.

"Confluence and Differentiation" depicts confluence as one aspect of blurred boundaries that often occurs in management groups. The positive values of conflict and differentiation in organizations are also explored.

"Polarization" examines the dynamics of differences further and allows us to discover in "extremes" valuable sources of energy and vitality. This chapter also provides a bridge to Section Three, "Power, Weakness, and Conflict."

For each subject, we conclude by describing a method or exercise that can help the reader check himself or herself on that dimension. For convenience, exercises are arranged so that they may be individually photocopied. With our publisher's cooperation, we are authorizing reproduction of the exercises for those of you who wish to use them with groups.

Three Ways to Go: About, Should, and Is

There are different ways of being in the world. You can:

- Make a model in your mind of the "right life" and keep trying to live up to it and eliminate the things that seem to interfere with it.

- Be in the middle of what is happening and rejoice at times, suffer at times, rest at times.

In Gestalt theory, a distinction is made among three ways of experiencing, interpreting, and communicating to others what goes on. Each of these three orientations produces greatly different results for the individual in terms of what he or she actually perceives and experiences, as well as in terms of his or her interpretation. This, in turn, influences the messages sent out to others and those received in return. These differences are particularly important in organization settings and account for a great deal of what we call "communication problems." Let's look at them:

- **About-ism:** Dealing with other people and events in your environment as abstractions. In the "About-ism" mode, you deal with situations, problems, other people, and perhaps even yourself as though you were quite separate from your feelings. Talking in the "about" way is talking as though you were an outsider observing others and yourself, rather than experiencing and being involved in what's going on *here and now.*

- **Should-ism:** Prethinking and then measuring your actions or even your thoughts against a set of standards you hold in your mind. You work hard at figuring out what you *should* think and do according to this set of standards, rather than getting your clues from your own internal feelings, ideas, and wants. Frequently, the fantasy that accompanies "shouldistic" behavior is: If I let myself go and did or said what I really felt like, there would be hell to pay both for me and those around me.

- **Is-ism:** Experiencing and communicating with the emphasis on becoming as aware as possible of your own unique nature and feelings, and acting accordingly. In the "is-istic" mode, spontaneity, naturalness, and freedom—in contrast to deliberation and good manners—are most highly valued. Is-ism deals with what *is* happening now. A key word is "I."

In discussing these categories, we want to stress that none of the above styles is always good or always bad; each has its usefulness at certain times. However, the fact is that most of us spend the majority of our time in the "about" or "should" mode and, except for rare occasions, feel uncomfortable or even fearful of allowing ourselves to acknowledge and deal with *what is*. Let's look at some of the positives and negatives of each of the styles we are discussing.

ABOUT-ISM

Talking "about" can be very useful, even essential much of the time. In writing this book, we are mainly talking *about* some concepts and ideas that we believe will be generally useful to our readers. In describing the elements of a reorganization he or she is considering, a manager would undoubtedly find it useful to talk *about* the general benefits and shortcomings of both the present and the proposed new structures. Talking about situations becomes less useful, and sometimes even dysfunctional, when the manager continually uses the about style to convey what seems to be a safe abstraction, instead of dealing with the concrete and immediate problem he or she is *now* having.

In talking "about," the personal pronoun "I" is seldom used; instead, words like "we" or "one" or "you" or "the organization" are substituted, thereby dissociating the speaker from his or her own statements. At the same time, the speaker also diminishes his or her potential impact on listeners, and it is often unclear to them (and even to the speaker) where he or she personally stands on an issue.

For example, we recall an executive who attempted to explain to one of his department heads his intention to transfer an important planning function into another department. In trying to justify the move, he used several reasons based on organization theory, concluding with, "The organization will benefit from the change and we will all be more effective." The department head, however, was unconvinced and dissatisfied. Only after several days of argument and mounting feelings of frustration was the executive willing to give his specific reason for wanting to make the change and to take a personal position, i.e., "I am unsatisfied with the way the function is being performed now." At that point, he and the department head were able to begin constructive discussions which eventually resulted in the improvement of the planning function in its present organization.

SHOULD-ISM

Should-isms are derived from the norms, standards, and preachments that all of us have heard from infancy on. Little girls, for example, are taught that girls *should* be quiet, demure, unaggressive, and so on; they are often taught as well that they should *not* (another form of should) show interest in machinery, seem to be too smart, or play football. Little boys, of course, are taught other shoulds: they should be strong, uncomplaining, responsible for protecting little girls, not be interested in cooking or sewing, and so on. As most of us are aware, our society has begun to seriously question these sex-role stereotypes, and these shoulds, which have so long been taken for granted, are now being widely criticized.

Shoulds also play a large part in determining management roles. Our ideas about proper managerial behavior—how you ought to act as a manager—can be gathered from a number of sources. For example, prescribed sets of rules may be provided formally by your organization. In some companies, these may deal not only with at-work situations, but also with personal conduct off the job. Sometimes the rules aren't formal, but "everybody knows" what's expected. Or, they may come as a set of folklore or traditions of good managership, or from your observations (frequently incomplete or even distorted) of other more-senior manager-hero figures, or from some stereotyped ideas of the "American Executive in action," or from one or more of the management training programs that have sprouted like dandelions all over the world.

IS-ISM

Being in the "is" mode means being aware of, recognizing, and dealing with what is happening right now. It doesn't mean giving vent to every impulse or feeling that crosses your mind or that you have to be compulsively honest in telling your secretary you don't like her dress, or your boss that you don't think she handled her last meeting with the board of directors very well. In fact, being compulsive about voicing your honest opinions in all circumstances would just be another form of should-ism. What being in the "is" mode does mean is that you become aware of how you really feel about what's going on with yourself and other people, and then make a conscious choice as to how or whether to deal with these situations. It means recognizing that you are angry with a subordinate, rather than telling yourself that you should not become angry with subordinates; it means recognizing that you feel down and discouraged; it means allowing yourself to feel jealous, antagonistic, and any number of other negative feelings when these feelings are with you, rather than telling yourself that you should not feel them. Again, whether or not you deal with the feelings is another matter that you can make a choice about.

One more aspect of operating in the "is" mode involves being willing and able to state explicitly and concretely what you want from others. As obvious as this may sound, it is surprising how many times in our consulting experience the simple act of both parties getting in touch with and clearly stating what they want of each other provides a concrete basis for a positive change in relationships. For example, we recently worked with a manager and one of his subordinates during a "difficult" performance counselling interview. After listening for a few minutes to an abstract discussion, complicated by years of working together, we asked if each were willing to express what exactly he wanted from the other. Quite simply, the supervisor wanted his manager to know that he believed the manager had made a faulty scheduling decision six months earlier. The manager, on the other hand, wanted the supervisor to accept and respect his desire to make needed technical contributions to a recent assignment he had given the supervisor. After the supervisor had the opportunity to tell the boss his opinion in a very direct way—which, incidentally, the manager agreed with—the basis for the ensuing discussion about how they would work together took a constructive turn.

Another way of saying all of this is that being in the "is" mode means talking straight and directly, *or consciously deciding not to.* Unfortunately, a good deal of the training managers have been subject to in recent years does not encourage straight talk.

NO ONE BEST MODEL

Many management-development programs, especially those that are human-relations oriented, prescribe principles for managers to follow if they expect to establish effective and positive relationships with subordinates, superiors, and peers. In many programs, the model of the "one best manager" is set up and training attempts to shape the student to conform to that model. Sometimes the "trainee" does not relate to the principles described in the model except to acknowledge them as theoretical information—"nice to know." At other times, however, a manager may attempt to change his or her behavior in the prescribed way, or at least to try it out.

Most training programs promoting the one best model are limited in their success because the trainees have not really internalized the recommended changes—that is, they have not really checked themselves to see whether or not, for example, being more participative really feels comfortable. Often the manager does not recognize what else is involved in adopting a new managerial style. If you are going to be a participative manager in your staff meetings, are you also going to be participative on the plant floor, at budget time, or when the time comes for reductions in force?

Mental decisions and resolutions about changing your managerial style continually require you to make *more* decisions and resolutions (also in your mind) each time an issue comes up. And what's worse, if you are plagued by the need for total logic and consistency in your own behavior, you may be in for a lot of trouble when logic and consistency say one thing and your impulses and feelings say another.

Heavy costs may be exacted in this internal battle between what your mind-model says you *should* do according to your newly adopted managerial ideal and what your feelings say they want you to do—especially if by force of will you turn off the feelings. Do that sort of thing often enough over a long enough period of time and you may join a long and illustrious line of fellow managers in a case of ulcers, heart disease, hypertension, or some equally popular disease of our times. At the very least, you can expect to increase your rate of spouse and children chewing-outs when you get home from work at night.

Another problem with grabbing onto somebody else's model for how you ought to act is that when you try to adapt yourself to these shouldistic prescriptions, other people (your subordinates and peers) may view your behavior as incongruent—out of line with other signals you are simultaneously sending. If, while saying to your subordinates, "I'd like all of us to discuss this policy issue and come to a consensus on what to do about it," you are sitting on the edge of your chair, glancing at your watch every three minutes, and grinding your teeth, they may think twice about jumping in and venturing new ideas for leisurely consideration. So, even when some managers try to follow the training prescriptions, they don't get the pay-off that seems to be promised in the management-development literature. Their performance and effectiveness do not improve, nor do their subordinates react to them in the positive way promised by the prescribers. We have known a number of managers who have experienced this "failure" and have then completely turned off to management training.

Theories about human beings are not necessarily bad, but they do need to be considered in the framework of *what is now*—not what might be if we could all start fresh again. People do not proceed directly from the womb into the organization in which they work; they spend considerable years in between having experiences and learning how to get along. And some learn to get along one way, while others learn to get along another way.

This applies to us and to you, and to everyone else you and we know who has been smart enough to live long enough to have a job or career. People are different. If you think about managers you have worked for and admired, you will probably find they come in a variety of styles and temperaments. Good managers, as well as the not-so-good ones, come in an assortment of models. Some are best at one thing and some at another. Frankly, we like it that way, it makes life more interesting.

On the following page, we begin with an exercise on "shoulds." Good luck.

Shoulds

SETTING

This is a self-oriented exercise aimed at helping you to identify and work on some of your "shoulds."

Probably few, if any, people in the world are completely themselves at all times. Most of us modify our behavior in a great many ways and in accordance with a variety of situations. By now, of course, you realize that we are not advocating that you as a manager *should* make a new resolution as a result of reading this book to always "be yourself." Our principle for change is quite contrary to that. After all, if you were to make that resolution and try to live up to it, you would merely be taking on another set of shoulds.

We believe that useful change in human beings occurs naturally. Paradoxically (there are many paradoxes in this book), the way to *allow* yourself to change and grow is to become aware of what you are doing now. It is especially important, too, for you to learn how you stop yourself from doing what you want to do and how you stop yourself from being who you are. The following exercise may help:

PROCESS

1 Write a list of the five or six most-important shoulds (or should *nots*) you have accepted yourself as a manager.* (More or less than that if you like—unless you feel you *should* make it five or six.)

2 For each item try to identify its source, that is, where the notion came to you from—e.g., from company policy, your boss, your early training, etc.

3 For each of the original items, write down specifically how you imagine you would act (either the same or differently) if you were to allow yourself to follow your own natural inclinations instead of the should or should not.

4 Write briefly *how* you stop yourself from following your own natural inclinations for each of the items. For example, you may imagine that following your own inclinations would result in your disappointing other people, such as your boss or subordinates; or you may think people in the organization would think of you as

---

*   The exercise can also be applied to you as a husband or wife, father or mother, son or daughter, etc.

eccentric, etc. Be as concrete and specific as possible. Name names and specific consequences.

5 Now try to put yourself in the place of the individual or individuals who would disapprove of or be disappointed by your behavior. Do your negative expectations stand up as well when you examine them from the perspective of the other person?

6 If possible and practical, arrange a time to sit down with one or more of the people you have identified and discuss with them appropriate parts of your list— that is, how you now operate vs. how you would like to operate, and get their reactions. Be especially alert to the probability that your expectations of their negative reactions may not be accurate. They may be much more willing to have you move toward the kind of behavior you would like for yourself than you originally thought. Also, be aware of the possibilities of reciprocation with the other person. Try to find out if there are some ways in which he or she would like to interact with you but refrains from doing. What are your reactions to this?

Look for potential new arrangements and tradeoffs that can enhance both your work life and your colleague's. Make notes of the results of your conversations. Short simple sentences are especially useful in your discussions with each other, particularly ones that begin with a straightforward statement of what you want of the other person. Encourage him or her to express briefly and clearly what he or she wants of you.

7 If you don't feel sufficiently comfortable to follow Step 6 with the actual individual involved, try it with a friend or colleague that you trust by asking that person to react to your items. Beware, though, not to fall into a pattern in which you give and receive advice on what to do. Honest, immediate reactions are usually more useful than advice.

8 After you have completed the above steps, take another look at your original list and see if there are some changes that you now feel prepared to try out. Don't push yourself too hard. Rather, start with some relatively easy ones, get some experience, and then go on to further work and discussions with others.

COMMENT

A way of enhancing this exercise when you feel moderately comfortable with it (you will never feel totally comfortable with it) is to ask others to join you in preparing their lists and inviting them, if they are willing, to work out their wants from you in similar ways. Taking several hours or even half a day away from the office with your own team on just such an exercise and working in an open way with each other can be a very valuable, productive means of improving life and effectiveness in your own organization.

In Section Four of this book, some additional exercises in this area that may prove useful in your work situation are provided.

On Pleasing Yourself

There are a number of ways
Of pleasing yourself
Or trying.
You can meet your standards
If you can
*   but can you?*
You can make everyone happy
Except yourself, of course.

You can climb
*   the Matterhorn*
*   the hierarchy*
*   the body of a lover*
*   over other men*
*   the ladder of abstraction*
*   or even*
*   down into the depths of*
*   your own self pity.*

I think those ways do not always
*   please well*
Tho some I have done
And still do.
There are other ways
Better I think
You can appreciate what you have done
And where you have been
Better still, you can appreciate
What you are doing
*   and where you are*
*   and who you are*

But best of all
You can give yourself permission
*   to be doing what you are doing*
*   to be where you are*
*   to be who you are*
*   to feel as you feel*
*   to be pleased*

Bless you.

Introjection:
Swallowing without Chewing

The best way to change is to become aware of exactly where you are *now*.

THE SOURCE

In the last chapter we talked about "shoulds" and how they affect your and our lives and ways of being in the world. At this point, we want to say a bit more about some of the sources of those "shoulds." To do that, we need to introduce another technical term, "introjection." Introjection starts long before a man or woman becomes a manager; in fact, it starts in earliest childhood. We might call it a kind of swallowing whole of other people's ideas, judgments, and styles. A classic example would be the rules of deportment and behavior that we absorb when we are children.

Kids introject lots of things, especially from parents, teachers, older kids, and even from their sports heros. You can probably remember some time in your life (maybe even yesterday) when you found yourself walking, talking, or otherwise imitating the style of someone you admired—and without being aware of it until someone pointed out the resemblance to you.

Many introjects are harmless and even fun; they last for a while and then get replaced by new ones or just go away. Others, though, are more serious. Psychotherapists continually encounter patients who have introjected large chunks of their parents' moral or value systems in ways that seriously interfere with their ability to lead satisfying lives of their own: the woman, for example, who keeps herself from a warm and full relationship with men because she has introjected her mother's distrust and suspicion of men and their motives; or the man who drives himself to exhaustion and frustration at work because he has introjected his father's ambition.

The point, of course, is not that either the mother's suspicion or the father's ambition are wrong in themselves. The mother may have had good cause to be suspicious for herself and the father to be ambitious for himself, but each lived in a different time and led a different life than their children, and what may have been right for them may not be for their offspring.

PROBLEMS WITH ORGANIZATION INTROJECTS

In later stages of your life, some more-sophisticated translations of these childhood introjects can get passed on to you and are reflected in the typical kinds of assumptions that people who work in organizations take for granted. For example, let's look at one typical introject and its component parts: The Good Manager. A good manager makes quick decisions and must appear decisive and self-assured at all times. He or she is a person who has a continuing interest in the work team and is always trying to get good working conditions for them and see that they are properly rewarded. A good manager should always wear the big company hat rather than be concerned about his or her own department or own future career, and so on.

One of the problems with introjects is that they are never fully assimilated—that is, you haven't truly chewed them up and made them a part of yourself. Rather, since they are somebody else's point of view, swallowed whole, they can be thought of as big undigested lumps that eventually begin to give you a kind of emotional indigestion. So, although we keep insisting to ourselves that we ought to follow these "basic rules," forces within us may be fighting against that. What if your personal decision-making style is slow and deliberate rather than quick? What if there are times when you are *not* sure of yourself? And what if, in actual fact, you are more concerned at the moment with your own career progress than with either your employee's comfort or the company's big picture? Do you just keep lying to yourself?

Introjects may keep you from recognizing your own internal realities about these things and accepting them as decent and legitimate ways of feeling. When this happens, you are probably either going to have to do a lot of artificial rationalizing to support your position, or a lot of self-denying, or both. And herein lies frustration, lack of fulfillment, and a lot of other unhappiness.

A third serious problem with introjects is that when you begin to react against them as a whole, you may find yourself resisting not only the "bad" aspects of the introject, but also the things about it that would be very useful and right for you as an individual. One manager we know had introjected the superaggressive style of his own boss, but, after attending a human-relations training program, came to the conclusion that a gentler, cooperative style was more constructive and "people oriented." On returning to work, he resolved to reject all aggressive behavior (a new introject) and for a while insisted on always orienting himself and his organization toward a collaborative approach, no matter what. Fortunately, as time went by, his good sense helped him to moderate his style to include both collaboration and competitiveness.

At worst, when you start to check your thoughts, feelings, and behavior in advance against swallowed principles (as in the above example), you may begin to cut off your genuine thoughts and feelings to such an extent that eventually you really can't tell how you think or feel. Or, you may begin to commit yourself to how you *should* feel so fully that you will not accept how you *do* feel.

Sometimes the same person may even introject images that are contradictory, making it impossible for the individual to feel fully comfortable or satisfied. For example, existing side by side with the introjected stereotype of the strong, firm manager who staunchly resists all influences and pressure in order to maintain his position may live the stereotype of the manager who is flexible and able to change with the times. But we can't be both flexible and unyielding at the same time, so no matter what action we take, we may be troubled by the feeling that we are violating an important principle of our integrity.

Finally, one can easily see how introjects can prevent us from achieving spontaneous and genuine contacts with other people, almost as though the introjects were screens or walls of alien material blocking a free exchange of ideas and feelings. Over the years these accumulated barriers combine into an elaborate matrix of "acceptable" behavior, which constantly cuts off and discourages the possibility of our finding out and being who we really are. And, to complete the cycle, our own restricted styles are noted by our subordinates and provide models for their behavior too—thus, we help shape the next generation of managers as well.

The "Shoulds" exercise in the preceding chapter can be helpful in identifying some of your introjects (see Step 2) and working with them.

Awareness, Contact, and Withdrawal

The quest for lasting solutions is hopeless. Life is a matter of living.

In talking about Gestalt theory we have used the terms awareness and contact. In this chapter, we are going to take a somewhat closer look at their meanings.

AWARENESS

"Being aware" seems a very simple process, but that may be deceptive. Stop for a moment and answer this question: *What are you aware of right now?*

Our guess is that, for many readers, the response to that question was fairly indefinite: "I don't know what I'm aware of"; or, "I'm not aware of anything in particular"; or a further question to yourself, "I wonder what I *should* be aware of?" For another large fraction of readers, we imagine the answer came out in the form of a thought: "I'm aware that I'm not sure of why they're asking me the question."

As we have said before, our culture, and especially that part of our culture that is centered in organizations, places extraordinary emphasis on thinking—rational, logical, systematic thinking. For many of us, this emphasis has resulted in an almost total reliance on our capacity to intellectualize. When we are confronted by an unfamiliar situation or even a feeling of discomfort within ourselves, our first reaction is most likely to ask ourselves or others, "Why?" But very often the answers we get do not satisfy our discomfort, or they only produce further questions, "Well, why that, or that, or that?"

What may be missing as we search our logical minds for "the answers" are parts of ourselves that are just not available through our thinking processes. To get a full, clear picture of our own needs, wants, and feelings, we must also be in better touch with other aspects of our awareness—that is, our sensory experiences and our emotional experiences.

SENSORY AWARENESS

Human beings are biological organisms with marvelous sensing instruments. We have the capacity to see, hear, smell, touch, taste, and to do each of these with subtle variations and in multiple combinations. Yet, except for certain special times, many of us seldom pay attention—that is, we are seldom aware of the continual flow of the products of these senses. Except when we are eating, attending a concert, playing a sport, or during other activities that by their nature demand the engagement of one or more of our senses, we actually seem to "turn off" our sensory experiences in favor of thinking. For some people the thinking process continues unabated even during obviously sensual events: some individuals think while they eat and hardly taste their food; others think even during sexual relations and hardly experience their emotional or bodily sensations. But, as we have pointed out, to adequately identify, act on, and satisfy our needs, we need to be aware of our whole range of sensations.

With the exception of some physically handicapped persons, all of us were born with both the capacity and the inclination to be aware of what we are experiencing. This was true in our infancy and through at least some portion of our childhood. Therefore, we have *learned* to shut ourselves off. Fortunately, we can learn to turn ourselves on again, too.

At this point, some of you may be thinking, "Well, I have been reading all this stuff about awareness, and it all sounds reasonable enough, but so what? Why should I turn on my awareness? What's wrong with having it turned off? Anyway, I have a hunch that turning myself on that way may make life more hectic."

Our reply: That's probably true, switching yourself from off to on may indeed be more hectic. It will probably also be more fun, more vital, and more interesting as well. You may get to know when you are feeling happy, sad, triumphant, threatened, affectionate, angry, and so on, and what you need to do to take care of yourself and your feelings. And if your awareness leads you to better contact with other people (we will be talking about that soon), it will probably also get you some livelier, deeper, more genuine, and stimulating relationships than you've had in quite a while—maybe than you've ever had before (on and off the job).

EMOTIONAL AWARENESS

The second aspect of awareness that many of us seem to have turned off is our sensitivity to our own emotions. Typically, in the early stages of our working with managers, when we ask, "What are you *feeling* right now?", the manager searches his or her *thoughts* for an answer. For instance, he or she may say, "I feel that is a hard question," or, "I feel that I ought to be able to answer your questions better," etc. Or the manager may reply, "I don't feel anything." The fact is, though, that *all* of us are always feeling something—we just aren't aware of it. We have lost touch with our feelings, sacrificed them in favor of our thoughts.

Stop again for a moment and answer this question: *What are you feeling right now?*

How difficult was it for you to get in touch with what you were feeling? Was it a relatively unfamiliar experience for you to get in touch with feeling interested, bored, anxious, antagonistic, satisfied, etc.? How tuned in are you to your physical sensations—for example, hunched shoulders tightness in your stomach muscles, wandering attention? Are your legs tight or relaxed? Is your breathing restricted or free flowing?

The turning off of awareness may be a problem for the organization as well as for the individual. If you are turned off, you may not be able to express either affection or irritation, appreciation or a sense of urgency. The turned-off manager's problem can affect others, for if the manager is unaware of irritation with his or her subordinate (or unwilling to deal with it), he or she does not finish with it. So the irritation continues as unfinished business and the manager may find less-direct ways of expressing this resentment, perhaps by treating the subordinate coolly, by withholding attention, by subtle snubs, or, at a more substantive level, by developing rationalizations for denying the subordinate a salary increase or a positive recommendation for promotion. Even if the negative expression is at the most-subtle level, it will probably have its effect on the subordinate who, in turn, will react first with confusion and subsequently with his or her own style of resistance or resentment. And so the circular process continues to build up and continues to create a distance between the two people.

CONTACT

Good contact requires awareness. Although the concept of contact is difficult to describe, the experience itself is remarkably clear when you are engaged in it. Contact is applicable to the individual, to relationships between people, and to other aspects of life that involve being in touch with people, ideas, or things that can be experienced with the senses.

Most commonly when we talk about contact, we are talking about contact between people. In brief, when two people are in contact, they are really seeing, hearing, and experiencing each other and what is going on *right here, right now.* When you are in good contact with another person, there are minimum interferences with your sensing processes.

When you are not in good contact, your senses are being interfered with—you are worrying, thinking of something other than what's going on here and now, making assumptions in your mind about what the effects of your words will be on the other person, and so on. When your mind is pre-occupied, of course, it is unlikely that you are really able to use your eyes and ears, to experience what is really happening in your immediate situation.

Good contactful conversation is usually characterized by a personal quality—the people conversing are involved with one another and the conversation contains excitement, presentness, and liveliness. Signs of non-contact or poor contact include boredom, impersonal discussion, a droning voice, talking about others, the distant past, or the far future, etc.

Most of us avoid real contact with one another and with ourselves as well in various ways. Two examples that are very prevalent in manager groups especially are: (1) intellectual discussions, and (2) self-neutralization.

INTELLECTUAL DISCUSSIONS

As we noted earlier, one way of avoiding contact is to abstract or generalize in an intellectual discussion, when what really needs to be dealt with is a specific point or the relationship between the people involved. Good contact most often leads to action; poor contact frequently leads to inaction or avoidance.

Very often this intellectual-discussion kind of avoidance is accompanied by physical signs as well. People talk *at* one another—that is, they deliver lectures or make speeches rather than talk to one another. Frequently, too, they do not look at one another when they speak, but focus on the middle of the room, the carpet, or the ceiling. For example, the superintendent of manufacturing says, "One of the problems with the engineering approach of this company is that our designs tend to be too sophisticated to be producible." As he speaks, he glances at the rug. What he really means is, "Doris [the manager of engineering sitting to his left], we are having a helluva time manufacturing unit number 9. I would appreciate it if you would get one of your engineers to redesign the fourth connector."

The superintendent of manufacturing may be avoiding contact for a number of reasons. For instance, he may not be entirely sure of his position and therefore fearful of a counterattack by the engineering manager; or, he may imagine that if he really made his request directly, the manager of engineering would be offended and react negatively. What the superintendent probably doesn't realize is that his message of dissatisfaction comes through anyway, and the indirectness of his complaint makes it unlikely that any corrective action will be taken. Further, the indirectness makes it even more difficult for the engineering manager to respond, and she will probably adopt a similar indirect or avoidant style in dealing with the manufacturing superintendent. If this goes on long enough, the two of them may build up an undercover feud that will be quite dysfunctional and unsatisfactory both to themselves and the organization. We have known feuds of this kind that have existed for literally years among members of an organization, never being explicitly dealt with.

SELF-NEUTRALIZATION

A second way in which contact is frequently avoided between people is through what might be called self-neutralization. Again, the reason for this self-neutralization may be concern about hurting other people's feelings or making an enemy; or it may be the result of an individual's desire to be "fair" and "accurate." In these cases of self-neutralization, the speaker may start out to make a statement about another person or situation, but then wash out the impact of that statement by producing exceptions to it, or providing mitigating circumstances or reasonable explanations. For example, the general manager says to her marketing director, "Bill, I'm not sure that our percentage of the market, especially in the new customer area, is as good as it might be. Now, of course, I realize you've had staffing problems, and general business conditions haven't been too good, but still, maybe we should have concentrated more in our West Coast regions, even though we did that some last year."

On the face of it, the general manager's statement seems quite reasonable and she appears to be a very understanding woman. The problem for the marketing director, however, is that it is very difficult for him to determine to what extent the general manager is really concerned and what her real message is. The actual complaint, if there is one, is never quite brought out and so cannot be dealt with. If, indeed, the general manager is really ambivalent and merely musing out loud, then she is not asking for a response or for follow-up action (and she is not likely to get it). If, however, she is trying to be delicate about voicing a real dissatisfaction, her message is not clear.

Failure to achieve real contact occurs frequently between managers and subordinates, especially when a manager softens the blow of his or her criticism of a subordinate's performance by "understanding the circumstances," or, on the other hand, by surrounding congratulations or praise of a subordinate's performance with careful qualifications. In an effort to be considerate and fair, or objective and accurate, managers sometimes dilute their messages to subordinates to such an extent that the subordinate walks away from the appraisal discussion without really knowing whether the boss believes he or she has done well or poorly

WITHDRAWAL

To understand and appreciate good contact, we also have to understand and appreciate the other side of the coin: good, complete withdrawal. It is unlikely that any one of us could tolerate being constantly in contact. For one thing, contact is frequently an exciting, involving experience and it calls for a good deal of energy. For another thing, good contact is also self-limiting —that is, good contact produces action and the ability to complete the business that needs to be completed. With the completion of that business comes a natural diminishing of the need for contact. And, as the need for contact and involvement diminish, either the need for withdrawal and pause increase or attention shifts to another focus.

As exciting and satisfying as good contact can be, it is important to realize that trying to cling or hold on to these feelings after they have naturally run their course is not useful. We have found in conducting a number of workshops that one of the temptations for many of the participants who have newly discovered the satisfaction and excitement of good contact is for them to try to hold on past the point of saturation and completion. To do so may actually bring a positive and exciting experience to a dull and sour ending. It is far better to recognize when your contact business is done and at that time to withdraw fully.

Good withdrawal involves clearly finishing your business with the other person and having that person finish his or her business with you, and subsequently either changing your attention to an entirely different focus or allowing yourself to rest without focusing your thoughts on anything in particular. Some useful guidelines for contact and withdrawal follow.

Self Checklist
for Contact

1 Am I talking about (e.g., in abstractions or generalizations) rather than dealing with (e.g., asking for what I want, being personal)?

2 Am I lecturing to the other person about what *ought* to be rather than dealing with him or her on what *is*?

3 Am I saying, "I can't," when what I really mean is, "I won't?"

4 Am I asking a rhetorical question, pretending that I am looking for information, when what I really want to do is to make a statement?

5 Am I saying "you, we, one, etc.," when I mean "I"?

6 Am I talking about the past when the issue is in the present?

7 Am I saying where I stand on an issue?

8 Am I saying "No" when I mean "No," or am I avoiding?

9 Do I stop when I am finished talking or do I go on and on with examples or anecdotes?

10 Am I "broadcasting" into the air, or at the rug, or to the group in general, rather than talking directly to the person(s) that I want to reach?

11 Do I send mixed messages (e.g., express anger with a smile on my face)?

12 Am I really seeing and hearing what's going on or is my mind thinking about future or past, or imagining what someone else is thinking?

Awareness

SETTING

It is difficult to talk about awareness in conceptual or theoretical terms, for awareness, at least the way we have emphasized it in this book, is almost the antithesis of conceptualization and theorizing. We talk about "being aware of what is going on" and that seems so obvious. It is obvious, and that is probably why it is so frequently ignored and neglected. Yet with development, there is potentially tremendous power in your own *obvious awareness*.

There are awarenesses in the areas of ideas, emotions, and senses. Most of you will have no trouble at all identifying ideas you are aware of—all we have to do is name the subject and you will have a catalog of your latest thinking immediately at hand. For example, what are your ideas about politics, about inflation, about managing?

In the area of emotions, though, it gets a little tougher—some of you would probably be lost entirely. Earlier we pointed out some ways in which people lose touch with how they feel about things and other people. Some of us have desensitized ourselves to even hearing or seeing any aspect of an event that would trigger a significant emotional response within us. You could call some people SOB's and they either literally won't hear you, or if they do, they will automatically decide you must be kidding, whether or not you are. Other people may let the message in, but immediately turn it into a piece of dead "data." Rather than having an emotional reaction, they convert the input into an intellectual form they can handle without involvement. Still others may both hear the message and feel its sting or caress, but they do not allow themselves to react overtly either by acknowledging or by taking action.* For many managers and other organization dwellers (as opposed to artists, for example), another desensitized area is the area of the physical senses. Just simply seeing, hearing, touching, smelling, and tasting are often blocked, usually by the process of too much intellectualization.

We have found in many training workshops that when we ask managers to focus not on what they are thinking but rather to report on what they are aware of (what they are experiencing right now), at first, most hardly know what we are talking about. Fortunately, with practice, they are able to reawaken the sensing equipment that has been

---

* Messages may, of course, be warm as well as negative, though for some people loving emotions are even more difficult to deal with than aggressive ones.

with them since birth. And when they do, the excitement, new perspectives, fresh approaches to old problems, and sheer enjoyment they experience make our work seem more worthwhile.

Increasing awareness seems to be a strong new focus in the human-potential movement and several recent books contain approaches and exercises for bringing about awareness improvement. The exercises outlined below are some basic, easy ones that you could try as a "beginner," just to see how it goes.

PROCESS

1   This exercise can be done with two, three, or four people. We think it's a good idea to do it the first time with some people that you know fairly well (husband, wife, friends) then try it with others. Start by sitting facing each other. Get into a comfortable position, either in a chair or sitting on the floor with adequate back support. Begin by just looking. After a moment or two of settling in, report to each other, in sequence, exactly what you are aware of at the given moment you're speaking. Each person begins his or her statement of awareness with "Right now I am aware of . . ." and reports whatever comes out. It is important that you report your awareness as it happens, rather than rehearsing an answer. For example:

Mr. A: "Right now I am aware of your red tie."

Ms. B: "Right now I am aware of my back against the chair."

Mr. C: "Right now I am aware of thinking." (When you find yourself thinking about something, it's not necessary or even desirable to report the subject matter, merely report that you are thinking, then let your thinking go and see what happens next.)

Mr. A: "Right now I am aware of feeling calmer."

Ms. B: "Right now I am aware of the sun shining through the window."

2   Don't try to build rational conversations or send messages to one another. In fact, if your interchange begins to assume an orderly pattern, it is likely that you have slipped into the usual "idea communication" pattern and are not really tuned into your immediate awareness. Remember, let it flow from within you. As the Buddhists say, "Don't just do something, stand there!" Concentrate on your senses: what you see, hear, feel, etc. If you begin to find you are bored, uncomfortable, or confused, just report that as well, and wait it out. Those things, too, will pass and you may be pleasantly surprised at what's on the other side.

3   After about 15 minutes, the participants can pause and, in a brief discussion, each can help the others emphasize where and how each tends to focus most of his or her attention—that is, is the person usually thinking, feeling, or sensing? Is he or

she generally focused on his or her own processes or imagining what's going on with someone else? Is his or her focus mostly internal or external? Those who have been predominantly in one particular mode, or set of modes, might try in the next round to do more focusing in the area that they have up to now mostly neglected. Again, the idea is not to strain to change, but to *allow* an easy shift of attention to occur.

4   After 15 minutes or so, if there are enough people involved, you may reconstitute the groups and try another round. We have used a similar exercise in relatively large groups, and have provided opportunities for people to change groups two or three times. This has usually been quite useful.

5   End the awareness exercise and allow all participants, either in subgroups or as a total group, to discuss their experience *briefly*. If you talk about how wonderful your experience with awareness was for too long, and with too many reasons, you are likely to dilute its impact.

COMMENT

What emerges, at least in the early stages of the exercise, will probably not be rational or logical, for we are not involved in a usual way of communicating. What frequently does happen after a while, though, and all on its own, is that people begin to communicate with one another in a totally nonintentional, unexpected manner that sometimes has deep significance for them. In watching this exercise in workshops, we have occasionally seen a group of three or four people with smiles or even a tear or two in their eyes who report experiencing strong feelings of calm, peace, and affection for one another, though they are not exactly clear about what has caused the feeling.

In attempting to use this approach, either for yourself or with a management group, don't expect too early or easy breakthroughs; most of us in organizations have a hard time allowing ourselves to be unintentional. Usually, it is necessary to remind people a number of times of the requirements of the exercise, and to allow them to try the process several times, perhaps in different subgroups, before they really begin to get the message.

Self-Boundaries
and Grounding

First you need to learn that you are in charge of what you
do; then you can discover that you do what you do because
you must.

One more idea from Gestalt theory that is worth looking at is the boundary
of the self. In a very literal way, each of us has a real boundary—our skin.
In a physical sense (disregarding for now the spiritual and metaphysical),
each of us is bounded by our skin; we physically end where our skin ends.
I am, or at least potentially can be, the world's greatest expert on *me*. You
are, or can be, the greatest expert on *you*. Neither of us really knows what
goes on inside the other's skin. We can imagine it, we can guess at it, but
we can't really know. Our boundaries are our limits. Yet, they are not
merely dead walls that surround and imprison us; rather, they are also our
sensing mechanisms. Our sense of touch is our way of feeling what is outside ourselves, our eyes are our way of seeing what is outside ourselves, our
ears are our way of hearing what is outside ourselves, and so on. Thus, our
boundaries are not only our limits, they are also our means for coming in
contact with other people and things that are not within ourselves.

CLEAR BOUNDARIES

A good sense of your own boundary and what is going on within that
boundary can be tremendously useful in helping you to know who you
are and where you are. People who have this good sense of their boundaries
and of themselves are often good people to be with: they tend to be comfortable with themselves, easy to communicate with, clear and direct in
their communication to others, and sure of themselves. (This last quality
may at times seem somewhat irritating to others who are less sure of
themselves).

Persons who are clear about their boundaries are most likely to know
that they themselves are the best experts on what is good for them and

what isn't. This does not mean they won't listen to others' opinions and ideas; in fact, they will probably be less defensive or "paranoid," and probably filter or distort incoming information less than most. Still, such individuals are confident that ultimately no one can influence their ideas or personality beyond the degree that they wish to accept that influence. They may open themselves to considering any input, for ultimately they decide which to accept and which to reject—they are in charge of themselves. Individuals with a good sense of their own boundaries can listen to the words of people with large reputations and people with small reputations, to people who speak loudly and people who speak softly, but neither reputation nor volume determines what they will believe. Their tests are conducted within themselves.

UNCLEAR BOUNDARIES

One of the ways in which many of us become confused and disturbed is by being unclear about our boundaries—where we stop and others begin. Out of this lack of clarity some such feelings as: *others* influence me too much; *others* threaten me; *others* put me down; etc.

A consequence of some recent trends in human-relations training that emphasize group processes and the building of group supportiveness is that many people have blurred their individual boundaries. So much concern has been given to the effect that one group member may have on another that many people seem to be continually worried about the effects of their words and actions on others in the group, as well as the effects of others' words on them. As we discussed earlier, there is a kind of game played in which people talk about the "right" things to do and say, i.e., things that will encourage other people's development; and the "wrong" things to say or do, i.e., things that may be damaging to others. In the pursuit of this game, many find themselves in a continual mind-screening process to determine in advance whether what they are considering saying will be OK or inappropriate.

As we have frequently mentioned, Authentic Management emphasizes the development of individual supports within each person rather than group supports. We strongly encourage each person to become increasingly aware of and confident in his or her own boundaries. In a practical sense this means that, when you talk to others, recognize that you have no way of really knowing what goes on within their minds, nor do you know what their feelings are. You may detect some signs of those feelings in the expressions on their faces or the posture of their bodies, but even then you can only interpret, guess, or imagine what these expressions or postures meant to them. Therefore, to really find out you must ask.

BEING GROUNDED

Being well grounded is the result of having a clear sense of your own boundary, a clear sense of what is going on inside, and a feeling of calm readiness for what is to come. It is knowing where you are: feeling solid, confident, and alert. A karate expert demonstrates a high degree of grounding. He stands with his feet firmly planted on the ground, his body balanced and steady. His mind is calm, clear, and focused on *here* and *now*. These same principles are highly applicable in organization situations too. When a manager is well grounded, for instance, he or she is relaxed, at ease, and yet prepared, with a mind focused on one thing at a time and a minimum of interfering thoughts. Significantly, good grounding involves physical as well as mental stability, for managers as well as for athletes. Well grounded, the manager can listen without feeling threatened, without imagining that someone is trying to manipulate or "do something" to him or her, and without interpreting or predicting hidden meanings in advance. If there is subterfuge or potential danger, the manager feels capable of dealing with it when the need arises. He or she is *in touch* with what is going on both inside and outside himself or herself. "In touch" is a valuable clue for good grounding. As we detail further in the exercise that follows, if you are able literally to feel yourself—physically feel your feet on the floor, your buttocks against the seat of the chair, and your spine against its back—you are most likely to improve your grounding.

LOSS OF GROUNDING

All of us lose our grounding at times during our interactions with others, but some of us are ungrounded almost all of the time. A number of signs can indicate loss of grounding: you do not know your own position; you do not know what you want or sometimes even that you do want something; your attention is focused almost exclusively on the other person or persons with whom you are engaged, and mostly you are guessing or imagining what it is they are really after. You may feel angry or anxious, or may try to please and/or try to avoid displeasing, often without really knowing what the ground rules for pleasing or displeasing are. Generally, you feel unsure, disturbed, or anxious, but sometimes you don't even realize *that* until a while later.

The ungrounded person is frequently involved in two different processes at once. First is the process of overt communications, as he participates in a back-and-forth conversation. At the same time, however, a lot is happening inside the person's head. As he or she talks or listens, the imagination is at work as well. Little thoughts, ideas and theories dash back and forth; the particular thoughts vary, of course, but they generally concern the kinds of things we mentioned above. And, since the individual is trying to do two different things at once, he or she is usually unable to do either one very well. Contact is impossible, because when attention is focused inward, the person literally does not hear much of what is being said, and what he or she partially hears is often misconstrued. Nor does he or she see the other person clearly.

In addition to this unsettled emotional and psychological state, the ungrounded person is unsettled physically: breathing is often constricted, the body is fidgety or tensed, and equilibrium is somewhat off-balance. You can probably recall physical signs like these in yourself and in others, and you may remember the disturbing and distracting influence they can have.

Self-Boundaries

SETTING

Being really in touch with your own self-boundaries is a subtle, but vitally important matter. Just how important it is can be related to the number of times you find yourself in situations similar to any of the following: talking extensively with others around a conference table, without quite knowing what's going on; being called on to make a presentation among a group of higher-echelon people and finding your mouth dry and your hands shaking with nervousness; or sitting in the office of a customer or high-level executive and searching your mind so desperately to figure out what he wants and what you should do next that you can hardly hear what he is saying.

All of us have been in situations like these and others that are at least as uncomfortable. We find ourselves unsure, without self-confidence, feeling inadequate, and continually searching for what to say or do next. Our boundaries are blurred and we have lost our grounding; in losing touch with the solid core of ourselves, we feel desperate and afraid.

Even in other less-pressure-laden situations, many of us are out of touch with ourselves. We have a question, or a problem, or an issue of our own, and yet we look everywhere else except to ourselves to find out what is right for me or wrong for me, good for me or bad for me. In our relations with other people, in both business and personal contexts, our questions are: What does *he* want of me? What does *she* expect? What are *they* thinking? What would *they* like to hear? And if in our engagements with others they, too, have blurred their boundaries, then they, too, are searching for what to say and do by asking themselves similar questions.

When this happens, there is no solidity of contact, nor is there much likelihood that any of those involved will emerge from the situation well satisfied. We have not had a genuine exchange between human beings who are willing to state where they are and what they want. We have not reviewed each other's positions and desires to see where they are compatible and where they are not, and we have not made solid arrangements with one another as needed. Rather, the outcomes of these blurred encounters are also blurred; they are typically vague, weak, and unlikely to engender much commitment from any of the parties involved.

Later in this book, we outline a fairly extensive set of steps for improving grounding and strengthening self-boundaries. For now, let's look at a few basic ways to check your boundary strength, and some of the simplest ways for enhancing it.

PROCESS

1   Through practice, become more quickly aware of when you have lost touch with
your boundaries. When you find yourself in situations such as those described
above, take a moment, as soon as possible, to recognize and acknowledge what
is happening. At first, the best thing you can do is just to acknowledge it: "I am
losing my boundaries."

2   Get in touch with your *physical* self! Especially, feel your feet on the floor, and
if you are seated, feel your buttocks on the chair and the spine against the back
of the chair. If you are slouching in the chair, sit up straight, though not stiffly.
Let your shoulders relax. When you have done that and really feel yourself, take
a moment and say to yourself subvocally, *"Here I am,"* and then repeat it to
yourself until you experience not only your physical body but the spirit of your
core self as well. Watch and wait and see if things begin to change for you.
Don't force it, just let it happen.

Usually, it takes a while and some amount of practice before these approaches
and those we will be talking about below become entirely effective, so give
yourself some time and allow yourself some practice.

On occasions when it is appropriate, especially when you have some time (for
instance, before an important meeting in which you imagine that you are likely
to be nervous and possibly to lose your grounding), get in touch with your own
anxiety. First, acknowledge your nervousness. Literally, get a feel of it: *Where*
do you experience your nervousness physically—in your chest, in your arms,
where? When you have located the physical feeling, stay with it, don't try to
change it or make it go away. Merely stay with it until it changes by itself.

One further thing you can try is to give your nervousness a voice. Focus your
awareness on the physical location of the nervous feeling and ask it what it has
to say to you. Then, let it speak to you through your voice. If you can, let it speak
out loud so that you can hear the words. Pay close attention to them.

3   Finally, when you find yourself really scared, ask yourself the question: "What is
the worst thing that might happen to me in this situation?" Then answer the
question. Do it either out loud or write it down on a piece of paper. When you
write, write without thinking or censoring, just see how it comes out and write as
as far as your pen or pencil carries you. Another good question to ask yourself
is, "What do I want *for me* in this situation?" Handle that one the same way as
the previous question.

4   For those who want to go a bit further and deeper, you can also try the following:
When someone says something "threatening" or "critical" to you, *listen*—let it
come in (e.g., "You are careless"). If it rings true, merely feel all aspects of it
you can. What are the concomitants of feeling careless—both in your mind and
body? No need to judge yourself, just notice.

If it is not true (you should know within a second or two), let it go. No need to defend or search yourself to see if it's true at a deeper level. Only what's readily accessible is relevant now.

If you have a strong "fight" or "despair" or other emotional reaction, experience it fully and at the same time let a small part of you stand to the side and watch you emoting—again, without judging. The truth or falsity of the accusation is irrelevant for now. Focus on the feeling.

As with many of the exercises in this book, it can be helpful to explore some of your discoveries about yourself with friends or with co-workers who are also interested in developing themselves.

COMMENT

There is only one thing better than knowing your own boundaries and being well grounded, and that is to work and interact with others who are similarly well boundaried and grounded. If, through the above suggestions and other approaches outlined in this book, you are able to help others in your work group (or family, for that matter) to achieve this state, you will be fortunate indeed. We have found repeatedly that it is a great pleasure to be in a group where relationships are based on strength and clarity rather than on dependency and game playing. Potentially, all of us can help each other grow and develop toward a freer and more vital life. To accomplish this, our agreement with each other needs to be not a collusion to sympathize with each other's artificialities and games, but rather a tacit agreement to deal with one another straightforwardly and with respect, though at times that may involve some discomfort.

Mirrors

Ed said
When humans found the mirror
They began to lose their souls
The point of course is that
They began to concern themselves
With their images rather than
Their selves

Other people's eyes are mirrors
But the most distorting kind
For if you look to them you
    can only see
Reflections of your reflections
Your warpings of their warpings

What then instead?

Do not look at yourself
    (except perhaps with amusement)
Feel yourself instead
As we did before mirrors
When we were young
And did not feel the need to please
But only to be
Experience how it is to be
Now

Where are your passions and desires?
Your knots and pains and anxious
    unattended muscles?
Where are your laughter and your tears
    that are deeper than your throat?
Where is what you want?
What you love and hate?
How do you reach and push away?
How do you waste your strength
    in self-holding constriction?
Keeping yourself against reaching
    and pushing away?

Be
And you will be involved in life
So involved in life
That you will afford no time
    or inclination
For staring with bulging
    or squinting eyes
At mirrors

Confluence
and Differentiation

Most of the time (maybe all of the time) everybody does exactly what he or she wants to do.

Some readers will be familiar with the term confluence in its geographical context: the confluence of two rivers is the point at which they come together from different directions and join in a single undifferentiated flow. Confluence, as a concept, is also applicable to relationships between people. Just as streams may join, intermingle, and lose their individual identities, so also may relationships among people.

Confluence may be, and often is, a very attractive and pleasing state for us. It represents harmony, peacefulness, and a sense of unity, qualities of life that most of us value. But that is only part of the picture. Confluence is only one side of the ebb and flow, the rising and falling of human affairs. On the other side there is differentiation, separateness, and turbulence, and these, too, are essential parts of experience in a full life.

Thus, our lives at best have a rhythm that moves us from times of stability to times of turbulence, from times of unity to times of separateness. When we get locked into one or the other state and try to maintain it permanently, problems arise.

CONFLUENT RELATIONSHIPS

Long-standing relationships between good friends or marriage partners provide numerous illustrations of overextended confluence. For example, consider the case of couples who have been married for a very long time, who apparently never argue or even disagree, and who seem to like all the same movies, books, food, friends, etc. The trouble in such relationships is that they often lose a good deal of the excitement they once had, and that may mean a loss of interest as well. The partners begin to take each other for granted sometimes to such an extent that they are hardly aware of the other's presence.

These relationships over time may provide stability, peacefulness, and predictability. These are comfortable qualities, but if those involved come to prize this comfort so highly that they strive to maintain it at all costs, they frequently (and often unconsciously) begin to withhold from each other all "negative" feelings for fear that their expression of those feelings might endanger the peacefulness of the relationship. When this happens, they may eventually find that their relationship has fallen into a rut and, in fact, that they have really lost both their individual personalities and their capacity for real contact with one another.

In some cases this state continues with a gradually increasing sense of dullness and dissatisfaction ("Is this all there is to life?"), until suddenly a crisis occurs—perhaps "another woman" or "another man." (Some marriage counselors see the other-woman/other-man syndrome as an unconscious attempt to heat up a cooling relationship—a sort of last-ditch effort to save the marriage.)

In many "smoothly run" organizations we have seen, confluence has become a prevailing condition. Having once reached a friendly and comfortable state, members of the management group become reluctant to be seen as troublemakers, boat rockers, or disturbers of the peace, and so they keep their negative or possibly disruptive ideas to themselves. As with individual relationships, however, this condition results in a withholding of potentially valuable feelings and ideas, and can produce a reluctant and safety-oriented organization in which little stimulation, creativity, or innovation occurs.

DIFFERENTIATION: BREAKING CONFLUENCE

Confluence needs to be broken intermittently by differentiation. We need to find ways to reassert our individuality for our own sakes, and for the organization's sake as well. In our view, well-run organizations do not always operate smoothly; bumpiness, difficulty, and conflict are also needed to increase organizational vitality and to teach members to work together in more than a single mode or tone. People need to be able to test themselves and each other. If an organization's members are unwilling to be negative, to buck the trend, and to take chances with one another, both the people and the organization will be limited and dulled.

What is needed to encourage and maintain a dynamic, creative, exciting organization is the recognition by members that cycles of peacefulness and turbulence, ups and downs, are natural and healthful. Conflict is not always something bad to be gotten rid of—it can be an exciting and energizing force that, if fully actualized and completed, may produce closer, more meaningful relationships within the organization as well as a more productive operating mode.

When we work with organizations as consultants we frequently say that our first step in the process of working with the management team is to help its members to learn to talk *with* each other rather than *at* each other. Our second objective is to help people to learn to fight with one another. What we are *not* saying, of course, is that everyone in the organization really needs to know the words "confluence" and "differentiation," but rather that people need to understand that conflict is not always an indication of a breakdown in communications, or an indication of dysfunctional rivalry or jealousies, or some other failure of the system to perform smoothly and efficiently.

And so you might respond, "Are these people kidding? Are they advocating people going around the plant punching each other?" No, we're not talking about people punching people (although we have observed some instances where a single punch or even a couple might have been considerably more merciful than the prolonged and bitter feuds that were carried on). In fact, though, conflict within organizations and among most people is mostly verbal, and sometimes it's even less overt than that— just a few vague expressions of disdain and time spent ignoring each other. The latter is probably the worst form of conflict—nonconflict— or rather avoidance.

Confluence

SETTING

The following exercise can be effective in a number of situations. It can be used among the members of a management group that has a long history of "getting along well," except that the members don't engage much in real debates about tough problems. It can also be used in a group that does have good working relationships and wants to do something to improve them still further. It can be used, too, between boss and subordinate, husband and wife, parent and child, and, in fact, just about any time a close relationship is important to two or more people.

As you will also note under number 3 below, the use of a third-party consultant is optional. The third party (not necessarily a professional consultant), can be quite helpful when he or she is tuned in. Sometimes someone who has a good feel for the two people involved and perhaps has read this book or been personally involved in some personal-development work can be very useful. Just make sure you don't enlist the help of someone who wants to solve *your* problems with *his* or *her* advice.

PROCESS

1   The exercise, or a variation of it, can be conducted in a group setting, with the group members pairing up in separated subgroups, or it can be conducted with just a single pair. If in a group setting, have each individual within the group identify someone with whom he or she has a relatively good relationship. (In the pair relationship, that's already done.)

2   Have each person separately make some notes of four or five things he or she likes about the relationship with the other person, and also four or five things not liked about the relationship—particularly situations or characteristics of the other person that "make me feel uncomfortable" or otherwise negative. Usually about ten or fifteen minutes is enough time for this part.

3   Have each person identify how he or she avoids talking to the other person about these conditions. Identify the predicted difficulties and risks in sharing these perceptions, and be as specific as possible. As we will emphasize later in the book, move down the abstraction ladder from the generalities to the specifics. For example, if the prediction is, "Joe would be upset if I told him what I thought,"

ask further, "And then what would happen?" Continue to ask, "And then what would happen?" of each response until the person has played out his or her imaginings fully, or until the point where they are no longer a hindrance. Both in this step and later the third party can be most useful in helping people get in touch with their vague "catastrophic" expectations versus the more likely and practical probabilities. The point here, however, is certainly *not* to try to change anyone's mind so that he or she is influenced to do more sharing than feels right. The right process in the Authentic-Management context is to help people get in touch with where they are now, and then to let this getting in touch have its own effect. That means that the person may decide to go further, or he or she may not. The choice is completely up to the individual.

4   After these steps have been completed separately, have the individuals get together in their pairs and alternately discuss their likes and dislikes, one at a time. It should be emphasized again that the written lists are not to be shared. Rather, people are given the opportunity to read or discuss the items on their list, one by one, going only as far as they want to.

From these discussions can come some good ideas for improvements in working relationships. Other exercises in this book may help to sharpen some of these new possibilities.

COMMENT

Actually, the above exercise is not likely to bring about any very heavy conflict, except in an organization of real tigers (in which case you hardly need the exercise at all). What it will do is rock the boat a little and perhaps give a number of people their first experience with the fact that you can discuss both positive and negative impressions with another person without (a) either of you dissolving in total embarrassment, or (b) the two of you becoming so upset or angry that you never want to speak to each other again.

In many organizations, especially the highly polished, large ones, overt conflict is difficult to find. People never seem to really get mad at one another, never give in to the impulse to shout from time to time. In other organizations, there's a lot of apparent conflict and a number of people may do quite a bit of shouting. But here, much of the time, it's not on-target shouting. Rather, it's some kind of competitive bull-elk dance in which the real issues, if there are any real issues, don't actually get addressed. We're not necessarily against competitive bull-elk dances, especially if those involved and those observing have a fairly good idea of what's going on. Frequently, however, more important things need to be argued about, and probably more people ought to be involved in the arguing.

As we said earlier, and as is illustrated in the "Case of the Unhappy Giant" on page 102, tremendous energy and revitalization potential are available in some types of turbulence. What we all need is more confidence (and that comes from practice) that good positive things are waiting on the other side of the battle, as long as one is willing to see the conflict through. If we can learn to fight well in organizations, we can probably learn both to like each other better and certainly to fear each other less.

Polarization:
Topdog – Underdog

The harder you push yourself, the harder yourself is likely
to push back. And that can make you damn tired.

In the previous chapter we looked at confluence and differentiation as two
extremes or polarities that exist in relationships between people. In this
chapter, we will be looking at a fairly typical polarity that exists not only
in interactions between people, but also within individuals—the topdog-
underdog conflict. The topdog-underdog is a classic polarity in Gestalt
therapy, and one that is especially relevant to managers. At this time, we
examine the topdog-underdog as a polarity that exists within the self,
i.e., within the individual manager; later in the book, we will look at this
polarity as it exists between managers and between management groups.

Each of us has within us a topdog and an underdog. Topdog is that
part of ourselves that tells us what is "right" and appropriate for our
behavior, and even for our thoughts. Most topdog positions are derived
from "shouldisms" that we have learned from parents, bosses, and other
authority figures in our lives. It is the little voice inside us that says you
should take that work home with you on the weekend so you can have
the report ready by Monday; or it's wrong for you to neglect holding that
counseling session with Fred, your subordinate; or you ought to be doing
a better job of budgeting than you are doing now, etc. The topdog can be
called conscience or drive or something similar, and its thrust can be and
has been for most of us very useful in our achievement orientation. Problems arise, though, when the topdog's demands are met by the resistance
of the underdog. The underdog is the resistant part of ourselves. He uses
his "weakness" as a subtle yet powerful counterforce to the topdog's
driving force. The underdog may resist in a number of ways. He may say
to the topdog's demands: "I want to but I am not able"; or, "I'd like to
and I'll do it tomorrow" (although of course he doesn't do it tomorrow

either); or, "I would if I could but I can't"; or, "Don't you know how busy I am?" or, "But, if I do that this will happen"; and so on.

Many of the unresolved, nagging issues that a manager experiences represent the battle between his or her topdog and underdog. The signs are indecision, confusion, and frustration: "Should I or shouldn't I?" "I should do this but I want to do that"; "On the one hand this, but on the other hand that."

THE COSTS

Perls has pointed out that in the contest between the topdog and the underdog, the underdog almost invariably wins, especially in the long run. But the winning or losing itself is not as important as the energy, frustration, and guilt feelings that so frequently accompany this internal battle of ambivalence. What is most troubling is not that you go out fishing on the weekend rather than finishing the report, but rather that when you do go out fishing you spend half your time feeling guilty about not being at home working on the report. Or, if you do wind up having a counseling session with Fred—because you think you *ought* to—you enter into it without the energy, enthusiasm, and interest that would make the session useful to both of you.

Another aspect of the problem of unresolved polarities is that the energy expended in the topdog-underdog internal battle is wasted energy. When we focus our attention and energy on the processes of the battle, we are not able to focus our attention and energy on the possibilities of new and creative thoughts or behaviors. For example, a manager may have within him a topdog who tells him, "You ought to inform Frank that he is not performing satisfactorily and not meeting your expectations," and, at the same time, an underdog who says, "Frank may be easily hurt by criticism, and you know that you ought not hurt other people's feelings." Such a manager may spend months or even years fretting about his situation with his subordinate, sometimes more inclined to let it go and other times more inclined to confront Frank. But, in this unresolved contest, there is seldom the energy or attention required to really address the problem of Frank in a new way. It would be far better if the manager either decided to have his confrontation with Frank or accepted that he was *not* going to deal with Frank, thereby freeing his energies for other matters. Of course, the irony here is that at some level of awareness Frank must already have an idea that his performance is not satisfactory to his manager, or at least that "something is wrong." Yet in the collusion of silence between them this matter does not get addressed, never gets concluded, and therefore drains important energy from both people.

WHAT TO DO

What then do we do about these polarities within us? As in the therapy process, the most important thrusts are toward clarity and completion. What typically happens in the topdog-underdog encounter is that the battle rages on silently inside a manager's head. The sides are not clearly drawn and the arguments for each side are not fully detailed and exhausted. What is needed instead is to delineate as clearly and completely as we can what the topdog part of ourselves is saying to us, and what the underdog part of us is responding. We need to be as thorough and as honest with ourselves as possible. We need to tap into our own spontaneity and impulse and allow ourselves to hear what is going on within us, even if it initially seems silly or irrelevant or not "responsible and adult."

At best, when we allow ourselves to freely explore the polarities—the extremes of our positions—we may achieve *integration*. Since this is not a book on Gestalt therapy, we will not deal with integration in as full a way as we might. For our purposes, it is sufficient to say that integration is not a compromise position, "somewhere between the extremes," and you don't usually get there by a nice, neat, rational process—integration *just happens* when it is ready to. It is often a new, creative, surprising answer that wasn't available to you as long as you stayed in your old, familiar, logical patterns. And it only becomes available after you give yourself permission to break out and explore more of what is going on within you.

Polarization

SETTING

SETTING

Following are some exercises that may help you to get in touch with your own polarities and give you an opportunity to practice working with them in a useful way. Recognize that it may take a while to get used to and good at using these approaches and, therefore, you may want to try one today, let some time go by, and try again a week or a month from now.

PROCESS

1 Think of a problem that is currently with you, one in which you are having some difficulty making a decision because of ambivalent feelings. Write the problem down in a few sentences—for example, Should I give Fred a raise at his next performance review or skip his increase this time?

2 Write a dialogue of the argument you are having with yourself about this question. Let the dialogue be spontaneous; don't censor yourself or worry about being silly or unreasonable. Only you will see the notes. Also, don't worry about which arguer is the topdog and which is the underdog; you may not know that until the whole dialogue has been completed. For example:

Me I: "You ought not give Fred the raise because his performance hasn't been very good this year."

Me II: "Well, Fred has been trying hard, it's just that he has been having a lot of trouble."

Me I: "You're not supposed to pay people more money for trying hard, you're supposed to pay for results."

Me II: "There are a lot of people in other departments in this organization that aren't doing any better than Fred and will probably get a raise this year."

Me I: "That's not the point, and you know it. Just because someone else is doing the wrong thing doesn't mean that you ought to do the wrong thing."

3 Continue writing the dialogue until you have either come to a conclusion or come to an impasse—that is, you feel that there is nothing more you are willing to say to yourself in either role. Put your dialogue aside for a while—maybe two or three hours—and go ahead and do something else.

4 When you are ready, reread your dialogue. To the extent you can, try to read it

with a fresh perspective, as though you were someone else—for instance, one of the writers of this book. When you reread the dialogue, underline those words and phrases that particularly catch your attention or seem important to you. See if you have gotten any new insights or come closer to reaching a decision. It may be useful to let a little more time go by—say, a day or two—and then go back and start a new dialogue or continue the old one. By this time, you may find that you have some quite new perspectives on the situation. *The issue may even have changed.*

5   Another way of doing this exercise is to find a place that is quiet and private. Set up two chairs that face one another and speak the dialogue out loud, moving from chair to chair as the speaker changes. It may be helpful to have a tape recorder going so you can listen to yourself afterward. When you listen to the tape, see if you can recognize in which chair you are most energetic, in which chair your voice is loudest and your points made most decisively, etc. When you believe you are clear about what you want to do, ask yourself how you are keeping yourself from doing it. For example, "I stop myself from telling Fred that I'm unsatisfied with his performance by imagining I would be impolite, and I shouldn't be impolite or hurt his feelings." Check it out and find out whether that "should" is really valid for you at the present time (though it may have been in the past). If you were in Fred's place, would you want your boss not to tell you about his dissatisfaction with your performance?

6   When you have concluded your own topdog-underdog dialogue, you may learn still more about your own attitudes and their relevance by using the dialogue technique (either in writing or with two chairs) in an imaginary conversation between yourself and Fred. Say what you would say to him if you decided to hold the discussion, and then what you believe he would answer. Don't be too concerned about accurately reflecting what Fred would *really* say, for there is no way of knowing that. What you are actually doing is getting a clearer picture of where *you* stand, both with yourself and with your projections of what goes on in Fred's mind and feelings. If, after you have finished the dialogue, you have some new ideas and you decide to really talk to Fred in person, *don't* get hung up with trying to duplicate the imaginary dialogue. Deal with Fred in a totally fresh way. Start by making contact.

COMMENT

Not much more to add. When we were kids they used to say that people who talked to themselves weren't necessarily crazy—unless they answered back. A number of the more-effective therapists, starting with Fritz Perls, have discovered in recent years that talking to yourself only with the silent thoughts of your mind can indeed be fruitless and even self-torturing. When you can bring your dialogue out into the open though, and give it the power of your voice or pen, you may well have started on the right track to personal clarity and freedom.

Power, Weakness, and Conflict

You can't win, you can't lose, and you can't break even,
but you've got to play because it's the only game in town.

A while ago one of the authors was asked by a colleague to join him in
consulting with one of his clients. The client, a highly successful general
manager of a building supply company, had just been offered the presi-
dency of a large retail chain organization. Taking over the new assignment would, as he saw it, require drastic changes in the company's way
of doing business, and likely the "reformation" or replacement of several
high-level people. That was the dilemma. This energetic, talented, and
essentially tough-minded general manager had about a year or so before
attended a sensitivity-training session, had been deeply touched by his
experience of warmth, affection, and support in the group, and had attempted subsequently to expand his knowledge by readings in organization development. Then, he had tried to apply the principles he had
learned to his own and other's relationships in his organization. The results of his attempts had been mixed. Some subordinates had responded
well to his openness and participative style; others had used the greater
leeway he gave them as an opportunity to become lax and ineffective.
Nevertheless, the general manager stuck devotedly to his perceptions of
what good human relations ought to be, and, in fact, his hesitancy about
accepting the new job offer had to do with his doubt that his management
approach would work with his new subordinates. As he put it, "I would
rather quit managing altogether than go back to my authoritarian ways."

After some exploratory discussion, it became clear that a certain
amount of misinterpretation had occurred in this man's understanding of
sound humanistic management practice. But in a larger sense a great deal
of what was troubling this executive we recognized as common among
many people who have been influenced by some of the conventional
human-relations training theories. He had come to regard his own power—
both his organizational position and his personal force—as something
uncomfortable, even bad. And so he worked diligently to restrain that
power for the sake of others whom he saw as less powerful.

Discomfort with power is certainly not new in our society. In politics,
for example, it is a commodity that many politicians deny having while
at the same time attributing excessive amounts to their opponents. The

situation we just described is not unique to the executive we worked with. For many people in various walks of life, self-doubts and guilt feelings frequently accompany the application of power, even in so simple a matter as giving orders to other people.

At the same time, we have also encountered a number of people at high organization levels who have, in fact, lost touch with their power and choose to avoid recognizing its existence. We recall clearly a group we consulted with that included three vice presidents of a major company, all of whom busily denied or avoided their authority to decide on changes in a set of organization policies, because they inferred that the company president reserved such authority for himself and their actions might offend him. (A number of the techniques the group used to avoid making decisions are recounted in the short parable that follows). In fact, the president wanted the group to decide on these issues and had implied this to them. As we learned later, he had not been entirely explicit because *he, too, was hesitant* about "placing demands" on the group. Thus, we had what almost amounted to an unintentional collusion of politeness and caution that produced a very ineffective task group.

In this section of the book we are first going to look at certain aspects of power and weakness in organizations. Following that, we will discuss conflict in a similar context.

In our culture we generally look on conflict as undesirable. With the exception of sports contests, we tend to regard conflict situations as problems that need to be resolved as soon as possible and our usual remedies call for rational and balanced approaches. From international relations through union-management relations to family relations, many of us see conflict as negative and harmony as positive. Still, despite our apparently strong general agreement against it, conflict goes on in the world and at home.

The same holds true of "extreme positions." In our society, moderation and the golden mean are spoken of positively and, for the most part, extreme positions are frowned on as unreasonable, disruptive, and contributing to conflict.

In the following pages, we will take a somewhat different perspective. In brief, we believe a great deal of human energy is frequently involved in these apparently negative dynamics and, if we allow ourselves, we can tap into these energy sources and discover that they are often convertible to very useful and enlivening purposes. We are not, of course, making a case either for wars or violent fanaticism. In fact, it is likely that if both conflict and extremes were more naturally accessible to more people in straightforward ways, less guilt and deception would be associated with them and there might be fewer wars and less violent fanaticism.

Eight Running Games for Executives: A Parable

One day when it was raining and there weren't very many people at the airport, a semiwise man of ideas came to Organizationville. He was called consultant. And he was semiwise because he knew a lot about some things and was quite ignorant about some others, and he didn't always know which was which. (If he had, he would have been a very wise man, indeed.)

At the airport the semiwise man of ideas was met by another semiwise man of action who was called executive. After greeting each other and eating an expensive and somewhat too-heavy lunch, which was the custom in such meetings, both semiwise men returned to the large and elegant office of the semiwise man of action and sat down to speak together.

"I am sorely troubled, O consultant," said the executive, "and that is why I have sent for you from over many miles and borders."

"So I expected," replied the consultant wisely, and he lit a large pipe with a curved stem and then appeared even wiser. "Tell me your dilemma and I will listen."

"In my enterprise," said the executive, "are many managers and executives who must each day confront and decide on many issues that come before them. If their decisions are good, the enterprise prospers; if they are poor, the enterprise suffers."

"So it is in many enterprises which I visit," said the consultant.

"True," said the executive, "but here there is another thing that happens, or, more correctly, does not happen. For the managers and executives of this enterprise too often make neither good nor poor decisions. Rather, they do not make decisions at all. And so the enterprise suffers as much—

and sometimes I fear more—as if the decisions were poor. Tell me, O consultant, if you can, something that you know about these matters that I may find useful."

"I will," said the consultant as he puffed his curved pipe slowly, "speak to you of eight running games for executives, and you may judge if that is useful or not."

"That I will do," replied the executive, "for I pay you much gold for your counsel and it is fitting that your words be useful."

And so the semiwise man who was called consultant began. "The first game is called *More Data Needed*. It is a delicate game but not difficult to play. When there is a choice to be made between alternatives and that choice is not clear, the executive may say such words as 'our information is inadequate' or 'we must wait until the trends are clearer in the marketplace' or 'the staff work here is insufficient in quantity or quality.' And so by playing *More Data Needed* the executives may easily delay deciding on a choice."

"Ah, of course," exclaimed the executive. "I saw such a game played last week in one of our departments. I shall note it down so as to more closely observe it next time it is played." And he noted the first game.

"The second game," said the consultant, "is called *It Never Should Have Happened in the First Place*. It is a game that is especially appropriate when facing difficult and unpleasant emergencies. When the executive cannot readily think of any attractive solution to the problem he may say 'If my predecessor, or my leader (or whoever else may be convenient) had done his job with more competence this problem would never have arisen.' A variation of this game is called *It's Not My Problem, It's Theirs*, which may be played between departments."

"Yes," sighed the executive, "I have certainly seen both versions played in this enterprise. It is not new to me, but I will note it down anyway so that I will be reminded." And he noted the second game.

"The third game," continued the consultant, "is called *Power, Power, Who Has the Power*, and is most often played in committees and study groups. When action must be taken which requires to a greater or lesser degree some departure from standard procedures or a change in conventional policies, words may be heard from committee members such as, 'Yes, I think it would be a good idea but it would take somebody higher up to swing it' or 'Well, we might do that except no one in this group has the authority.' This game, by the way, may be played at any level in the organization. I have seen vice presidents who were most skillful, and while I have never witnessed it, I would expect chief executives play a version of it too."

"This game, too, I have heard about indirectly," said the executive rather quickly, "I'll make a note of it while you tell me about the fourth game."

"The fourth game," said the consultant, "is known as *Waver*, and it, too, is most often played in meetings. *Waver* is a subtle game and requires more skill and precise timing than most. It has the advantage though of being visible only to the keenest eyes. The object in the game is for a group who wishes to avoid making a decision to cycle back and forth between two or more alternative decisions without ever quite coming to a conclusion. The test of skill, of course, is to see how close to a decision they can come and still not quite make one. Thus, to the observer, and at times to the group members themselves, their deliberations appear cogent, relevant, and purposeful, except at the final instant they are able to switch to a different track. Championship-calibre *Waver* players may make the game last for weeks or perhaps months."

"Hmm," said the executive, "I can remember sitting in for a while at a meeting of my division heads. They were discussing capital investment, though they never quite completed their discussions. If I am not mistaken, they were playing *Waver* then. I'll make a note of this game too."

"*What Will Harry Think*," said the consultant as he tapped the ashes from his pipe, "is the name of running game number five. It is a very simple one that may be played by any number of players and needs no special court or field. Where courage or trust are low among executives and anxiety or suspicion are high, a course of action may be delayed at least for a short while by worrying about what Harry would think. Harry may be a superior or even a peer, and no one, of course, takes the trouble to ask Harry what he would think for that would defeat the purpose of the game. Instead, the players speculate on his reactions and so may find many reasons to avoid reaching a conclusion for a while. If the players wish to extend the game, options are available, for once the question of what Harry would think is finally decided, they may ask what Martin and Roy and John would think as well."

"Yes indeed," smiled the executive, "and Peter and Paul and Saint Sebastian too. I have seen this game played very often and it has just as often annoyed me very much." And he noted the fifth game on his list.

"The sixth game," said the consultant, "is called *Yeah, But* . . . and it is frequently a competitive game. The play is basically in two strokes. Player number one proposes an idea, or the solution to a problem, or an action to be taken and his opponent responds, 'Yeah, but . . .' and then fills in one or several reasons why the idea, solution, or action won't work, or is not quite adequate, or has been tried before and failed. The game is often played by in-group members in response to ideas proposed by others outside the group. If it is played well, those in the group can successfully resist the penetration of any new ideas. There is another interesting version too, played most often by those who ask for advice or help from others while at the same time being firmly determined not to change their present styles. As the advice is given by player two in response to the apparently sincere request of player one, player one 'yeah, buts...' each offer. Played skillfully, player one may frustrate any number of advisors, either concurrently or sequentially, to the point of distraction and then walk away complaining sadly that no one in the world can solve his problem. Which does, of course, make his problem a very superior one to the run-of-the-mill variety most of us have."

"Well," said the executive, "there's another one that I am only too familiar with in both versions. There are two divisions in this enterprise that are constantly rejecting each other's ideas and have been for years. And we have a comptroller who is exactly like your example. I myself have tried to help him many times. I certainly want to note this game."

"The seventh game," said the consultant, "is a sad one. It is called *Wash Out* and it may be played by a single player or a group. It is usually played when there is a lack of confidence in a person or an organization and sometimes when there is even a lack of hope. The game goes like this: An individual or group face a problem or requirement to be met and come up with an idea or approach. But unlike the *Yeah But*... game, they need not wait for an opponent to contest or diminish the worth of their conception. Instead, they do it themselves. *Wash Out* is the game of self-defeat, the game of unworthiness and despair. The game that ends in loss before it has begun."

"I have seen it, too, in this place," said the executive, "and my heart has been heavy. As I watched it played, I wished there had been something I could do," and he noted down game number seven.

"Before I go on to game number eight," said the consultant, "there is something I would like you to tell me, O executive."

"Yes," asked the executive as he glanced up curiously from his list, "what is it?"

"I would like to know your judgment of the usefulness of those things I have so far told you. Has what I have said of the seven games been worth the large amount of gold you pay me?"

"That," replied the executive after several moments thought, "is a difficult question to answer. Your explanation of the games has been interesting and well put, though I must say that most of these things I knew before, and, in truth, I see these games almost every day played within this enterprise." The semiwise man of action paused to ponder. "Yes, I must admit that I am hard put at this instant to say whether you are worth your gold or not. Perhaps your explanation of the eighth and last game will tip the scales one way or the other."

"Very well," said the semiwise man of ideas, "I will continue. The eighth game is the game of *Consultant*. It is usually played only by those who are very high in an enterprise, for only they can afford the large amounts of gold that this game costs to play. *Consultant* may be a useful game if it is not played too often or too long. But when it is played as a substitute for doing what needs to be done, it is not at all useful. *Consultant*, after all, is a game of talking and listening and not a game of doing. Therefore, sir," the consultant leaned closer to the executive as he spoke, "my words and your notes of them may indeed be interesting and well put, but if you do no more with them than you have so far with your own experiences in this enterprise, *Consultant* will be no better a game than any of the previous seven."

The executive smiled. "Now I will answer clearly your question," he said, "what you have told me is indeed worth the gold I pay you."

When the semiwise man of ideas left the semiwise man of action at the airport on the following day, the rain had stopped and, while the clouds were still dark and rolled heavily above them, on the horizon a small but clear streak of blue sky peeked through.

EIGHT RUNNING GAMES FOR EXECUTIVES: COMMENT

We think the preceding parable deserves some further comment. It turns out, of course, that there aren't merely eight running games, there are probably dozens, and if you consider individual styles and variations, probably hundreds can be identified. The question, for both the manager as a participating member of a decision-making group and the consultant as a facilitator of group effectiveness, is: What can be done?

One helpful step is just to be alert to the existence of the games, and to be able to spot at a fairly early stage when they are being played. Much of the time, the executives who participate in these games are not aware that either they or others in the group are playing them—the games are not usually deliberate ploys. Actually, it would probably be better if they were. As a matter of fact, the participating manager or consultant's main thrust in dealing with these avoidance techniques ought to be to help the players become fully conscious of what they are doing (or avoiding), how they are doing it, and whether or not they want to continue.

Following are a few hints on recognizing and dealing with the running-game phenomena:

- Help those in the group to come into the "here and now." Make sure that the blockages or barriers to the decision-making process aren't leftovers from past situations. If unfinished business between two or more members of the group seems to be interfering with the progress of the meeting, it will probably have to be dealt with first, or at minimum, recognized and acknowledged by those involved, with an agreement to put it aside until later. (In Section Four, the exercise section of this book, we have outlined several approaches for helping people focus on the present.)

- Get clear on whether or not people really want to make a decision. What is in it for them to decide? What is in it for them *not* to decide? Is someone at a higher level of the organization expecting a decision from the group? Will the decision really have any action consequences for people in the group or others in the organization? Is it actually just as well if the group has an opportunity to explore its various points of view, make its comments, get some ideas of each other's positions, and then just retire, rather than really having to make a decision?

Over some period of time we have observed an interesting difference between people. As a friend put it, some people seem to be "ammunition wagons" and some people seem to be "rifles." Ammunition wagons enjoy collecting data and information—the more information, the better they like it, and the more they enjoy themselves. They tend, however, to get very uncomfortable over the prospect of being incorrect in anything they do; the idea of being wrong is almost intolerable. So, consequently, they soon recognize that if you don't make a decision, you obviously can't ever be wrong.

Rifles, on the other hand, don't seem to worry much at all about being incorrect, nor are they terribly oriented toward collecting information. They are action takers. They see their self-concept or reputation as tied into how effectively they take action. They can be incorrect about subject matter without worrying about it, and they tend not to be too concerned about making mistakes in some of their actions either, as long as the majority of them, or the important ones, work.

- One of the most frequent reasons for avoidance, of course, is that making a decision may involve some risk. Yet, often for those involved, the risks are vague and unclear. The consultant or manager participant can make a useful contribution if he or she can help the group both collectively and individually to focus on the question: What are the risks specifically? And, of course, What are the risks in *not* making a decision?

■ After sitting for a while with a group that is being avoidant you ought to have a fairly clear picture of where the point of avoidance is. This can frequently provide some clue to what they are avoiding. Another potentially useful intervention is to take a moment to stop the action of the meeting and help the group to recognize that they are avoiding. Then, don't be in too much of a hurry to move them along. Rather, take some additional time to explore the process of avoidance and its basis more thoroughly. The more fully and frankly group members are able to recognize and be explicit about their concerns and misgivings at this point, the less likely these factors will reoccur again at a later point in the deliberations. (For some techniques that may be useful here, see the exercise in Section Four, "Going Further In.")

■ Be ready to recognize and deal with problem situations that exist between only a few of the group members, and yet whose effects are blocking the work of the entire group. There may be competitive situations, feelings of threat, etc. that are not being dealt with straightforwardly. A temporary postponement of the meeting, giving those involved in the difficulty an opportunity to work out their needs in a separate session, may in the long run save considerably more time than the delay.

■ Finally, when all else seems to have failed, *be ready to give up*. Frankly acknowledging that the group has been unable to perform its function effectively may be considerably healthier than pretending that something useful has been done. Confronting the members of the group with your own statement that you are ready to acknowledge your own inability, as well as theirs, in reaching a decision can be very sobering to the group. I have seen cases where this action stimulated frank self-assessments by other members of the group, and subsequently a turnaround in what had previously been almost totally ineffective work. We are by no means suggesting this be used as a ploy. When you say it, you ought to mean it. That doesn't imply, though, that you aren't ready to hear other group members' reactions and go further if some new encouraging signs emerge.

The Myth
of Omnipotence

You aren't nearly as powerful as you think you are and
other people aren't nearly as weak.

If you are like many managers we know, the most formidable barrier to
freely expressing yourself in the organization setting is probably fear.
This fear takes many forms: fear of others and of how they might affect
you and your career; fear of how you might make mistakes, and so im-
peril your image as a modern, competent manager; and, not least, fear
of offending or hurting others.

One of the most important areas of study in examining organization
behavior is the manager-subordinate relationship. In this relationship,
probably more than in any other, both managers and subordinates frequently restrict the potential range of their interaction and their possible
capacity to enjoy each other as well as work more cooperatively toward
their common purposes.

DEMOCRATIC LEADERSHIP

For many years, an important focus for theories of management has been
the area of direction and control. A whole range of management philos-
ophers and theoreticians of varied backgrounds have all advocated caution
in the manager's use of direction and control. Cases were and are made
for participating, permissive, or otherwise moderated styles of supervision.
By now it has become clear to almost every manager or supervisor who
sees himself or herself as "beyond the dark ages" that bosses are not
supposed to be domineering and authoritarian—or at least, if you are,
you are not supposed to be seen that way by your subordinates.

Clearly, a dictatorial or oppressive style of management is no longer
generally acceptable in the United States. But we believe that the real
basis for this truth is not found in philosophical images of theoretical

democracy; rather, it stems from the high probability that most people who work in present day organizations are unwilling to tolerate oppression. They will find a way of rising up against it, either overtly through some form of rebellion (like strikes) or covertly through some fears of sabotage.

For many managers, though, the ideal of "democratic leadership" has not served as a useful model. Their attempts to regulate their own behavior to make it fit the ideal have been strained and unnatural, and frequently received with discomfort and suspicion by their subordinates. If a person's behavior is authentic, it must reflect his or her own internal, personal realities at any given point in time, not somebody else's prescriptions of what he or she ought to be like.

THE COSTS OF RESTRAINT

In the practice of psychotherapy, therapists repeatedly encounter the guilt- and anxiety-ridden patient who tortures himself with fantasies of how he has abused or injured others. In this way, the patient achieves a state of such self-mistrust or self-hate that he becomes unable to interact with those around him and can only turn inward. His vitality and excitement are lost as he spends his energy in restraining and punishing himself.

In an organization culture where the exercise of direct power is disapproved by the norms of the organization, many people in positions of authority may experience a comparable (though, of course, less extreme) problem. They may become vaguely uncomfortable or even terribly concerned about the "awesome force" they have over other people. We call this pattern the "myth of omnipotence."

The myth of omnipotence can be a paralyzing specter. Managers who are too much concerned about their power to harm may begin to withhold or divert energy, spontaneity, and thrust in order to avoid hurting others. This withheld thrust has adverse effects on *both* the withholders and those from whom they withhold.

In the course of our organization consulting work we have encountered many cases in which managers struggle painfully to force their behavior to conform to an image of managership in which they are continually benign, nonauthoritarian, objective, encouraging, and facilitative toward subordinates. At the same time, they hold back their own wants, convictions, and desires to move things ahead. "Negative" emotions toward subordinates, such as irritation, criticism, impatience, and so on, are withheld, because a "good manager" (like a "good parent") is not supposed to express such things to those who look to him or her for guidance.

Believing the myth of your own omnipotence might boost your ego if you could, at least subjectively, feel superior to and more capable than your subordinates. But the typical manager seldom enjoys that feeling of superiority, even at a subjective level; instead, he or she struggles with constant ambivalence and lack of fulfillment.

Perhaps more important, your subordinates also may suffer from the ambiguity of the signals you send out. On the one hand, your words are encouraging, patient, and reasonable; on the other hand, however, the expressions on your face, your tone, your body signs (e.g., fidgeting, tension, etc.) almost invariably show through and are perceived by your subordinates. These contradictory signals are seldom if ever dealt with, and so the disbelief, confusion, and frustration of both you and your subordinates go on and on.

ASKING FOR HELP

Of course, the other side of the coin must be considered too. All of us, at some time in our lives, feel the pangs of doubt, confusion, uncertainty, and anxiety. If you believe, however, that living up to your role of manager requires that you hide these supposed "signs of inadequacy" from your subordinates (or superiors, for that matter—or perhaps worst of all, even from yourself), then here again you are denying a part of your own humanness. You are also avoiding a real opportunity for meaningful contact between yourself and others, as well as an opportunity to ask for and get help.

In organizations where asking for help is generally considered a sign of weakness or inadequacy, we have seen several consequences. Both individuals and departments tend to be isolated, secretive, and suspicious of one another. Neither problems nor solutions are shared. Frequently, while people may work hard, their overall effectiveness is less than it might be. The ideas of others are often rejected as "not-invented-here" even when those ideas might be useful. Interaction among peers tends to be guarded, and sometimes limited to talk about how well things are going.

In one company we were called into, a whole division had almost collapsed before the division general manager was willing (or desperate enough) to provide a realistic report to his peers and his president about the state of the organization. It was generally agreed that if the general manager had been willing to ask for help earlier, his organization might well have been saved. And, after our post-mortem analysis of this situation, other high-level managers in the company admitted that this reluctance to talk about problems was a common characteristic among them.

The myth of omnipotence can be worn like a big cloak—button it up and you can pretty well cover up the outlines of yourself. By keeping yourself muffled, you can protect everybody else from what you might do to them if you weren't covered up, and you can also protect yourself from what everybody else might think if they could really see you. If everybody wore their omnipotence cloaks, then everybody would be safe from everybody else—but very lonely.

FULL EXPRESSION

In our work in organizations, we have found that it is far healthier for a manager to express his or her feelings, negative as well as positive, and to candidly say what he or she wants or even demands. With your full expression, your subordinates can more completely experience you and what is important to you—they don't have to guess. They can then accept or contest it (and you) as they see fit. Interestingly, when you have fully expressed yourself, you will probably discover that you are more ready and able to listen to others' expressions as well. From this interchange of full expression and full reaction, both you and your people can grow in a meaningful way.

First, in your relations to each other, you learn to know one another more richly and authentically, and through a heightened awareness of your feelings, both you and they learn to know yourselves better as well. Secondly, with repeated practice and greater familiarity between you, the substance of different ideas and perspectives can also be more adequately tested and new, more-effective ways of working together can be developed.

We have worked with several high-level managers, long inhibited by their images of the good human-relations participative manager, who were finally able to fully and spontaneously release their pent-up feelings. When the breakthrough comes out in strong expressions of anger, affection, dislike, or whatever, there may well be an initial shock that is uncomfortable to everyone (including the consultant). But with time and the courage to stick with it, those involved work it through. They are able to deal with each other's strong emotions much better than they were able to handle the avoidances and phantom expressions of their past relationships, and eventually they may achieve a vital, robust, and mutually satisfying relationship in which both manager and subordinates are far freer and more energetic than before.

It is, of course, possible that some managers, if encouraged to fully express themselves, would turn out to be intolerable tyrants. In our experience, however, there are few such people. In the context of psychological theory, the "intolerable tyrant" may well be a person suffering the myth of his or her own personal helplessness. As an act of self-defense, the individual tries to control completely all those around. In therapy, as such individuals are able to confront their feelings of helplessness and come to recognize for themselves that they are not as totally helpless as they believed, the tyrannical behavior begins to change. At any rate, we suspect that a straightforward undisguised tyrant is easier and better to deal with than a disguised one.

CHANGE

Many of us think about change as the key process of organization development—and we think of it as something to get *someone else* to do. In the Authentic-Management framework we see change, especially in relationships, occurring in several ways:

- Change in *other's* reactions to an individual's behavior when they understand his or her context and purpose more clearly, and/or increase their willingness to deal with the individual in *his* or *her* context.

  One example of this I recall occurred in a team-building session in which a powerful and vocal manager who had been perceived by many of his subordinates as harshly critical and punitive was encouraged in the group setting to intensify his behavior even further. As he "did his thing" (using an Authentic Management exercise), it became clear to all that what was going on was his very vocal expression of his own frustrations ("keeps me from getting ulcers," he later explained) rather than punishment of his subordinates.

- Change in the individual's feeling about himself or herself when the person fully experiences and acknowledges his or her own behavior (e.g., lessening of self-contempt or feelings of failure). Frequently, of course, when people feel better about themselves, others feel better about them too.

  In illustration of this point, we recall an individual organization member who was accused by his peers and manager of being frequently sarcastic and at the same time aloof. His initial response to this criticism was to deny it. However, as we worked together, he eventually acknowledged that his sense of humor did run to the ironic, and, in fact, he tried to control it but sometimes slipped. He disapproved of himself on this score and so "pulled back" whenever he became aware of it. (It was this withdrawal that made him seem aloof to others.) Again, utilizing an Authentic Management method, we asked him to dramatize his ironic humor by engaging "ironically" with each member of his group. He did so, and after some initial sheepishness, was delighted with his own performance. The others were too. In later contacts with the group, we learned that a positive change in relationships continued long after our session. Though he still made ironic (or sarcastic) comments to others, some of which occasionally stung, he was no longer seen as aloof and most people appreciated his wit.

- Change in actual behavior when the "unfinished business" that stimulates that behavior is completed (e.g., finishing up with past resentments and projections, and so allowing new and clearer perceptions of others to emerge).

One case that illustrates this change involved a long and growing conflict between a department head and his senior subordinate. After we worked with them for a while, the subordinate acknowledged that he resented his manager because he believed he himself should have been promoted to the department-head position several years before. Later, in a two-chair polarization exercise in which he dialogued with his boss, playing both his own and his manager's parts, he slowly and steadily struggled through his unfinished resentments (of *himself* primarily) and later gradually began to make real contact with his boss.

- Change in the response of the individual to others resulting from clarification of what they want from him or her (e.g., the person really recognizes for the first time that he or she is being asked for help and cooperation, rather than being criticized).

- Acceptance of status quo—no substantive change but a reduction of tension as those involved finally accept *what is*. Interestingly, many times this act of giving up, by reducing countervailing pressures, actually seems to precipitate later substantive change as well.

- A combination of two or more of the above. This, of course, is most frequently the case.

The Case
of the Unhappy Giant

A couple of years ago we were asked to consult with the high-level manager of a large staff group. This man, who we will call Dick Taylor, had developed a strong, even passionate, commitment to human-relations values. Included in these values, as he saw them, was the requirement for him as a manager to be fair, rational, and helpful to those who reported to him. Most of the time Dick operated in this way quite readily and naturally. He was, however, an individual of great personal force, with strong emotions and subject to occasional moodiness. Those who reported to him recognized these qualities and had gradually grown accustomed to them, though, as might be expected, some were more and some less comfortable with his style.

Over a considerable period of time this strong, able manager grew increasingly discontent and unhappy in his relationships with several members of his staff, and the staff members, in turn, were also bothered. The problems they had can be illustrated by the typical interactions that went on in Taylor's staff meetings. These were generally conducted in a fairly free-flowing style with the floor pretty much available to anyone who wanted it. Sometimes the meetings were quite businesslike and, at other times, they were mostly a series of rambling discourses punctuated occasionally by concise irrelevancies.

For the most part, Taylor and his staff were fairly satisfied with both the focused and the "nonproductive" discussions. From time to time, however, and for no very apparent reason, Dick would suddenly jump into the discussion with all the force of a safe dropped from a ten-story window. Usually he landed on one of about three or four members of his staff, and frequently—though not always—his attack was logically sound. It was not so much the substance of what he said as the vehemence and unexpectedness that seemed to most affect the people who were his targets.

The responses of those who were jumped by the boss varied: some replied by defending their position with counterlogic; one used humor, including self-deprecating comments to reduce the tension; still another acted out and sometimes verbally expressed his feelings of being punished by the boss. Whatever the response, though, what most frequently seemed to happen was that after a round or two of exchange Dick would stop talking and would settle into a glum, silent slouch. When that happened, the entire group would fall into a long awkward pause, without reaching any real solution of the issue.

After working with the group for some period of time, we found ourselves in one meeting face-to-face with the classic pattern. An important proposal for a change of policy had been made by one of the staff, and tentatively supported by two others. Taylor's reaction was quick and strongly negative. He accused all the proponents of being panicky, unrealistic, and out of touch with the organization's needs. After the typical pattern of responses from these staff members and another round or two of exchange, Dick lapsed into grim silence.

As consultants to this manager and his staff, our task was to help the group focus on their interactions with each other and ways these could be improved. Here was our opportunity to deal with their problem as it was happening. We had a number of alternatives: (1) we could try to shift the group's attention back to the "strictly business" content of their issues and discourage their getting involved in personal issues;* (2) we could intervene in such a way as to focus even more sharply on the disruptive, inhibiting effects of Taylor's outbursts; (3) we could analyze or encourage the group members to analyze the reasons for and consequences of their interaction pattern; or (4) we could intervene in a way that *encouraged the fight to continue* (without having any clear idea of what the outcome might be). Admittedly with some hesitancy, we made the fourth choice (primarily by allowing our own spontaneous feelings of resentment and antagonism to surface). We expressed our own discomfort first, then asked Dick to follow through with his criticism—in fact, to really get into it even more fully.

After some hesitation, Taylor began, at first with some awkwardness but soon with great enthusiasm, to blast a number of his staff. At the same time, the people he attacked were encouraged to respond, even counterattack if they felt like it. Soon other members of the staff also joined the

---

*   This was really not a choice we considered seriously. Ignoring or excluding personal dynamics from consideration in an ongoing work group seldom produces useful results.

fray, usually on the side of their colleague. This free-for-all style was allowed to develop into a roomful of shouting people that more resembled a disorderly convention of longshoremen than a staff meeting of high-level corporate managers. And the outcome was marvelous.

As the group reexamined its interaction process some time later, members recognized that this turbulent meeting (and a few others since) had produced for the entire group a greater sense of vitality, excitement, and personal relatedness than they had felt for many months, and that this feeling had carried over into subsequent staff meetings as well. In addition, the manager reported that their fights had brought him a new sense of respect for the staff members who stood up to him. In subsequent encounters other staff members also began to stand their ground more readily.

What was the basis for our encouraging the fight to continue? First, our choice was mostly intuitive rather than theoretical, arising out of our immediate feelings and our willingness to risk making a mistake. As we had worked with the group over some period of time, it became clear to us that the manager was quite aware of the effect of his "attacks" on his staff members, perhaps too aware. Why, then, did he, an enlightened, human-relations-oriented manager, continue this behavior?

The answer is simple: the feelings behind his behavior were part of him—part of the whole of his humanness, power, and emotionality—those same qualities for which his staff and many others respected and trusted him. What then could be done? To preach self-control or even temperance to Taylor hardly seemed worthwhile (whether the preaching was overt and direct or through the more subtle use of group feedback). Even if he resolved to stop his verbal interrupts his feelings would still be sensed by others and would float like a pervasive phantom among them all. No, the answer was not for this manager to back away from his impulsive behavior, but rather, *to go further into it.* The point was not to cut himself off with guilt feelings about abusing his subordinates after an exchange or two, and then settle into melancholy self-blame. Rather, it was to stay engaged with them in battle until it reached its natural conclusion—until he and they had the opportunity to fully experience and possibly to finish the unfinished business between them.

Over time some major positive effects came from this new style of engagement for the group: the entire staff became more comfortable with the boss and each other, and Dick Taylor began to *enjoy* his relations with his people more than he had before. We believe that the experience Taylor had in allowing himself to follow through on his aggressive impulse rather than holding back was a significant one in his own growth. He discovered that, lo and behold, his "victims" did not perish from his onslaught, but rather, seemed to grow stronger. Conversely, we saw evidence of a similar positive effect in the subordinates' discovery that they were able to handle whatever the boss threw at them and to come back swinging.

CONSULTANT'S FOCUS

In this section, we would like to speak especially to organization-development students and consultants; of course, we don't mind at all if the rest of you join us, too.

In most organizations, the interaction style just described would not be an easy one for people to initiate and pursue without help. Generally, most organizations have too much of an overlay of historical norms and traditions of "appropriate behavior." Here is where organization development and the third-party consultant can be of great help. The consultant can concentrate on assisting managers and subordinates to fully experience and express "where they are"—both on issues and in relationship to each other. He or she can highlight their interpersonal process and help them to discover their own vitality and the satisfaction and excitement of full expression. The consultants can also help them to become aware of *how they stop themselves* from completing their experiences, and of their own predictive (usually catastrophic) fantasies—e.g., the manager imagines, "If I really let myself go I would oppress, overpower, do terrible damage to my subordinates," while the subordinate thinks, "I must be very careful because this is a very dangerous environment." When these murky catastrophic expectations have surfaced, the consultant can help the people explore and test them against reality, and finally work out individual arrangements between people that will allow them greater self-expression and fulfillment.

While many of the processes we are describing probably seem quite similar to typical O.D. consultation theory, in practice there are important differences of execution. Confrontation and "owning feelings" are, of course, common concepts in O.D. In our experience, however, many O.D. consultants facilitate confrontation only to the point of emergence of an identifiable problem (e.g., manager A does not listen to subordinate B or the manager of one organization repeatedly fails to solicit the advice and involvement of other managers with whom he "ought" to be interdependent, etc.). In some organizations the surfacing of such complaints—the fact that they have finally been brought out into the open and acknowledged—can be a major step, but frequently the consultant then moves too rapidly to the task of problem solving. Thus, with the consultant's help, the manager acknowledges his fault and resolves to "listen more carefully" to his subordinate; or action items are prepared and task groups formed to develop new processes to assure better coordination between the various organization subunits, etc. The trouble is that this premature movement into problem solving may be addressing symptoms rather than causes and may produce solutions that are superficial and temporary at best.

The Authentic-Management mode encourages stronger, deeper, and more concrete (as contrasted to abstract or generalized) interactions. Most importantly we emphasize *staying with* the transaction until both parties have *completed* their business with each other. The individual or contesting parties are encouraged to dramatize and perhaps even exaggerate their behavior—to become fully aware of *what* they are doing and *how* they are doing it (not why). The manager who does not listen is encouraged to go further into his or her nonlistening mode, to discover and be explicit about what he or she is doing *instead of listening,* to identify how listening is avoided, and to complete whatever needs completing before full attention can be given to listening. The subordinate who is not listened to may be encouraged to discover how he or she keeps from being heard (i.e., from talking louder or more forcefully, from *demanding* attention, etc.). The managers of the noninteracting organizations are encouraged to state clearly what each wants (or even demands) of the other, with emphasis on meeting their own "selfish" needs rather than because it would be "good organizational practice." And each manager is encouraged to respond "yes" or "no" to each demand. The reaction to this "selfish"-demand-oriented process is frequently quite. remarkable. Paradoxically, these heated exchanges generate more respect and positive feeling between the contesting parties than a raft of cool, rational, for-the-good-of-the-company sessions. The ultimate decisions also seem to be more viable.

The Tyranny
of the Helpless

You aren't nearly as weak as you think you are and other
people aren't nearly as powerful.

The other side of the myth of managerial omnipotence is the tyranny of
the "helpless." Organization-development theory has for most of its relatively brief history stressed the support of the less powerful—the subordinate, the reticent team member, etc.—and the solution of disagreement
through rational processes. In the context of our national culture and
traditions, this is not surprising. Unfortunately, however, some of our
approaches have attempted to help the helpless by providing an easier
world for them through advocating the restraint (usually by "self-control"
and under the moral pressure of "human-relations rightness") of the powerful manager or team member. We believe this approach is wrong. Not
only does it foster the inhibiting omnipotence myth and guilt feelings of
the manager, as discussed earlier, but it can also be experienced as a con-
firmation of the person's own inferiority—a kind of invalidism imposed
on the individual who is granted the so-called benefits of other people
holding themselves back for his or her sake. Better by far to help the
"helpless" one to discover, use, and rejoice in his or her strength and
ability to move forward independently, rather than to have others take
turns pushing the patient's wheelchair.

Robert W. Resnick, a Gestalt psychotherapist, makes the point this
way:

*Many therapists see themselves as members of the "helping
professions" engaged in the "helping relationship." Beware! Such
people are dangerous. If successful, they kill the humanness in their
patients by preventing their growth. This insidious process is
somehow worse realizing such therapists typically want the reverse.
They want their patients to grow, to live, and to be, and they*

guarantee the antithesis with their "help." The distinction between true support and "help" is clear: To do for the other what he is capable of doing for himself insures his not becoming aware that he can stand on his own two feet. . . .

Relationships between some individuals within organizations have many of the characteristics of a topdog/underdog conflict. The apparently powerful, assertive person makes demands on the ostensibly weaker underdog, but somehow, the demands are never quite met. And while the topdog's pressure may be great, the underdog's ability to divert, deflect, or delay is often greater. So-called weak parties in a variety of relationships may have very great, though not immediately apparent, advantages in their ability to resist without attacking, and to use the strong person's own strength against him or her. We have worked with a number of teams in which one or two members, undoubtedly without conscious intent, skillfully manipulated the apparently stronger members of the group, including the boss, into "helping" them. This helping takes many forms. It can be protecting the quiet member, taking his or her side in a competitive situation, being more sympathetic to that person's problems and inabilities to meet commitments than would be the case for other members of the team, etc. One of the most harmful accommodations to the weak party involves others holding back their forcefulness and vitality in order to keep from offending or upsetting the person.

OGRE BUILDING

A variation of the underdog game is ogre building. Almost all of us in organizations have the capacity to build ogres fearsome enough to scare ourselves half to death. The ogre may be a supervisor, especially one at a higher level than those we are accustomed to dealing with, another organization, or, perhaps most insidious of all, "the system." Ogres can be very useful sometimes in helping you to avoid doing what you don't really want to do anyway. We do not object to the use of the ogre for that purpose, if, indeed, you are conscious of what you are doing and you really want to do it. More frequently, however, most of us are not aware of what we are doing and our ogres are not so clearly useful. They are compounded of some degree of organizational reality, plus our own projections and predictions of dire consequences. Organization-development methodology is frequently useful in dealing with ogres, especially the mutual ogres dreamed up by internally competitive organizations for each other. We believe that more can be done, especially in helping individuals to discover their courage and capacity to confront and deal with their own ogres.

In the therapeutic process mentioned earlier that addresses topdog/ underdog conflicts, the first step involves heightening polarization. The individual increases his or her awareness of both these internal forces— especially *the power inherent in his or her underdog position.* A sense of excitement, pride, and energy often accompanies this new awareness. Later, when the person has fully experienced his or her own extremes, he or she may move naturally to an integration—i.e., the individual is able to regain access to those submerged or renounced parts of himself or herself, and eventually becomes able to utilize, as the situation requires, a more-complete spectrum of behavioral potential.

The Case
of the Second-Class Citizens

A case that illustrates the points we have been discussing in the preceding chapter involves a large government agency we worked with. We began with a team-building session between the top management group (including the chief and his central staff) and about a dozen field supervisors, each of whom headed a local service office. The pattern of complaints, and there were many from each side, was clear and repeated. The central staff complained that those in the field seldom seemed to be able to respond to requests for new information, nor did they often try out proposed new .methods developed by the central staff for use in the field. When they occasionally did try out the recommended procedures, it was in a most cursory way that practically assured the failure of the new approach. Finally, after repeated efforts, the central staff people quietly abandoned their efforts to direct the field supervisors and adopted what they felt to be the more-modern management approach of asking the field people to submit their own ideas for innovation and improvement. This approach fared no better.

What we noticed as we heard the presentation of this information from the central-staff people was their almost complete lack of emotion. This pattern had been going on for about a year and *must* have produced frustration for the agency chief and his staff, yet in listening to the presenters we heard only careful neutrality, infinite patience, and dispassionate though devoted interest in "objective problem solving."

It took considerably longer for the case of the field supervisors to emerge. Their first responses to the complaints of the central staff were rather desultory and almost apologetic. They had very heavy work loads, many new people to train, spent a great deal of time on public relations, and so on, all of which limited their ability to concentrate on new approaches. Besides, they felt it was quite unlikely that they could develop any new methods that would really satisfy the central staff, since the central staff people were "obviously so much better informed about the latest trends" in their specialized field. Similarly, the information emerged that in the past year a few of the field supervisors felt they had attempted to institute some of the recommended new approaches of the central staff, but had not done well at it. And while they had not been overtly criticized by the staff, they had "felt" disapproved of.

As consultants, we recognized alternative approaches we might take. First, we could try to help the field supervisors by encouraging the central-staff members to examine their Olympian posture and how their cool paternalism put down the supervisors. They could then explore ways this pattern might be changed into a more encouraging one. Second, we could pursue the problem-solving approach by helping the total group to recognize specific areas of weakness in the supervisors' skills. Training programs for building those skills could then be developed. Third, we could encourage the field supervisors to go (in the Authentic-Management sense) even further into their complaints. We chose the third.

We requested that the supervisors elaborate further on their grievances against the staff. The result, after some initial hesitancy, was a veritable flood of complaints, many dating back years. In essence, the field supervisors reported they felt like second-class citizens, without influence or power in their dealings with the staff. They didn't know what the staff meant by "innovation," and what's more they didn't much care. (They did, however, have some good ideas from time to time which they put into effect without fanfare, seldom telling the staff anything about them.)

When the venting had subsided, we asked the field supervisors to talk about how they characteristically dealt with the staff. After a slow start the supervisors rolled out a substantial list of "passive-resistance" and "playing stupid" techniques. In a little while they were laughing and enjoying their catalogue immensely—and so were the central-staff people, who prior to this time had perceived themselves in the superior position, and so very much "responsible" for the oppressed feelings of the supervisors!

Some time later, after the supervisors had become aware of the way in which they exerted their own resistive power in their dealings with the staff, we were able to turn successfully to the possibilities of developing different modes of interaction between the groups. Now, however, they were able to do so not as impotent sufferers, but as equals. Interestingly, one of their demands was that *the staff be more clearly demanding.* Their experience in the past, they reported, had been confusing. Since the staff (in their efforts to be "understanding") had been so tactful in making requests, it was almost impossible to tell what was really important to them and what wasn't.

Many other aspects of this case emerged and were dealt with in this and subsequent meetings, including our attention to the operating styles of the agency chief and the central-staff members, the identification of real developmental needs for both staff and field personnel, and so on. We were clearly better able to deal with these other problems later on because we started where we did.

CONSULTANT'S FOCUS

In the organization consulting process, especially when dealing with complaining people—those who see others and/or their environment as oppressive and preventing them from doing what they want to do—it is a good idea for the consultant to begin working with the client in a way that concentrates on identifying the client's strength. That may not be easy, as the complainer's strength is not readily apparent. On the contrary, he or she usually spends much of the time denying having any strength at all. All power belongs to "the others"—the boss; his or her more influential, articulate, or aggressive co-workers; or, most oppressive of all, "the company."

As consultants, we begin by being suspicious of these complaints. This is not to say that we think the complainers are intentionally deceptive, nor do we doubt that widespread inequalities of power and opportunity for certain classes of organization citizens do exist. Rather, we have found that most people do possess some form of power, even if that power is passive, resistive, or a withholding kind that is used to manipulate others, often by triggering feelings of guilt among the more active and assertive people with whom they deal.

In the consulting approach we advocate, the primary step is not to help people embark on self-improvement programs. Rather, it is to encourage them to recognize and appreciate where they are now, so that the consultant may help them find their own unique paths forward to change and growth. It is also important to recognize that this change and growth, at best, will occur naturally rather than being forced either by external pressures or models. Paradoxically, natural change in an individual does not preclude his or her boss or others from exerting power or expressing their wants strongly and explicitly. What is explicit and up front is seldom harmful, though it may be difficult to deal with. Covert, withheld, or truncated expression often is harmful. In most circumstances, the consultant will do best to encourage in both individuals and organizations the full recognition and completion of their negative feelings rather than premature objectivity or problem-solving approaches. By the same token, the consultant can set an example by offering a clear and explicit statement of what *he or she* wants and how *he or she* feels.

We in the field of behavioral science have placed great emphasis on the negative consequences of authoritarian management for both organizations and individuals. In voices sometimes gentle and sometimes determined, we have addressed the power figures in organizations and called on them to depart from old patterns, to risk a new approach, and to allow greater and more-meaningful participation in the organization's affairs by those lower in the hierarchy. Many of us have made substantial contributions in helping managers to recognize and exercise their responsibilities toward their subordinates. This has, in the main, been good and worthwhile. The time has come, though, for us to begin to address subordinates as well. We need to help manager and subordinate become aware of the alienating and vitality-sapping consequences of both "playing helpless" and "playing helpful." We must question ourselves and encourage others to question unthinking acceptance of and adaptation to someone else's rules of good human relations, without regard to how these rules feel inside of us.

We believe it worthwhile to urge ourselves and others to take new risks —risks of greater self-assertion, more spontaneity, and more willingness to experiment with power and competition, as well as trust and cooperation. If we in O.D. do indeed believe in a wider distribution of power, it would be well for us to stop trying to deny power's existence, muffle it, wish it away, or disguise it under velvet wrappings. Rather, we can encourage as many people as possible at *all* levels of the organization—from highest manager to lowest subordinate—to discover their own power and use it.

Power may be felt as power-over
And if so it will be oppressive
Oppressive to its victim-prisoner
   and
Oppressive to its wielder-jailer
For the jailer is not much less
   the prisoner than the prisoner

Power-over must be held tightly
   and
Carefully with tense alert
It must be handled, manipulated
   outside the self, now constricted
   now relaxed a little.
Power-over therefore is not strength
   but a binding
Power-over may be clutched desperately
   or greedily
But it is not loved even by its holder

Power-in is love
Power-in is strength and a free heart and
   great joy
It is easy amusement and readily available
   love
Power-in is potency
And if I have it
   even in great quantities
That does not preclude your having it too

Rather,
If I am easy with my power that may
   help you to be more easy with yours
And God, what two of us together can do
   with easy power is beyond reckoning!
We could free the world

Conflict

The best way to stay scared is to keep yourself from finding out exactly what you're scared of.

So far we have been talking about strong people and helpless people—or at least people who play those parts. Let us now consider the situations in which the roles are played, particularly those scenes of high drama—conflict. In Authentic Management and in its Gestalt-theory base, conflict is seen as a natural function, as much so as harmony. If we are each willing to be ourselves, we are probably going to agree on some things and disagree on others. If we desire and move toward action—that is, putting our different views into effect—then at some point our views will be in conflict. When such conflict is dealt with openly and fully, it need not be damaging. More likely it will be positive and vitalizing to the organization.

AVOIDANCE OF CONFLICT

As Robert Phillips once put it, "In organizations it is usually not conflict but the avoidance of conflict that causes most problems." In many organizations with which we have consulted, Phillips' observation seems to be borne out. What we frequently see are long-standing "undercover feuds" between individual managers or even entire departments. Almost everyone knows they exist (e.g., "You know, the Accounting Department and the Personnel people haven't really talked to each other for years"), but no one does much about it. As a result, the organizations interact with each other only when they absolutely have to, and then only in guarded and restricted ways. Any possibility for innovation or cooperative improvements in their processes with one another is very limited. Indeed, in some situations a liaison or coordinator must be appointed to mediate between the two units —ironically, an officially established job in which the incumbent has a vested interest in keeping the two organizations apart!

Many different reasons are given for avoiding conflict. Frequently we avoid engaging in a potential conflict situation because we imagine that in such conflict we will be weak and inadequate while our opponent will be strong and effective. These fantasies about ourselves and others may not be limited only to people, we may also see ourselves as oppressed by "the organization" or "the system." There are, of course, times when substantial differences do exist in the power and the fighting ability of people, but more often, just as we carry myths of omnipotence, we also carry myths of helplessness.

ASSUMPTIONS ABOUT CONFLICT

In the Authentic-Management approach to dealing with conflict, we generally start with some assumptions. These include:

- Conflict between individuals or organization units is as natural as co-operation, and both are essential to healthy functioning.

- Conflicts often represent opportunities for energizing those involved and may also be opportunities for creative changes in relationships and processes.

- It is extremely difficult to bury conflicts successfully and the emotional and operational costs of making rules (whether formal or informal, self-imposed or externally imposed) against conflict are usually too high.

- Typically, the largest barriers against dealing with conflict straightforwardly are imagined catastrophic predictions of the outcome. And, most often, these predictions are vague, general, and unreal (though they may inspire quite real fears).

- Suppressed or disguised conflict is almost always more harmful to people and organizations than the possible temporary discomfort and turbulence often involved in confronting the conflict.

- It is generally *not* useful to push people into dealing with their conflicts. Rather, they can be helped to become more fully aware of their real issues, their positions on those issues, their hopes and fears associated with confronting the conflicts, their willingness or unwillingness to engage in conflict, and their readiness or unreadiness to deal with each other.

CLIENT READINESS

In dealing with conflict, the Authentic-Management approach provides some useful guidelines. First, determine as clearly as possible whether those involved in the conflict are or are not ready and willing to deal with one another. In most cases, this can be accomplished quite simply, by asking them. If they are reluctant, then the basis of their reluctance can be explored. In this exploration the parties should be encouraged to be specific and concrete, *but not pressured to change their minds.* Some useful questions to ask are: What are the *worst* things that might happen to you or your organization if you were to deal with _____ about your disagreements? What are the *best* things that might happen?

In addition, it is generally best to engage a consultant or third party who is not involved in the issues or the disagreement. He or she may then lead the participants through the steps noted above and those that we shall be discussing.

When the willingness and readiness of the parties have been sufficiently explored, it may be clear that one or both are not willing or ready to engage. If this is the case, we need to recognize their right to avoid, and they ought not be pressured or persuaded to go beyond where they are ready to go. An invitation can be extended, however, for them to come back if and when they are ready. Even this preliminary exploration of readiness often has a valuable and positive effect. The explicit recognition of hopes and fears frequently helps those involved to gain a more realistic perspective, and an increased feeling of potency often results from clearly saying, "No, I'm not ready to go further," and having their statement respected. People who have clearly declined to go further now frequently come forward at a later time and clearly assent.

FROM ABSTRACT TO SPECIFICS

In moving forward with the conflict encounter when both parties have agreed to engage, there are a number of ways to help the parties sharpen and clarify their issues and thereby improve their possibilities for a successful outcome. Those involved should be strongly encouraged to present clear, concise statements of their positions. These statements should be as brief, specific, and concrete as possible, rather than abstractions or generalized descriptions. For example, rather than an argument about effective spans of control based on theoretical principles of organization, each party should be encouraged to specify *which* particular organization unit or members he wants to have reporting to him, when, where, and what particular benefit that will have for him. The greatest payoff can be achieved by going beyond the ritualized, polite abstractions of typical organization talk to an explicit statement of needs—without anyone having to justify his or her position with noble, unselfish motives.

FROM IMPERSONAL TO PERSONAL

We encourage personal rather than impersonal arguments, for people's individual beliefs and desires need to be specified and addressed with as much legitimacy as official policies and procedures. In our consulting we have found many times that when we encourage discussion at a deeper level than the cliches and generalizations of organization talk, the real issues turn out to be people's feelings of insecurity, lack of trust in one another, or questions of competence, rather than organization principles.

We recall one argument in which an operating department insisted on asking for written guarantees of adequate support procedures to be provided by a service unit. The argument went on for some hours with no satisfactory outcome. When the focus of the discussion was changed, however, to talking about *who* specifically in the service organization would provide the support, several names were mentioned as possibilities. When the manager of the operating department indicated that two of the names proposed would be quite satisfactory to him, and the support organizations agreed to provide those two people, the discussion with respect to written guarantees of procedures quickly tapered off and was no longer an issue. After the discussion, it was clear that the primary concern of the operating-organization members about procedures was based on their anxiety that adequately competent people might not be provided to service them.

SUSPENDING CAUTION

In the early stages of exploring a conflict situation, especially when a consultant or third party is available, the people involved in the conflict can be encouraged to suspend for a while their sense of caution. Again, in contrast to conventional advice in conflict situations, we like to encourage people to gradually let go of their "walking on eggshells" posture and take a few chances. A more thorough and creative exploration generally results if those involved are encouraged (though not pushed) to allow themselves and each other some extravagances, unreasonableness, and even irresponsibility in stating their points of view.

We have frequently found it useful to inspire and encourage a kind of lighthearted, playful atmosphere among the participants, so that the situation, rather than evoking super caution and restraint, takes on a lighter, more-boisterous quality in spite of the so-called serious disagreements. When people get into this spirit, they take themselves and their problems less somberly and the more fluid and easy atmosphere that results frequently encourages more creative and satisfying resolution.

CATASTROPHIC FANTASY

In a similar spirit, we recommend that participants in conflict speculate *explicitly* about the predicted outcomes of their actions. We might ask one of the participants: If things don't go your way, what's the worst thing that might happen? And then what would happen if that happened . . . and then what would happen?

In each iteration of the question we attempt to help the participant move more and more toward specifics rather than generalized phantom concerns. In the process, we both often discover that his or her vague catastrophic fantasy is much less terrible when looked at closely and concretely, and/or the person can safeguard against the threatening aspects of the situation with some relatively simple specific actions.

For instance, in working as consultant to the executive group of a smaller organization that was about to merge with a larger organization, we were aware that the members of the executive group were very alarmed about the future. We asked them to state their most serious fears. As they reported these concerns, we listed them on the blackboard. They included comments such as: "We will be swallowed up"; "They will put someone in charge of this organization who will exploit it to their benefit and to our detriment"; "They will change us, and we will lose our purpose."

After completing the listing of concerns, we began a second round of questioning. We asked, "What do you mean by they will swallow you up? How will they do that?" The response to these more specific questions were considerably less alarming. The members of the executive group gradually realized that it was highly unlikely that their organization could or would be "swallowed up," because of the nature of its function and its necessary operating patterns.

When later we further explored the concern about a parent-organization takeover, they were able to formulate a specific proposal calling for an organization directorship that would include as chief executive a member of their own group and as second in command a member of the parent organization. This was sufficient to reassure them with respect to maintaining the integrity of their organization and was perfectly acceptable to the parent organization. It was apparent, however, that if they had gone no further than their original generalized fears, they would have had very little basis for working with the larger organization to reach an agreement. It was only when they moved down the abstraction ladder to specific concerns and a realistic view that they were able to formulate their proposals and obtain satisfaction.

COMMUNICATIONS VERSUS SUBSTANTIVE DISAGREEMENT

As almost anyone who has read a management text or even the Sunday supplement knows by now, a considerable amount of conflict between people arises from breakdowns in communications. Frequently people talk past one another, and what appears to be an argument is, in reality, a missed communication. At other times, difficulties and apparent disagreements seem to arise more from semantic problems—that is, different understandings of the same words—than from substantive differences in position. However, while recognizing the importance of communications, we need to be careful not to fall into the trap of thinking that all conflict is the result of communications failures.

Some issues are indeed substantive disagreements. Often, both communications difficulties and substantive differences contribute to a conflict, and it is important in working with the conflict to distinguish between the two and to isolate the issues that are substantial from those that are a matter of words. This can best be done, as we have indicated in so many instances, by moving our focus down the abstraction ladder from general concepts to specific people, things, and acts.

UNRESOLVED CONFLICT

Finally, in dealing with conflict, we need also to acknowledge that, unfortunately, we cannot always expect a happy ending. Many of us have had a number of positive experiences in working with conflict situations, using approaches such as we have discussed. We have helped people to bring out their issues fully and we have discovered that conflict resolution and personal satisfaction seem frequently to result. And so there is a temptation to keep pressing for agreement and happy endings, sometimes past the point of good sense. It is important to recognize that it is legitimate, appropriate, and normal for human beings to disagree from time to time, even after full discussion and engagement.

When this happens, it ought to be looked on as one step in a process, with at least a couple of possibilities for the next step. First, the parties could decide to go elsewhere to get a resolution (i.e., the next higher level of management); second, they could agree to allow the impasse to exist, with both parties *explicitly* recognizing that while they have not reached agreement, they will suspend, at least temporarily, their need to get resolution. At times, this agreement not to agree seems to work slowly to dissolve the issues. Somehow, after having fully expressed their positions and invested their emotions in the disagreement, its content becomes less important and the area of conflict actually seems to diminish over time without ever having been resolved.

BEYOND MODERATION

In the preceding paragraphs we have talked about the usefulness of bringing out extreme positions rather than attempting to constrict our thinking automatically to the reasonable and moderate position. In conflict situations, as well as in our quests for creativity and the development of new approaches, allowing ourselves the luxury of considering extremes can be a bold new adventure with high payoff. It is easier to reach far out to extravagant positions initially and then moderate as required than to start from our conventional "moderate" positions and move out into really creative new positions. This, of course, is one of the principles of brainstorming and other forms of free expression that encourage temporarily letting go of self-censoring and self-regulating.

CONSULTANT FOCUS

In working with conflict, both as participants and as consultants, we have learned to beware of the temptation to achieve premature resolutions or papered-over agreements so that "everyone can be friends again." We have already said that few people are comfortable in conflict situations; interestingly, the degree of discomfort is frequently greater for the spectator or consultant viewing conflict than for those actually involved. Especially for the consultant, it is important to become aware of your own degree of comfort or discomfort with conflict, your own catastrophic expectations, and how you make yourself uncomfortable—that is, what are *your* fantasies or imaginings about the course and consequences of what is happening? For example, do you fantasize: If this goes any further the people may physically attack one another; or, If they continue this way they will never speak to each other again; or, If things go wrong they will blame me for it, etc?

There are many ways in which people (including consultants) tend to divert conflict. Frequently this involves changing the subject, making a joke out of the interaction that's going on, cancelling out feelings (for instance by saying, "I'm sure you don't really mean that, now do you"), and so on. In our experience, frequently the people most nervous about arguments are those who are observing rather than those engaged in the arguments. If you take time to check with the participants about whether or not they are feeling anxious or concerned, you frequently discover that they are not, and that you may be experiencing the highest level of anxiety in the room.

As we noted earlier in the chapter on "Self-Boundaries and Grounding," it is important for each of us to recognize and distinguish our own feelings in a situation rather than attributing those feelings to others.

Authentic-Management Exercises

In this section we are including a number of additional Authentic-Management exercises and techniques that can be used by both managers and consultants. The exercises can be divided roughly into three categories. First, there are approaches for developing and improving skills in basic areas, such as contact and withdrawal, shouldisms, polarities, etc. A few of these are primarily oriented to individual development (comparable to the exercises already covered earlier in the book) and others are for use in group or work-team situations. Second, a number of exercises are for use in specific problem situations that frequently arise in organizations. Third, a few relatively unconventional techniques that explore some different ways for a manager (or nonmanager) to approach his or her work are included. The section concludes with an outline for an introductory Authentic-Management workshop of one or two days.

In another sense, this section is devoted to demonstrating in an operational way some of the "what and how" of AM consultation—especially its emphasis on using what is happening (rather than measuring what is happening against someone's model of what ought to be happening). We hope that this central theme will prompt other consultants (and perhaps some managers) to create their own exercises. Good luck.

Contact and Withdrawal I

SETTING

The critical importance of awareness and contact has been emphasized throughout this book. In consulting with organization groups, we have found that almost invariably for really solid work to be accomplished, those involved need to be in contact with one another. When there is no contact, there is abstraction, generalization, and frequently avoidance of the real issues that need to be addressed and the action decisions that need to be made.

To illustrate, we recall the early stages of a recent consulting engagement when a general manager we know said to his industrial-relations director, "John, what I'm wondering about is whether the industrial-relations organization is a suitable function within which to incorporate the affirmative-action program of this company. Perhaps the circumstances and special requirements of these minority problem areas ought to be centered in a separate function."

After we had worked with the two people for a while and real contact had been established, the question became: "John, I'm wondering if you have the clout to give this company a real affirmative-action thrust. I think whoever does this job will need to push on some of us, *including me,* and you don't seem to be doing much of that lately."

As you can see, contact isn't always easy and pleasant, but it is necessary if we are going to know where each other stands. In the case we are describing, by the way, the contact had some difficult and even awkward moments for both people, but in the long run each was a great deal more satisfied. As the general manager later explained, he had fully intended to place the affirmative-action program under a special administrator reporting directly to him. His initial comments had been intended as a prologue to soften the blow. As we learned from the industrial-relations director later, if their conversations had concluded at this noncontactful low, he would have felt very dejected indeed, since the industrial-relations organizations of other companies in his city almost all included the affirmative-action program.

In this particular case, when the general manager made contact with his industrial-relations director and told him what his real concerns were, the two men engaged further in a lively discussion about the causes of the industrial-relations director's recent seeming avoidance of forceful engagement with other members of the executive group. The details of that conversation are too extensive to report here, but it is sufficient to say that when specific cases and instances were discussed, and the two men were able to exchange what their desires and expectations of each other were, a new "working concept" was developed and affirmative action was placed within the industrial-relations organization on at least a trial basis.

Contact grows from awareness. In training awareness, we are helping people to get in touch with what is going on with themselves and others *right now*. Our aim is to help them to tune into a vast array of fresh and relevant stimuli in the realm of ideas, emotions, and sensations. With practice, these can be brought to bear in the creative solution of both straightforward and complex problems. We are encouraging people to let go, at least temporarily, of their persistent intellectual mind-models, and to experience freshly, as though for the first time, the other person or situation. From this experience comes new perspective, excitement, and the possibility of new approaches and solutions.

In contact, at its most basic level, we are saying, "Sharpen your awareness of what is going on right here and right now with you and the other person with whom you are engaged."

PROCESS

1   When working with a group that seems to be avoiding getting down to business or is having a somewhat difficult time in making meaningful contact with one another, ask all of the people in the group to talk to only one other person at a time, and to talk *directly to* that person. Further, when they do speak, ask them to say only what they *really want to say* and say it in a statement of no more than a sentence or two.

Another instruction useful for enhancing contact is for each speaker to address by name the person to whom his or her statement is directed. When responses are made to the initial statement, they should also follow this same format. This process of interaction can be carried on anywhere from a few minutes to a significantly longer period of time.

It is worthwhile to note not only the increased relevance of these briefer communications between people, but also the quality of the intervening silences. In most groups, silences can be very disquieting, primarily because of what people imagine the others in the group to be thinking. In a group where there is good contact, there tends to be less nervousness, and when this is the case, quiet periods can be appreciated.

2   After a certain period of time in the above framework, when relatively good contact has been established and people are speaking directly to one another, these rules may be set aside and group members may be allowed to speak to each other in longer statements and without addressing each other by name. The good contact should carry over into the more ordinary mode of discussion,

however, and group members can remind each other if and when some begin to stray into noncontactful abstractions.

3   When group members have acquired an adequate understanding of good contact, they may then be helped to learn about good withdrawal as well. Withdrawal may take at least a couple of forms, the most common being the ordinary device of taking a break for coffee, a walk, etc. Slightly more elaborate and quite useful other techniques can also be used to enhance withdrawal. It may be suggested to people that they stop their encounter at a convenient place, close their eyes, and imagine that they have gone away to some favorite spot, such as the mountains or the seashore. During the next few minutes, they imagine themselves just sitting around enjoying the scenery, far away from the people and the situation in which they have been involved. After a while they can be asked to come back to the present, a fresh contact may be reestablished, and work on the issues or problems started over.

By and large, withdrawal is an insufficiently appreciated function. Contact and withdrawal are important aspects of human rhythm. Good withdrawal makes for good contact, just as good contact makes for good withdrawal. Withdrawal can be restful and reinvigorating. It is especially relevant at the conclusion of a long and arduous argument or problem discussion when a breakthrough has finally occurred and some points have been resolved. Too often, most of us tend to hurry on from one conclusion to the beginning of another task without pause.

4   Another useful point for withdrawal is during a tension-producing deadlock. When nothing else seems to be working and people continue to rehash the same points, a brief period of withdrawal can be quite productive.

5   Finally, a helpful personal guideline for reestablishing vital and meaningful connections with others is to give yourself permission to talk for as long as you really feel that you are in contact, involved, and interested. Then, when you recognize that your contact is declining, *stop* rather than continuing to make small noncontactful talk. In explaining your withdrawal to others, a brief comment, something like, "Say, I feel kind of saturated now with what we've been talking about. Let's take a short break," can be quite useful. What you are likely to find is that the other person will readily agree. Most of us can sense another's diminishing involvement in conversation whether or not we know a thing about contact and withdrawal.

COMMENT

In the context of the above exercises, as well as the more ordinary processes of daily life, it can be very useful for you to get in touch with your natural patterns of contact and withdrawal. Each of us has these rhythms and many of us frequently ignore or override them, sometimes with negative consequences.

We suspect it will not be difficult for you to remember some recent conversations you have had, either in a business or social situation, in which you found yourself initially interested in and attentive to what the other person was saying, and then gradually found yourself drifting away, until you were only partly hearing the conversation or not hearing it at all. Think about conversations with friends, family, and others that you know well—many of us have learned how to either partially or almost totally tune each other out.

Contact and Withdrawal II

SETTING

This is a contact-enhancing exercise primarily for use in a workshop setting; however, it can be used in other situations as well. The exercise utilizes the "Self Checklist for Contact" (see page 61). Prior to beginning this exercise, copies of this checklist should have been distributed and fairly well discussed with the participants.

PROCESS

1   In the workshop setting, participants should identify someone with whom they have a problem of some kind, based on past associations. If the group is composed primarily of people who have no past associations, individuals may pair up with others with whom they tend to feel uncomfortable, even if it's just based on a first impression. People who are unable or unwilling to identify others that fall into either of these categories may choose someone who they just want to get to know better.

2   Generally subgroups will consist of two pairs. (Exceptions may be made if three or more people are involved in an issue.) Members of one pair should begin to discuss their problem with each other. In this process, they are encouraged to share their nonintellectual awareness with one another and to practice the suggestions contained in the "Self Checklist for Contact."

3   The second pair in the group observes the interaction, and may from time to time share their own awarenesses and brief observations when the process seems to be bogging down or diverted. Care should be taken so that the members of the observing pair do not excessively disrupt the interactions between the working pair.

4   After fifteen to twenty minutes of the interaction, at an opportune point, either the trainer or a member of the observing pair may call a temporary pause, and at this time the observers may make observations of the contact and communications process they have observed according to the guidelines. The observations should be brief and responses by the active pair should also be brief.

5   The active pair then resumes interaction for the remainder of the assigned time. All members should keep in mind the rhythm of contact *and withdrawal* so that, as necessary, those involved may break contact for a while.

6 At the conclusion of the assigned time, the observers may provide a final brief commentary. The group should take a short break and the observers should begin their own active engagement, while the formerly active pair becomes the observers.

COMMENT

A good deal can be learned here in both the observer and the active participant roles.

Shoulds II

SETTING

This is another version of the exercise we outlined in Section Two. Here, it is somewhat more formalized and can be used with pairs, trios, or quartets. Depending on the subject matter and purpose, it can be used among managers in the same group, between managers from different groups, between managers and subordinates, etc. The purpose of the exercise is to help people explore—first within themselves and then with others—some significant ideas for enriching their lives at work.

PROCESS

1   Participants form into groups of from two to four. Orient the group either toward:
   a a general exploration of the shoulds each participant has adopted toward his or her job; or
   b the shoulds associated with handling a particular problem area (if your purpose is to look at the way group members are approaching that area).

   In either case, we suggest that you point out that no one will be asked to share any ideas, thoughts, or written material that he or she doesn't wish to share, and that the exercise will probably be most useful and enjoyable if it is approached in a lighthearted spirit.

2   Each participant in the group spends about five to fifteen minutes alone, listing the three to six most important shoulds (or should nots) for him or her in the context of (a) or (b) above. Then, for each should, indicate what you would do if you didn't have that should—i.e., your natural inclinations. (Incidentally, this could be the same as you're doing now or something different.)

3   The group meets together again and in sequence each member shares, to the extent he or she is willing:
   ■ What his or her should is and what he or she would do if that should was eliminated.
   ■ How he or she stops from doing what he or she wants to do. Be specific.
   ■ Whose rule is the should: parent, society, boss, organization? Is it a real rule, or one that is self-imposed? What would happen if he or she bent or broke it? Be specific.

4 Others in the group react based on their feelings and observations, rather than by giving advice. For some useful guidelines, see "Functions of Observers" in the exercise called "Polarization—II."

5 After you've done all your sharing, take a break. Get some coffee or a beer, or lunch, and don't think about the problem for a while.

6 When you reassemble participants, take a fresh look at their shoulds lists. Do you have any new perspectives on any of them? Are there some different ways of viewing the situations, your opportunities, and how to deal with them? Discuss these new ideas with others in the group. If there are things some members haven't been able to get any new perspectives on, that they still feel concerned about, discuss those, too.

COMMENT

If ideas emerge that people want to go further with, they may want to take some additional time later to negotiate with one another (or with others outside the group) on how to make some changes. The "I want . . ." exercise can be useful for that step.

Polarization II

SETTING

Basically, this is similar to the polarization exercise we outlined in Section Two of the book. The main differences are the setting and the inclusion of other people. This out-loud dialogue technique can be extremely powerful and effective, not only for getting breakthroughs on tough problem situations, but also for helping people to rediscover and reown characteristics of themselves they have until now disowned. Doing their rediscovering with another person or two to share the experience also encourages the reopening of genuine human-being-to-human-being engagement. We all find out (or at least those of us who are willing to) that we don't need to use our roles, titles, policies, procedures, and other assorted organizational armament quite as much as we thought we did; we don't need to hide ourselves from ourselves and each other quite as deeply.

This exercise can be used most easily in a workshop setting or with a work team when people are really interested in their own individual development and in building closer interrelationships. It can be used in other settings as well, of course. In any case, it should be introduced only after the people involved have gotten to know each other fairly well and feel relatively comfortable.

PROCESS

1   In pairs or trios, each participant identifies and makes note of either:
    a A problem he or she is having with another person (boss, co-worker, subordi-
    nate, etc.); or
    b A problem he or she is having himself or herself (ambivalence about a decision
    to be made, dissatisfaction with some aspect of his or her personal life or
    career, etc.).

2   After some introductory discussion, one participant volunteers to work first. The
    working participant sets up two chairs for a dialogue between himself or herself
    and the other party to the problem, or between the two aspects of himself or her-
    self. (See the exercise "Polarization" in Section Two, page 82, for guidelines.) If
    the working participant has any discomfort with the presence of observers, they
    should discuss the specific discomfort briefly—but fully—until it is taken care of or
    other arrangements are made.

3   The person working begins and proceeds with the dialogue while the observers contribute as outlined below. Usually the person who is working should switch back and forth between chairs fairly quickly. *Note:* No one should feel compelled to start or continue this exercise if he or she doesn't want to. He or she can stop at any time.

4   After a designated period of time, say about one-half hour (with some additional cushion time) or earlier if the first participant concludes before that period, take a break. Then, repeat the process with the next volunteer.

FUNCTIONS OF OBSERVERS

1   Relax! Don't try too hard to figure out what's going on and what the solution is. The best thing you can do is just be there and allow yourself to "be with" the person who's working.

2   Help make sure both you and the person who is working do what you need to do to deal with any initial nervousness or embarrassment. The best approach is to tell each other where you are before he or she starts.

3   Your interruption of the dialogue should be minimal. When you need to speak, do so *briefly*. You can help by doing the following:
   - Suggest "switches" when the worker has been in one chair too long and seems to have bogged down.
   - Encourage him or her to speak *briefly* and directly to the other chair rather than to make speeches.
   - Encourage the worker to stay in the present and deal with current thoughts and feelings rather than the ancient past.
   - Encourage him or her to talk in a *personal* and specific way—who, what, when where—*not* in elaborate explanations of "why" or generalizations about the "big problem."
   - If the person seems to be bogging down in confusion, you might ask him or her to tell the "person" in the other chair what he or she wants *right* now. Suggest the worker start a sentence with, "Right now I want . . ." and see what comes out spontaneously. This may be quite surprising and helpful.
   - If something the worker says *really* seems significant to you, ask him or her to repeat the phrase once or twice to make sure he or she hears it clearly. (Don't overdo this.)

4   If during or after the dialogue you clearly sense the worker is experiencing nervousness or embarrassment that is seriously interfering with the process, ask about it and encourage a clear acknowledgment of what is going on. Remember, it's okay for the worker to stop at any time. It's usually very helpful if you share your own feelings, too. Remember, keep it brief.

5 Don't try too hard to solve the problem or get it resolved. What's important is a full and *alive* exploration—even if it ends in an impasse. Often the resolution comes to a person hours, or even days, later.

6 It's hard to describe when the exercise is finished, beyond saying your eyes and ears will tell you. Chances are you will get a feel for it after some practice. Again, check it out with the one who is working.

7 Keep a few notes of your own reactions and feelings while the person is working. At what points did you feel good, bad, excited, bored, etc.? Share your feelings with the worker at the end, but again, don't overdiscuss.

8 Enjoy yourself.

COMMENT

The process of the dialogue sometimes proves quite amazing, and it is occasionally difficult to fully understand from a strictly rational viewpoint. Life, it turns out, just ain't always all that rational.

As an observer, or even as a participant in this exercise, you are going to be very tempted to guide your worker to the "right choice." If he or she has been holding back from confronting some antagonist on some issue, you are probably going to be rooting for him or her to tell the SOB where to get off. If the worker has been having a difficult time with an intimate friend or loved one, you will be hoping for a reconciliation. Well, root and hope as you may, *you really don't know* what would be best for the person or the others involved. Those of us who have been in this business for a long time are still continually surprised at the startling twists and turns of human affairs. For some it is best *not to confront*—at least not now. For others, it is best *not to reconcile,* but perhaps to separate even further.

There is no way for any of us to really know these answers beforehand. Certainly, we cannot know better than the person what is important and healthful for him or her. So, that is the clue: Help the individual to arrive at his or her own answers by looking within. And, in the process, watch and perhaps you will learn something new and even profound.

Focusing on the Present

SETTING

Following are a number of approaches for helping to focus on the here and now. These can be useful in many situations and serve several purposes. First, for people to be available, their attention needs to be with what is going on. If they are not available, they cannot receive information, cannot be influenced, and cannot do much about influencing anyone else. Have you ever given a talk or made a presentation before a group of people, talked for twenty minutes, feeling fully informed and very clear about your subject matter, concluded your pitch, and then stopped and asked, "Any questions?" At which point, some guy in the third row raises his hand and asks about subject matter you clearly covered ten minutes earlier. You've no doubt then said to yourself, "What's happening? Is it me, or have all these people gone to sleep?"

Well, the likelihood is not that they have gone to sleep, but rather that they haven't arrived yet. For instance, the guy in the third row might well have spent the first ten or fifteen minutes of your presentation not hearing a word. Instead, he was still thinking about a conversation he had with his boss in a meeting just prior to this one. The woman in the fifth row, by the way, may not be here either. She may be into the future, considering what to say to her general foreman about the schedules for the rest of the day.

Second, almost all of us have been involved in long, elaborate, and confusing group discussions and meetings. Things frequently get so involved that after a while it's clear that no one in the room remembers what the original subject was. Well, it may or may not matter what the original subject was, but for anything effective to be done, the group needs to focus in on some single subject that is *relevant now.*

And finally, in most cases we can think of, it is difficult for a management group to proceed in the business of making plans for the future if the group members don't all have some common basic understanding about where they are now in the present.

These exercises for focusing on the present will help in situations such as those just described, and in many others as well. Both in management workshops we conduct throughout the country, and in consulting with management teams within companies, we very frequently use the techniques discussed below at the beginning of the session and periodically thereafter. In fact, "going around the room with a right now" is very familiar parlance for a number of management groups we have worked with, even when we're not there.

Besides helping to bring people into the present, these exercises provide an opportunity for the members of any group to acquire in a very short time and with very few words a snapshot of the ideas and concerns of their fellow members. In brief, everybody gets to know where everybody else is very quickly.

PROCESS

1 *"Right now I . . ."* This is a very simple process. The consultant or any other member of the group says, "Let's do a right now," or "Let's go around the room with a right now," etc. Our bias is that whoever calls for the round begins it with his or her own statement.

That may, in fact, be, "Right now I'm wondering what everyone else is thinking." Or it might be, "Right now I'm confused," or "Right now I want to take action," etc. Then, proceeding to his or her left or right, others begin to make their right-now statements in sequence.

A couple of cautions: People should be strongly encouraged to become genuinely conscious of *right now,* rather than to use that expression as the introduction to a long intellectual assessment, speech, or commentary on what's happening in the group. Second, it should be considered perfectly legitimate for anyone to say, "Right now I have nothing I want to say," or to report, "Right now I'm blank."

At the end of the round, a number of actions may be taken as a follow-up to the information that comes out, and that, of course, will depend on what was said. We have seen several occasions when the use of this simple technique has changed the whole character, direction, and feeling tone of a meeting. Groups have gotten back on track, or onto a new and more profitable one. Again, while the phrase may be a little awkward for some when the approach is first tried, people get more and more used to it and generally find it beneficial. With time, it often becomes quite comfortable and easy to use.

2 There are any number of variations of the "Right Now" exercise that can be useful, and you can invent on the spot to meet a specific need. For example, if you want to focus in on particular dimensions, you might try each person saying, "What is bothering me right now is . . . ," or "What I want to do right now is . . . ," or even "The most important point that's been made in this meeting up to now is. . . ." Go ahead and invent some more and let us hear from you.

3 *Quaker meeting.* This is an approach actually modeled after Quaker meetings— people speak when the spirit moves them. The approach may be called for at the beginning of a session, or after people have received a lot of information, or after they have been involved in discussion over a long period of time. It is especially worthwhile when the manager or consultant wants to determine what is

going on with members of the group in a somewhat deeper way than typically occurs with the "Right Now" exercise. This method can be most helpful when there is a desire to get a reading on the deeper emotional or intellectual tone of the group.

The group is asked to begin by sitting quietly for a moment and then, "as the spirit moves them," to speak (if you like, stand and speak) a single word, or a phrase, or at most a sentence about whatever comes into the speaker's awareness at that moment. It may be useful to ask group members not to censor themselves any more than they absolutely have to and not to rule out what they might pre-judge to be an irrelevant comment. Rather, let it all come out. The consultant or manager may make public notes (on the blackboard) of the phrases and words as they emerge, although it is likely that after the process has gone on for a while, the general tone in the room will be apparent without any special effort needed to systematize what is reported.

COMMENT

Not much more to be said.

Hopes and Concerns

SETTING

This exercise can be used frequently in both small and large groups.

Probably just about all of us have spent some time in bad meetings. Meetings can be bad right from the beginning. Sometimes even before a session begins, the attendees know it's going to be bad.

One of the principal reasons for ineffective meetings is that people come to them with different expectations, different purposes, and different wants, yet often the differences aren't noticed or worked out. Sometimes the person who called the meeting knows from the start that things don't feel quite right, but he or she really doesn't know what's wrong or what to do about it. The following approach can help significantly.

PROCESS

1   When the group has settled down, the person responsible for the meeting asks each participant to take a few minutes to write down: (1) the one or two things he or she would like to get out of this session; and (2) the one or two things that are the worst that could happen if the meeting goes badly from his or her point of view. In both cases, the emphasis is on the *individual participant.* You are not asking the person to report what would be best or worst for the total organization, or the company, or other people in the group, but *for him or her.* Participants are also told that they are willing to share, but no one needs to report anything he or she does not want to.

2   After everyone has had an opportunity to write a list, the meeting leader or consultant, if one is being used, asks them to call out their hopes and concerns to the extent that they are willing to do so. The consultant lists these, probably in abbreviated form, on large newsprint—one list for hopes and the other for concerns. In doing the listing, be sure to stay as close as possible to the original words of the participant—don't "sanitize" it. There is more vitality in, "I'm afraid this meeting will turn into a dog and pony show," than in the revised "The meeting may not be constructive."

3   When everyone has had an opportunity to call out his or her input, allow a period of time for people to really study the lists. Strongly consider the possibility of

devoting at least a part of the meeting's agenda to some of the most common and important themes on the lists.

Unless it is inappropriate because of the subject matter of the meeting, the leader or consultant makes it clear that he or she is *not responsible* for other people getting what they want from the meeting. Rather, the leader encourages people to take responsibility for themselves and indicates that he or she will try to provide a climate and the necessary resources for them to pursue their desires. Of course, the leader will represent his or her own function and own needs in the group.

We strongly recommend that the consultant or manager pay particular attention to the "Concerns" list, especially if the items are serious. For example, if a number of people are concerned that the meeting will be "as ineffective and useless as the last one we attended," that concern should be addressed. You need to find out *how* it was ineffective and useless and what they believe can be done to make it better. Ignoring the problem won't make it go away. On the other hand, on occasion we have seen groups turn around and go forward with a new sense of purpose after they've had a chance to voice and explore their complaints and either get clearer explanations or develop a revised way of working together among themselves.

4   During the meeting, the manager, the consultant, and the group may periodically refer back to the posted lists to see how well they are realizing their "Hopes," and whether or not they are getting into the difficulties they anticipated. Action can then be taken to enhance or correct the process of the meeting in accordance with the manager's and the group's intentions.

In the closing moments of the meeting, we like to ask people to take one more look at their own particular items on the lists and to indicate briefly how well they think they have done.

COMMENT

The "Hopes and Concerns" approach can have some additional helpful effects that are not immediately obvious. For one thing, the manager and other participants get a clear picture at the beginning of the session about where everybody else is and what they want to get. Many times, the lists themselves provide the most relevant and up-to-date basis for developing an agenda—in some ways considerably more useful than more-structured or formal information gathered in advance. In addition, the very act of expressing their concerns helps most people to move forward from attitudes of frustration or despair to greater energy and commitment.

I Want ...

This is in all probability one of the most important exercises in this book, for it involves developing the ability to transmute some of the "about-isms" in your life into some "is-isms." We are moving down the abstraction ladder from the vague and general to the specific and concrete. In Section Two, we gave examples of the differences between discussions *about* things and concrete action requests in the *is* mode.

The single and simple instruction in this exercise is: *Ask for what you want.* This is really the only thing you need to learn, and a tremendously important lesson it can be. In the following "Process" section we provide some guidelines for how to get at it.

PROCESS

1 Next time you find yourself in the middle of a conversation and things aren't going well—that is, they don't seem to be going your way, people don't seem to know exactly what you want, and you don't seem to know exactly what they want—STOP! And then, start your sentence with something like, "Look, what I really want is. . . ."

If you can, really let yourself do this fully, even if at first you have to plan out a bit what it is that you want to ask for. And after you have made your request, pay attention to the response and stay with the engagement.

2 For a somewhat more-structured variation it's a good idea to have a consultant or third party available. In this case, both parties to the negotiation are told the purpose of the exercise—for example, you would like to help get a clear statement of positions on the subject being discussed. To do this, each person is to ask the other very directly for what he or she wants. The other person then has the clear option of saying either: "I am willing to give that to you," or "I am unwilling to give that to you." A third possibility would be, "I would be willing to give that to you under the following circumstances." Asker and responder may rotate as negotiations continue.

Be sure each participant speaks briefly and concisely. Most of the time all of the reason for the requests have already been discussed. If they haven't been, then discuss them briefly and go on to the actual request: "What I want from you is. . . ." Don't let explanations divert clear answers. Similarly, with responses, make sure that very early, preferably in the first word, a clear "yes" or "no" is voiced.

3   One further variation of the exercise each of us can try is: "What's in it for me?" We have mentioned before that much of the time the great clarifier is *self-interest*. Many of us spend a lot of time complaining about having to do things we don't want to do. Our point is that each of us *always* has a choice, so next time you "have to" make out that thirty-five page report check yourself on what's in it for you. Do you *really* have to do it to keep your job? To please your boss? (What's in that for you?) Do you actually sort of enjoy doing it (including the complaining)? Might you not be able to cut it down to ten pages? You may even find that the strongest part of the requirement is really habit and you may want to check out whether or not that's a good enough reason for you.

COMMENT

If any of the above variations work for you, you might try turning some other people onto this approach as well. They may thank you for it later on. If you do decide to offer your assistance to others, remember: Don't thrust it on them if they don't want it.

Finally, without any reluctance about being redundant, we want to again stress that asking for what you want is one of the first and best steps toward authenticity.

If I Were King

SETTING

This approach can be especially useful with high-level managers, particularly those who have had long-standing relationships with each other in their organization. It can be used either with a single manager or with groups as described below.

Several years ago, one of the authors met with a man who had just been appointed vice president and general manager of a very large organization. In his mind, his promotion seemed to afford almost as many problems as opportunities. Since he had been selected from among a group of his peers, several of whom thought they were qualified for the job, he felt that he needed to be very careful not to antagonize or upset any of those who now reported to him. He knew that his own success depended on their support and effective performance.

As we talked, it became clear that this intelligent and highly competent man was holding himself back, almost to the point of paralysis, out of his concern for the reactions of those who now reported to him. He scarcely allowed himself to think of some of the changes he wanted to make in the organization and its operation.

To relieve some of the heaviness of this situation, we suggested to him that he play a game. The game was "If I Were King." As a result, within twenty minutes he had developed (he spoke and we made notes) a list of eighteen items he wanted to initiate or change in the organization. When that had been done and he reviewed the list, he almost immediately determined that he could begin work on ten of the items without delay. In the case of four others, he decided he would first need to do some preliminary groundwork but the items could be carried out, and he finally decided to abandon the remaining four, at least for the foreseeable future.

When, as a consultant, you encounter a manager, or even an entire group of managers, who is cutting off personal creativity and force by anticipating negative reactions, potential hurt feelings, or other forms of resistance, you may want to try the "If I Were King" game.

PROCESS

1   As king, the manager is asked to say spontaneously and explicitly what he or she would do if given complete sovereignty and freed from any concern about the possible objections or resentments of others. As the manager speaks, the

consultant takes brief notes that can be referred to later. The idea here is to introduce what may be for many a refreshing new viewpoint, and so make available some dynamic and vital ideas that had previously been inhibited by the manager's own self restrictions. After these have been brought out, it will often be found that:

- Many of the vaguely anticipated negative responses from others are more imaginary than real when they are dealt with concretely.
- Often, with some relatively slight modification, a good idea can be made acceptable to others in the organization.
- If the idea is important enough, it may be worthwhile and appropriate to put it into effect, even if it must be carried out over the objections of others.

2 One variation of this approach can be very useful, provided that the top manager of the group is confident and secure and those reporting to the manager have relatively good relationships among themselves. This method can involve an entire top management team, with members given the assignment of developing and presenting to the whole group a short list of what they and their organizations would do differently if each was made king and did not have to worry about the reactions of boss or peers. Each manager in the group should prepare a list separately on newsprint, so that it can be presented to the whole group later on. Each manager may even include on the list the things he or she would insist that peers do if he or she were in charge.

This exercise is most effective if initiated on a spur-of-the-moment basis rather than as a carefully prepared assignment. The idea is to encourage a spirit of fun and free exchange among the participants and thereby to tap into previously suppressed sources of energy. As king, each manager should be encouraged to be extravagantly selfish in his or her demands on others, at least for the moment.

3 After the presentations have been made, take a break, then have the group come back and look at the lists in a more-serious way. What do they suggest as real possibilities? Can some modifications be made to render some of the outlandish ideas practicable?

COMMENT

This new clear expression of individual manager desires will probably generate surprisingly positive reactions among fellow managers. At minimum, the shared experience will produce a new high-expectation base from which to derive necessary modifications and compromises, rather than a self-restricted low-expectation base from which they have operated in the past.

We Believe –
You Believe

SETTING

This is an intergroup exercise, particularly useful for conflict situations. It can also be adapted for use between two individuals. For this exercise, we recommend inclusion of a qualified consultant.

Polarities exist within a single individual (e.g., topdog—underdog), in interpersonal relationships, and in intergroup relationships. One of the shortcomings of some conventional human-relations practice is what we call "premature problem solving"— that is, an attempt to resolve *apparent* issues too quickly, sometimes before the real issues have had a chance to be fully developed. Usually this occurs because of the discomfort many people experience when they are witnesses to conflict situations. As noted before, people who are observers to an argument are frequently much more distressed by what is going on than are the people who are involved in the argument. When we check later, we find that those who were the contestants found the argument exciting and involving.

At any rate, when premature problem solving occurs, the consequences may be avoidance of the real problem or an intellectualization of the problem that removes it from the here and now and makes it an abstraction. Ostensible resolutions or compromises are often developed which are not sustained when the parties return to the everyday pressures of their working environment. For example, in some conventional organization-development intergroup exercises, logical solutions to the presented problems (which may not be the real problems) are reasoned out, or future "action items" are identified to be discussed and dealt with later by subgroups of the participants. Often, however, in the press of the organization's daily business, not very much follow-up occurs. Many of the premature resolutions do not stand up and the parties return to conflict, perhaps at a more covert level. Some people are left with a vaguely troubled feeling that they have failed or that the other party did not keep his or her part of the bargain.

In other cases, the failure to fully express and explore the polarities before attempting the resolution may result in both the consultant and his or her client's mistaking the presented problem as a cause rather than a symptom. And so, the underlying real problem never emerges clearly. Thus, while symptomatic relief to the presented problem may be prescribed, new symptoms emerge later because the underlying cause was never dealt with. Most consultants who have had repeated contacts with a client over a long time span can recall going back to help the group work on a new version of a problem that was supposedly solved "last time."

PROCESS

1 After appropriate introductions and prework have been concluded, the consultant describes the exercise to the groups involved. We have found it quite useful to give a full explanation, including the intentions behind each part of the process, so that people can be assured that they are not going to be tricked or manipulated.

2 The two groups are instructed to meet in separate rooms and in a period of time—probably from one-half hour to an hour, depending on the issues—they are to prepare on newsprint two lists. The first list should be headed "We Believe" and should contain their position on the essential issues of the argument between the groups. On the "You Believe" list, their perceptions of the *other* group's position on each issue should be shown. Items should be brief, but the groups should be encouraged to list them in clear terms, even allowing for some exaggeration. The idea at this time is not so much to be reasonable or fair-minded as it is to be fully expressive. These lists should cover all of the most important issues of difference between the two groups. Each group selects a spokesperson.

3 Both groups return to the central meeting room and the two spokespersons present their groups' lists. Questions may be asked by the other group's members for clarification, but arguments should be delayed until both spokespersons have completed their presentations. Each group should then identify the items both on its own and the other group's lists that it feels most strongly about—perhaps two or three of these.

4 Members of both groups should then be informed by the consultant that for a specified period of time (it might be a half-hour to an hour and a half, depending on the extent of disagreement) it is free-for-all time. People may say to each other whatever they wish, including statements, accusations, denials, etc. However, these ought to be made briefly and in a direct form. As this portion of the meeting proceeds, the consultant's function is to monitor and encourage the brevity and directness of the interchanges and to pay careful attention so that he or she may discover underlying issues. (Remember the "I want . . ." approach.)

5 By the end of the period of time indicated, if the participants have been kept to brief and direct statements, the arguments will probably begin to be repetitious or redundant. If that is not the case, then the consultant may want to extend the free-for-all. Remember, the idea is to encourage the participants to "get it all out."

6 At this point, the consultant slows down the action and provides an opportunity for all members of both groups to make a final statement for this period of time.

Statements may be about anything, but they should be brief, direct, and, wherever appropriate, addressed to a particular individual.

Based on his or her observations up to this point, the consultant may then comment on the functioning of both groups and even individuals within the groups. Depending on what has occurred during the preceding time, he or she may encourage and work with particular people to clarify their positions, check out hypotheses, and all those other things that consultants do.

Some time may be taken after the consultant's comments for members of both groups to discuss the observations offered. They can also share some of their own observations with respect to their interactions so far during the meeting. During this segment, members are instructed to change their focus from the subject matter of their debate—for awhile, they are to talk only about themselves and their interaction. The point here is not to encourage them to feel unsuccessful or guilty about their battle; rather, it is to help them to see its processes clearly and, if possible, to discover the excitement, humor, and even the fun in it. When this segment has been completed, the group should take a break, with members of both groups encouraged to intermix. In fact, when possible, pairs of people consisting of one member from each group could be encouraged to go off and have lunch together and discuss the morning.

7   When the total group reassembles, members are asked to summarize briefly the most-important points of difference (perhaps two, three, or four). In this process, the consultant should be alert for such sources of conflict as: real versus imagined disagreements, catastrophic expectations, differences growing out of inadequate communications, failures to fully express what each group wants of the other, missing elements in the dialogue that may be crucial, and goal differences as well.

8   After the issues have been developed and the polarities fully expressed, the consultant should provide an opportunity for the participants to attempt a re-definition and resolution of their points of view and feelings. This may be done in open meeting if the groups seem to be ready for this, or they may once again separate in order to further discuss where they are *now*. When discussion has been completed, the groups are asked to prepare a brief list of *specific requests* they want to make of the other group.

9   When the subgroups reassemble as a total group, the spokespersons present their requests in the format, "We want you to . . . ," and the members of the other group then have the opportunity to reply, "We are willing to do that," or "We are not willing to do that," or "We are willing to do that under the following cir-cumstances. . . ."

After both groups have had an opportunity to present and respond to the requests, a summary is prepared of the agreements and disagreements. For the items of disagreement, the groups have the option of specifying how they will obtain resolution, which can include presenting the issue to a higher authority for decision, or explicitly allowing the difference of opinion to continue without taking action until some future date, or some other arrangement, as long as it is explicit.

OPTIONAL

10 An additional step can be used at an appropriate place in this process, especially if the issues are difficult and not much progress seems to be occurring. The consultant may suggest that one of the groups subdivide itself with half of its members playing themselves and the other half playing representatives of the opposing group. These subgroups then dialogue for a limited time (say about twenty minutes or so) to see if they can develop some new ideas for resolution. If possible, this should be done with the members of the opposing group present in the room, but sitting in an outer circle. Again, the spirit should be light and enjoyable if possible.

After the first group has completed its exercise, the opposing group may move to the center of the room, divide itself similarly, and deal with the same issue or another one. When both have completed this phase, they will again have the opportunity to discuss possible mutually satisfactory resolutions.

11 *A variation.* A simple on-the-spot variation of the "We Believe—You Believe" exercise is for the consultant to list quickly on his or her flip charts the points made by one of the contesting parties. The consultant may then ask the other party to go down the list, item by item, indicating when his or her position is indeed in opposition to the person who originated the list and when it is in reality the same or similar. In our use of this approach, we have noted frequently that many differences are more imagined than real. After a brief mutual exploration, parties in disputes are often able to eliminate a majority of their supposed differences and center in on the few that remain.

COMMENT

In using the above exercise, as well as other of the more-elaborate ones, the consultant would do well to keep his or her primary energy and attention focused on *what is happening in the room,* rather than rigidly adhering to a preplanned design. In our experience, many opportunities for new and creative variations grow out of the real requirements of the situation.

Paradox

SETTING

For us, the authors, one of the most intriguing concepts that has emerged as we work in this field has been *paradox*. What we have learned, and it has occasionally been an uncomfortable learning, is that things do not always work in a linear, logical way. In fact, sometimes to get where you need to go, you have to travel in what seems to be the absolutely wrong direction.

Most discoveries about the workings of paradox are probably made accidentally. For instance, instead of trying to turn a bad situation around, sometimes we elect to stay with its current direction, with little more to guide us than hope and faith—and then, lo and behold, something good comes out in the end. It's a surprise to everyone, they all congratulate us for being brilliant consultants, but actually *we* are just as surprised as everyone else. For us, it's a matter of trusting the process of what *is* happening, rather than trying to change events to fit some idealized model we may have in our heads about what ought to happen. A good example of the workings of paradox is contained in the Herald Project case, discussed in the following section of the book. Here a management team finally got out of its doldrums (complaints and catastrophic predictions) by getting further into them. We have seen many other less-dramatic examples as well, some of which will be illustrated in the following five aspects of paradox.

PROCESS

1   *Saying no.* We believe it is very important in working with an individual or with individuals in groups to help them to recognize very early in the process their ability to be in control of, and responsible for, their own behavior and fate in the group. One important step in demonstrating this is to help people get in touch with their ability to say no, both to the consultant and to each other. One of the ground rules we talk about quite explicitly and almost immediately when working with people in a personal-development group or a work team is that, as we see it, we have a right to ask anyone in the group to do anything we see fit. *And,* at the same time, he or she has the right to say yes or to say no. The same ground rule applies for group members' interactions with each other.

There are some useful ways to help implement this ground rule. If, as a consultant, you ask a group member to say or do a particular thing (for instance, to participate in an exercise) and you detect he or she has some reluctance even though ostensibly willing to proceed, ask the person to try saying, "Yes, I am willing to do what you ask." And then, after a moment, to say, "No, I am not willing to do what you ask." The person should try out the statements *without predetermining* which one will be valid for him or her. It may be useful to have the individual repeat the pair of statements in the same format several times until the valid option becomes clear. There is an old saying that goes, "Think before you speak." We have a new one that goes, "If you want to know what you really mean, speak before you think."

A while back, we conducted a workshop with about fifteen management participants. During the two days, everyone got involved except for one man. He sat back, obviously interested, but also obviously reluctant. Just before the end of the workshop, he abruptly announced he wanted to get involved and work on an issue he had. Something about his tone of voice, and his previous behavior during the workshop, made us feel that he might be volunteering only as a response to his own pressure on himself. So we asked him to try the "Yes I want to get involved—No I don't want to" exercise. He did so, and it was immediately clear from the tone of his voice, both to himself and the other members of the group, that he did *not* want to participate any further than he had. We all recognized this, accepted it, and the workshop ended.

About three months later, at a company-sponsored party, the same man approached one of the authors and smilingly held out his hand in greeting. He said, "You probably don't remember me. I was in a workshop of yours several months ago. I didn't do much except that I learned to say no." At this point his smile broadened further, "That was really a valuable thing to learn for me. I've been saying no to more people ever since, and it sure feels good."

The point of this paradox is that only when you have learned to say no fully, can you learn to say yes fully. If you can say no, then indeed you are in charge of your own behavior and your own fate. Then, when you assent, you are doing so not because there is no other way out, but because you want to. In working with a group, it is of course important that the members get in touch with the legitimacy of saying no to each other, as well as of saying no to the consultant. The other side of the coin is for them also to become aware of the energy and power in freely saying yes.

2   *Problem relationships.* Most of us have either been involved in or observed long-standing problem relationships—competitions, feuds, etc. Many of you who are consultants have also tried to work with people who are enmeshed in these problem relationships and you are aware of the great difficulty frequently involved. Sometimes, after what appears to be a temporary success, a softening of the battle lines, only a short time elapses before the contestants are back at it again.

We have found it useful to explore some options before attempting to encourage the parties to resolve their differences. It may be quite useful to examine and to help them consider: "What is in it for you to keep your relationship *just the way it is?"* The question will probably be startling at first and frequently, the immediate response is a denial like, "What do you mean? There's nothing good about this relationship!"

Don't give up too soon. Keep at it for a while. You might say, "Well, that's probably so for the most part, but just for a moment let's explore, if there *were* something in it for you, what do you think it would be?" With a little light-handed encouragement, the participants may find that some aspects of their supposed problem are beneficial or satisfying (even though these may not be immediately obvious). For example, two strong, competitive managers we know derived mutual stimulation and a sense of excitement from their periodic clashes, though neither was fully aware of it at first. Incidentally, the rest of the management team also got some vicarious enjoyment watching "those guys fight." After the benefits have been fully recognized, acknowledged, and appreciated, the consultant may then, if it seems warranted, encourage the participants to explore: "What is in it for you to change your relationship, and how?"

A similar principle is also involved in working with people who seem to be hope-lessly stuck—in a business problem, for example.

As a counselor, you work with them, pouring huge amounts of energy into trying to help them break free and see their other options. But try as you may, nothing happens. A good question then is, "What's in it for you to stay stuck?"

3 *Reversal.* Reversal is closely related to the previous approach. Again, it is most useful when, after long and arduous work by both consultant and client, nothing seems to be happening; the bind and impasse remain. The client is saying, I want this or that to change, but seems unwilling or unable to effect the change, or identifies so many obstacles or burdens in the path of change that the situa-tion appears hopeless.

When this happens, ask the client to try the reverse—that is, ask him or her to say, I don't want to change this situation! He or she may be reluctant at first, and you, in fact, may feel a bit uncomfortable even suggesting it. (How could anyone not want a promotion or not want a more positive relationship with the boss, etc.) But again, as we've said before, life does not always proceed in what we construe to be a logical and orderly manner. Some experience with this and the other paradox approaches may provide you with a few fascinating new insights on the way life sometimes works.

4 *Resentment—appreciation.* Elsewhere we have touched on resentment and appre-ciation as a way of dealing with negative feelings. In this section, we are going to talk about its paradoxes and how to explore them. In a two-party conflict situ-

ation, especially where the real core issue is unclear, an exercise in which both people have an opportunity to voice their resentments of each other in brief, clear, energetic terms can be very useful.

Following the full expression of the resentments, those involved may be asked to express their appreciation of each other in the same format. During this process, the consultant should be on guard, so as not to encourage an artificial "let's shake hands and be friends" ending. On the other hand, he or she ought to be particularly alert for paradoxes. For instance, the accuser may, in fact, appreciate the same qualities in the opponent that he or she also resents. When the consultant has some inkling that this might be the case, he or she can raise it as a possibility or perhaps "feed the accuser a line"—i.e., suggest that the accuser try out a phrase such as, "I resent your aggressiveness and domination *and* I appreciate your aggressiveness and domination." The speaker may be surprised to find that the statement holds true, even though he or she would never have thought of it. (Of course, the consultant should also provide a clear opportunity for the speaker to *deny* the validity of the "fed line" immediately after saying it.) Each participant should also be assisted in getting in touch with the reality and legitimacy of the paradoxes he or she feels. They are not unnatural.

Another use of this same intervention may be in the midst of an antagonistic exchange between two individuals concerning a *quality* of one or the other or both. In this case, the consultant may interject himself or herself into the process and ask the contestants to reverse their statements, that is, to switch from saying, "I *don't* like the way you dominate these meetings," to saying, "I *do* like the way you dominate these meetings." This, of course, is the reversal idea we spoke of earlier.

The consultant should be aware of the possibility that frequently the very qualities being criticized by one party in the relationship may be those qualities that *that individual* possesses, or qualities he or she disapproves in himself or herself or has tried to repress. For example, when one person says to another, "I don't like the lighthearted way in which you treat this serious subject," it is possible the person has denied some part of his or her *own* capacity for humor. We want to emphasize, however, that these examples are possibilities rather than certainties, and therefore the consultant ought to be ready to give them up quickly if the client denies their validity.

5   *Going deeper in.* The idea of going deeper in, whether it's deeper into a problem, deeper into a fear or concern, or deeper into any negative situation or attitude, is not an easy one for most of us to accept. By training and perhaps even by natural inclination, we tend to avoid or escape from pain or discomfort. Perhaps most crucially, most of us want to be in control of what is happening or about to happen in our environment. If we can be in control, we can shape events so as to avoid danger or at least minimize its impact on ourselves. Yet, for some kinds of learning, for the possibility of self-discovery, and for the recognition and realization of our own and other's potential, we have to be able to let go of our control from

time to time. We have to allow ourselves to flow with the stream of events for a while rather than denying or fighting it, simply trusting that something positive will eventually happen.

The Herald Case (see Section Five) provides an example of "going deeper in." When this author suggested to the project manager and the group that they become even more explicit about their prediction of losing the proposal to another company, he did *not* know what would happen. All he knew was that since a great deal of the group's attention was focused on the probabilities of losing, that was the area in which we needed to work, even though it was uncomfortable. This same principle holds true in any number of other difficult organization problems. What we are suggesting is that the next time, or at least the time after next, when you run into an "impossible" situation—the feuding managers or departments, the apparently demoralized work group, the apparently stifled subordinate or disillusioned manager—try helping him or her or them to *go further into* their difficulties, rather than immediately looking for ways to escape. Some of the approaches we have outlined here and in other parts of the book should be helpful.

Voice and Body Awareness

This segment is primarily addressed to consultants, although it will certainly be relevant to any person who wants to increase his or her own comprehension of life experiences and his or her perceptions of what is going on in the world around. At times in this book, we have noted the limitations of trying to understand everything that happens in a rational-logical-cognitive framework; while rationality and cognition are useful for many purposes, there are large areas of our lives in which intellect and theory do not lead us to truth. In fact, they do quite the reverse, and lead us away from what is real in our experience, diverting us into our heads in a search for intellectual models that will "explain."

Many times, there is a great deal more truth inherent in the tone of a person's voice, in the expression on a person's face, or in the set of limbs and body than there is in a person's mind models about the way a situation ought to be interpreted. Many times the feelings we can sense within our bodies may provide us with more significant indicators of what we are experiencing than the words we may be saying or the thoughts that may be going around and around inside our heads.

Our emphasis so far has been very much on each person learning individually what is going on within *himself or herself,* rather than using what has come to be called the clues of body language to figure out what is going on in someone else. We believe this point is extremely important. We do not advocate the "use" of body and voice awareness for everyone, and we certainly do not advocate "using it on" anyone else. When you have become familiar, accepting of, and comfortable with recognizing and paying attention to your own body and voice signs, then you may be able to help others become more aware of and comfortable with theirs. The point in focusing on body posture and voice in the Authentic-Management framework is *not* to analyze or interpret for another person what his or her body or voice are indicating. Rather, it is to help others focus their *own* awareness on what they are doing or experiencing in their bodies and voices, and to get their own messages from those clues.

PROCESS

1 Heightening awareness of body and voice is, of course, relevant and potentially useful in just about any consulting or counseling situation. Our recommendation is that it be introduced into the consultation work (assuming the requirements we

specified above have been met) gently and gradually. The consultant would do well to say a few words about his or her focus on body and voice beforehand; in fact, we like to first ask the permission of those we are working with before we begin to comment. Further, we have also found it best to begin in this area by commenting on our own awareness of ourselves. For example, "I find myself feeling a little 'tight' as I begin to work with this group," or "As you tell me about your experience with your assistant, John, I find myself smiling a bit."

After a while, you may share your awarenesses of what you are observing with the other person as well. For example, if while a person is talking in a very low and controlled voice you become aware that her voice has changed from its previous tone or volume, then you might say, "I am aware that your voice has changed. It seems to be lower and the words seem to be coming more slowly. Are you aware of that?"

Most of the time you will have accomplished your purpose merely by bringing your observation to the other person's attention. The person will likely get his or her own message quite quickly, and you may then ask if he or she is willing to share this new awareness. If, on the other hand, the person is either puzzled or antagonistic to your observation and says something like, "So what?" or "What does that mean?", you can respond by indicating that you do not know what it means, that you are not making any interpretation or analysis of the observed behavior, but rather that you are simply sharing your awareness of it. If the person finds it useful, fine, and if not, you are willing to let it go. The process is similar when focusing on body signals—for example, when a person clenches his fists while talking about something, or leans forward intently in his chair, or physically pulls back, etc. Again, most of the time, it is only necessary to point out your awareness of the action and to let the individual deal with your comment as he or she chooses.

2 When you and your client have worked together for a somewhat longer time and the legitimacy of recognizing body and voice signals has been accepted, you may want to try a further step. In cases where the body signal does not trigger an immediate insight to the client, you may ask that he or she stop for a moment and exaggerate or intensify the signal—for example, tighten his or her fist still tighter, or repeat a particular comment in a loud voice, then still louder, etc. After the client does this, wait quietly for a moment or so afterward and then see if some new message comes through. *Don't overwork this process.* If the messages do not come through within a moment or two, then they are probably not there, or even if they are, the client is not ready yet to hear them.

Some of the more common body and voice signals to be alert to include:
- changes in voice volume or tone—from loud and strong to quiet and weak, or visa versa at key points in talking;
- the verbal expression of anger, frustration, sadness, etc., while maintaining a smile; or, more frequently, talking *about* negative situations with a smile;

- clenched fists, tightly folded arms, stiffness in the body, and other signs of physical tension;
- the raising of a hand to cover or partially cover the mouth or grasp the throat.

Frequently, though *not always,* these may be signs that the client is keeping from saying certain things.

3   A still more-advanced use of body signs, which should be used only after considerable experience, involves the following process. After identifying the particular body signal, ask the client to place all awareness in that area and then to "give voice" to the signal. For example, after both you and the client have identified the clenched fist, ask him or her to concentrate awareness there and speak for the clenched fist: "If it had a voice, what would it say to you [or whoever else might be the focus]?" The approach can be carried still further to the point of conducting a dialogue—e.g., when the finger is covering the lips, ask the client to have the finger talk to the lips, and then have the lips respond. Continue as long as it feels right.

These approaches can be tremendously useful in providing new insights, but again should be used by consultants who are sufficiently experienced to feel comfortable with what they are doing. The experience comes with practice, and one of the best people to practice on is yourself.

COMMENT

Tuning in to your body (and thereby tuning out of your head for a while) can be a major step in expanding the range of your consciousness. For those of you with an experimental bent, who have the courage and liveliness necessary to let go of your need to control yourself and all the world around you, even for a little while, this can be an entry point to a rich and rewarding new vista.

Many of us are locked into our heads—more specifically, locked into our intellectual computers and their accompanying theory storage compartments. We have been busily accumulating and storing theories, models, and other forms and concepts since early childhood. And when we have a problem or a situation to deal with, many of us know only how to search through the storage and try to find something that fits the occasion. Sometimes it works, other times it doesn't. When it doesn't, frequently we keep grinding and regrinding within our minds, repetitiously (and sometimes desperately and futilely) trying to find a fit.

Going Along with You

SETTING

Human beings are continually involved in a natural process of change. They don't have to try to be, they just are. All other living things are continually changing, too. Without any deliberate resolve or intention, they unfold and develop according to their inherent natures and characteristics.

Frequently, however, we humans, especially in Western cultures, have inhibited and discouraged our natural growth and change processes in favor of trying to force ourselves into predetermined "correct" patterns. Our intention here and elsewhere in this book is to help you get in touch with the ways in which you prevent yourself from developing. Then, when you are ready, this awareness will help you allow yourself to change. This is not an easy process for most of us, for it is an unfamiliar approach and is based on faith in your own inherent nature. That is exactly what we are trying to encourage—that you trust yourself more.

One of the things you will discover in getting in touch with yourself is that you are not constant either in focus, interest, energy, or capacity—something you've probably noted already in your day-to-day activities. What many of us frequently do with that discovery, however, is to fight it. We try to force ourselves to conform to a set of standards we think we ought to meet. If we feel tired one day we blame ourselves for that; if we lose interest in making out a report that is a regular part of our work, or in preparing a budget for our organization, we blame ourselves for that and try to force ourselves immediately back onto the "right track."

The costs of this constant pushing are high. We spend a great deal of energy fighting and criticizing ourselves into frustration and irritability. What is less obvious but equally true is that when we push ourselves in a direction and toward a goal that does not feel right, at least at the moment, we deprive ourselves of the opportunity to discover something new about ourselves—possibly some new direction that we might find appealing, or some new stimulus, potential, or creative spark that might be discovered, if, instead of pushing, we allowed ourselves to go along with our natural inclinations.

About now we can hear some of you saying, "If I let *myself* go with my natural inclinations, I'd just goof off for the rest of my life." That response represents your prediction about yourself. Catastrophic predictions are one of the ways in which people stop themselves. In the practice of psychotherapy, as well as in our own experiences in consulting with managers, we have learned that people's predictions about themselves are frequently incorrect—especially their catastrophic expectations.

There's only one way of checking that out, though, and that's by trying it a few times. (What have you got to lose? You can always go back to the old way.) One small word of caution: Don't expect immediate success the first time you try one of these exercises. It takes a while before any of us get to trusting ourselves sufficiently to let go a bit of the tight reins of self-control.

PROCESS

1   So, if you're game, next time you find yourself confronted with an unappealing task—one that you very clearly don't feel like tackling at the time—rather than force yourself, acknowledge that there's where you are. In fact, it will help to say out loud, "I really don't want to do this now." Then, wait for a moment, relax, and see what comes to your attention. Perhaps it will be the desire to close your eyes and just relax for a while. If that's it, do just that—close your eyes and let yourself "go away." A good way of doing this is to think about some pleasant place where you've been—the mountains, the seashore, etc. and in your fantasy reconstruct the scene with yourself in it. Enjoy your trip and your time there for as long as you like. You don't have to worry about overstaying, for automatic processes within you will guide you back to the present when it's right to come back. (A trip like this may take a minute, two minutes, five minutes, or ten.)

2   When you return to the real world of your desk, check to see if you don't feel more refreshed and more inclined to go at the task that needs to be done. If not, stay loose for a while, see what other thing or situation claims your attention, and follow that new claim for a bit. Even if it seems irrelevant or silly, allow yourself to go along with your own inclinations rather than choking them off. Stay with whatever occupies your awareness until you have finished it. You may be pleasantly surprised about where it leads you.

COMMENT

In working both with individuals and with teams, we have found that exercises such as this frequently produce creative new ideas and approaches in very unexpected ways.

Meditation and Letting Go

SETTING

What we would like to do now is to go a little further than you might expect in a management development book and talk a bit about meditation and letting go. If we need a reason for that (for being a little unconventional, that is), we can mention that in our experiences in working with many managers in many different organizations, we have frequently found them very interested in learning some techniques to facilitate achieving good, deep relaxation in about fifteen to twenty minutes. While we would not want to guarantee absolute accuracy, we have heard that fifteen to twenty minutes of meditation is equivalent to about a two-hour nap. Our own experiences and the reports we've had from managers we have worked with on these techniques have indicated that they are, indeed, very worthwhile.

Meditation can be valuable in a number of contexts. Close your office door, ask your secretary to hold off all calls and visitors for twenty minutes, and you may emerge (after a little practice,that is) very refreshed and ready to go. Meditation is also an excellent preparation for dealing with complicated problems. Try it sometime when you have gotten bogged down with a tough one, nothing seems to be working, and you're getting awfully tired and discouraged. It's like taking a break, or going home to "sleep on the problem." You may find that when you return from your meditation break your focus will be sharper and clearer and that you may have access to fresh approaches that weren't available to you before. Meditation is also useful in achieving a more calm and peaceful state and in getting ready to deal with other people, whether in business or personal situations. Try it, you'll like it. Allow yourself to get into the habit; about ten to fifteen minutes in the morning before work, and then another ten to fifteen minutes in the evening, perhaps soon after you get home, may help after a while to make a significant change in reducing the tensions in your life.

PROCESS

1   Find a quiet place (though it doesn't have to be absolutely noiseless) where you are not likely to be disturbed. Select a comfortable, straight-backed chair and sit with your spine in a relatively straight line, with your shoulders relaxed. Your feet ought to be flat on the floor, shoes off (if you can allow yourself to be informal with yourself). The back of your left hand should rest in the palm of your right hand with your thumbs lightly touching.

2   Begin the meditation with a relaxation exercise. Slowly and thoroughly, as you sit
in your chair, focus your awareness on the soles of your feet as they are in contact with the floor and feel any tensions or tightnesses in the muscles. If there are
tensions, feel them fully, perhaps even intensify the tensions a bit and, when you
feel ready (usually a few seconds), let them go.

Next, go to the tops of your feet and repeat the process—that is, focus your
awareness on the tops of your feet, become aware of any tensions or tightnesses
there may be, intensify them as much as necessary, then, when ready, let them
go. Step by step, do the same thing with the rest of your body, working upward
to your ankles, your lower legs, your calves, your knees, etc.

Pay particular attention to your buttocks, your anus, your chest, your shoulders,
and various parts of your face. End with the top of your head, really seeing if you
can experience your scalp. For many of you who have let your bodies become unfamiliar territory, it will not be easy to really feel these parts of you at first, but as
time goes by and with practice, you will become increasingly sensitive and aware
of your*self*.

3   When you have completed the body-relaxation exercise, begin to count your
breaths, both inhalations and exhalations (with proper diaphragm breathing, your
stomach should move outward when you inhale and inward when you exhale).
Don't strain. Begin to count, one on the inhale, two on the exhale, three on the
inhale, four on the exhale, and so on until you have reached ten, then start again
from one. The point is to focus your attention only on your breathing and the
counting. If you lose track of the counting, *don't stop to scold yourself* or analyze
where you went wrong, merely begin from one again.

You will find it very difficult, especially at the beginning, to keep from thinking all
sorts of random thoughts, such as, "I wonder what the purpose of this is?" or,
"When I get through here, I'm going to have to go see my boss," or, "I really
seem to be doing well," etc. Don't try to stop the thoughts (you can't anyway).
Merely observe them, let them pass on, and refocus on the counting. Think of
these thoughts as logs floating down a slow river—you can watch them pass without trying to hold onto them or do anything with them. Eventually, they will come
less frequently and be less insistent, and so it will be easier to let them go.

4   After you have been doing the breath counting for a while, and when it seems
right for you, you can try a "mantra." Mantra is a Sanskrit term for a word or
phrase that is helpful in meditating. Some American mantras that we have used
with managers and they have found useful are "I am" and "let go."

When you begin the mantra, say it out loud, though in a low tone. For instance, on
each exhale of the breath, say, "I am." After a while, let the phrase pass from
your lips to the inside of you until it becomes a soundless sound deep within you.
As you repeat it inside, you may hear it with your body, feel its rhythm, experience

its vibration within you somewhere—stomach, heart, head—whatever place is right for you.

With the mantra "let go," you can follow the same procedure. What you need to realize is that you are saying "let go" to yourself; you are saying let go of ideas, let go of thoughts, let go of troubles, let go of worries, let go of interesting ideas, etc. If you find that you keep getting flashes of brilliant new ideas that you are afraid to lose, keep a notebook near you, jot them down quickly, then forget them and get back to letting go.

5   When you are finished meditating (and most of the time you won't have to be called out of it—your own bio-clock will keep time for you), take a moment to be with yourself and to look around. You will probably notice some changes in your environment. Colors may be brighter, images sharper, sounds clearer, and so on. But then again, those are common reactions with some people; for others, there are still other reactions and your reaction belongs to you.

COMMENT

For almost everybody, meditation takes some time to really get into. To have it work for you, you will need both desire and patience, at least for a while. After a time, meditation becomes a very natural and regular practice for many people.

Then again, if you try it and find you don't have sufficient quantities of either desire or patience or both right now, let it go. Perhaps you will come back to meditation again someday later when it and you are more right for each other.

Authentic Management: Short Introductory Workshop

A one- or two-day experience. With one trainer—about ten to fifteen participants; with two trainers—twenty to twenty-five participants. Suggested exercises are described elsewhere, as indicated.

8:30–9:00 Informal hello. Ask participants to get in touch with *how they feel about being in this room now.* Workshop leader shares own feeling and asks for several others to volunteer brief comments.

9:00–9:30 Participants circulate in small spontaneous groups. Share with each other "how it is to be here now," get to know each other. Ask them to be alert to how their feelings change as they talk about them.

9:30–10:15 *What is Authentic Management? What is today about?* Some introductory comments by trainer. Description of the day (or two). Briefly cover theory of awareness and contact, in contrast to getting stuck in mind-models.

10:15–10:30 Coffee break

10:30–10:45 Demonstrate "Awareness" exercise, then provide instructions to participants (see "Awareness" exercise, page 62).

10:45–11:45 Subgroup in trios for "Awareness" exercise. Recompose subgroups once or twice. About twenty minutes per group. Trainers circulate to provide coaching.

11:45–noon Reassemble total group and share experiences briefly. Avoid overanalysis of experiences.

Noon–1:30 P.M. Lunch

1:30–2:45 Theory on "About-ism, Should-ism, Is-ism," with emphasis that "Is-ism" + awareness = contact, and more-effective action possibilities. Distribute "Self Checklist for Contact" (see page 61) to group. Go through each item with them. Allow time for questions and comments (*brief*).

2:45–4:45 Provide instructions for next exercise: "Contact and Withdrawal" (see "Contact and Withdrawal-II," page 129). Subgroup in quartets for exercise. Trainers circulate. (Coffee break between first set of pairs and second set).

4:45–5:15   Reassemble total group and share experiences.

5:15–end   Summary of day, wrap-up, bridge to second day, if scheduled.

Note: In the workshop, as elsewhere, use your judgment. If other subjects and exercises seem more relevant for the group you are working with, try substituting.

SECOND DAY

There is a substantial range of possibilities for designing this second day. With a foundation of awareness-and-contact experience, participants may go forward in several directions. Some possibilities are outlined below, but we suggest the trainer also consider other options mentioned in the book.

8:30–9:00   Brief review of previous day's learnings and bridge to what will be covered today.
"Right now I am aware . . ." (see "Focusing on the Present" exercise, page 136). Move quickly around the room, trainer starts. (Later trainer can explain purpose and uses of this exercise.)

9:00–9:30   Briefly cover relevant theory, according to your selection. Possibilities include: polarization, self-boundaries, introjects, should-ism, omnipotence, confluence, etc.
Allow time for coffee break.

9:45–Noon   Utilize exercise corresponding to theory. Most probably useful here are "Polarization" (page 82), "Shoulds" (page 49), and "Confluence" page 76).
Consider reversing order of exercise and theory input. (*Note:* When presenting theory, it is a good idea to share a few personal examples from your own experiences—e.g., share some of your shouldisms.)

Noon–1:30   Lunch

1:30–end   Again, a number of possibilities are available including another theory and exercise combination.
We suggest, however, that the trainer seriously consider inventing his or her own format for this period—perhaps right-on-the-spot! Consider ways in which the learnings can be translated for use in on-the-job situations. Perhaps invent some simple simulations (e.g., a performance-appraisal interview, or a meeting with the boss, etc.).
In the last hour or so, especially encourage people (perhaps in subgroups) to explore ways they may use what they have learned back on the job.

Does Anyone Know What's Happening?

(OR, SOME ADVICE TO MANAGERS ON HOLDING MEETINGS)

There just aren't very many managers who don't conduct and get involved in a lot of meetings. For many managers, meetings are simply a large pain, both in terms of the time they take and in terms of how ineffective they are for accomplishing what they're intended to accomplish. That, of course, brings us immediately to a starting point:

1.   An awful lot of managers don't really know what an awful lot of the meetings they call and conduct are really supposed to do. Especially with respect to regularly held meetings—staff meetings, for example—they haven't thought about the purpose for years. So that's the first step: know what you want to get out of your meeting—and it is *your* meeting, you know. From an Authentic-Management point of view, we'd like to add some other suggestions to this first one.

2.   When you're discussing an item on your agenda, whether it's a formal agenda or not, first be clear yourself and then make it clear to your subordinates what you *want* from them.

- Do you want them merely to hear what you have to say?
- Do you want them to follow up what you're saying and *take action* afterwards?
- Do you want them to discuss your proposal and add their ideas?
- If it is to be a discussion about an item that requires action, what, if anything, do you want from them in the way of decision making?
- Are you reserving the decision-making authority strictly for yourself, or are you asking them to participate in the decision?

- Do you want their recommendations or do you want only to hear their exploratory discussion?

Let us make it very clear we are not advocating any of the above options as *the* right way to manage. We have frequently said that for us a good manager has access to all of the possible options and uses one at one time and another at another time. What he does do is make it quite clear to his or her people exactly what is wanted, so no one ever has to guess.

3. When you have some action you want one or more of your subordinates to take, be explicit about who you want to do what, when. If you're asking for volunteers, make sure you've gotten one. We've seen, and we're sure you have, any number of cases where people wound up saying to one another afterward, "Well I thought *you* were going to do that."

4. Check to see after each item of consequence on your agenda, particularly discussion items, that everybody has finished with what he or she wanted to say. As a friend of ours put it, "good endings make good beginnings," and a clean completion of one item on the agenda means that people can really be ready for the next one. When the completions aren't clean, people may spend five to fifteen minutes or more continuing to wonder about the previous item.

5. If you and your group are into developing a plan that you want to take action on, then recognize all the steps required. For instance, what steps have to be taken (by whom and when) from: (a) the decision, to (b) the development of a sufficiently detailed operational plan, to (c) the actual implementation, to (d) completion?

6. Check at key points in your meeting to see how you and your group are doing. In the exercise section we have proposed several ways in which this can be done. A hint: when you call for "going around the room" to get people's reactions, start by sharing your own position. There is nothing like a demonstration of being up-front to encourage other people in the same direction.

7. When members of your group, including yourself, are engaged in a hot debate, make sure that before too much time goes by you or someone else in the group gives a clear summary of what the various positions are and who is holding them. Also make sure the summary is perceived as accurate by the relevant group members. If you know what the positions are, you can focus on the differences and what to do about them. Again, you and

we have seen and been involved in many cases where the voices in the room were very loud but the positions were very vague. (The exercise section also contains a number of suggestions about handling differences in points of view.)

8.   Get better at handling tough, controversial problems, especially those involving outside people or organizations. Help yourself and your people to learn to mobilize quickly for what needs to be done—whether it be competition, appeasement, compromise, cooperation, or surrender. In fact, in our view, a good manager will at various times in the course of his or her work be involved in all of them, and without getting terribly hung up about it. At this point, we must of necessity talk at this general level, but we hope your reading of this book, combined with your own creativity in adapting what you like to your own particular situation, will help.

9.   Whenever you can, break out of the "closed society" stance. If you've got a problem, consider utilizing not only those in your own department, but others as well. Service and staff groups, even other operating groups, usually have resources available. We know a number of managers who at this point would respond with, "Not on your life! If we call any of *them* all we'll get is a lot of second guessing, interference, and less help than bureaucratic hindrance." After that we would probably hear at least one or two old war stories about "the last time I tried that," or experiences of some fellow manager in an adjacent department. A lot of that kind of response is true, but we also know that most managers don't utilize all the options open to them. Most of the time you can negotiate for what you want, including the manner in which you get it, especially with staff organizations. Try making them a proposal and, if they have a counterproposal, listen to it and see if you can come to some agreement. If not, you can say to us, "See, I told you so."

Another somewhat different approach, though still along the lines of opening up your department's society a bit, is to consider inviting key people from organizations with which you interface to sit in with your group from time to time. This can be particularly useful when your group is discussing its work arrangements with their organizations. Again, in some groups, that's probably "sure death." But we have seen a number of cases in which the chance for people to sit in on each other's meetings has produced remarkably good results. They get to know you a little better and you get to know them a little better, and that usually helps. (You might even get to the point of asking them for their input on plans that affect their operations.)

10. Related to the above, but more internal, develop ways to get work done, even high-level work, by using others. Many times during our consulting with management groups we have seen good ideas tabled, avoided, or taken on with so much reluctance that everyone in the room knew there would probably never be any follow-up. The reason, of course, was that everybody had too much to do and the additional work would just have made the whole thing impossible.

But, if you think about some of those bright young men and women in the next echelon down who have all that energy and desire (especially when it comes to doing a special assignment for the people upstairs), you have a whole new set of resources. At least sometimes, the work that would otherwise require a top manager can be reformulated in such a way that a lower-level person can do most of it, at least up to the point of decision making. One of the nice things about this (assuming for the moment that the organization isn't bogged down by "politics") is that the lower-level people get a chance to show their stuff to the brass and you and your group get a chance to see some of these bright young men and women in action.

Out Loud

Own what you feel, whatever it is
Your feeling is not your enemy
   for it is part of you
And you are not your enemy.

Rather, your feeling is a child of you
That sometime ago you disowned
She is trying to return to you again
Tho, like an unsurely loved
   and upset daughter
She may wear a spiteful face and
   clamor too much
And so seem less endearing

If you do reclaim your feeling
This daughter of yourself
She/you will grow together
And ultimately
   be totally loved

A Case Study: The Herald Project

SECTION FIVE

A Dedication: To the real Dick Wilson, the most authentic manager I know.

SMH

A Case Study:
The Herald Project

In this section, we discuss the initial phases of an organization-development effort in which one of the authors was, and still is, involved. This project, which we will call the Herald Project, is being conducted in a large aerospace organization. The author was an internal consultant (i.e., an employee of the corporation) and was introduced to the project manager by the company's director of marketing, who believed there was a need for organization-development work. Since this initial contact, the author has continued to work with the project on a number of occasions over several years.

Since our objective in recounting this case is primarily to illustrate Authentic-Management approaches in action, our plan is not so much to relate specific techniques and methods (especially since these are covered extensively in previous sections of the book), but rather to provide for the consultant-reader a feeling for the style, emotional tone, and thought processes that primarily shaped this particular consultant/client relationship. In this context, I have decided to talk about the case from a first-person standpoint and to share not only a picture of the events as they occurred but also my own feelings, thoughts, and observations as we went along. In addition, I am including a comment section in order to highlight some particular points.

FIRST MEETING

I was introduced to Dick Wilson (this and subsequent names have been changed) by the director of marketing, Bob Landis. Bob had known both Wilson and myself for some time, though Wilson and I had never met before. We had a relatively brief time, only about a half hour or so, in which to say hello and talk a little about the project. Wilson was in the midst of a very busy period and therefore had scheduled another meeting to follow ours with his assistant manager, Bob Tucker, and Landis. He subsequently asked if I would like to sit in on the upcoming meeting, and I said yes.

Wilson explained that the Herald Project was still in the proposal stage—that is, we were one of two aerospace organizations currently in the midst of a frantic effort to complete a proposal to NASA to design and build a highly complex space satellite. We were involved in a big (over 90 million dollars) and difficult effort. A further complication was that Wilson had only recently assumed the leadership of this project. He was a replacement for Harold Lawson. Lawson, who had been the proposal manager during the project's initial phase (this was its second phase) was still attached to the proposal effort, but his present position, as we will discuss later, was quite unclear.

My initial impressions of Wilson were that he was extremely bright, energetic, and strong. During the initial meeting with Landis and myself, he probably did about 75 percent of the talking.

In the midst of our discussion, Wilson's secretary announced that Bob Tucker had arrived and Wilson asked her to have him come in. After a very brief introduction and without any special preliminaries, Wilson began the business of the meeting. During the course of this meeting of four, I observed over a period of time that again a great deal of the talking was done by Wilson. He talked about his concepts for organizing the project quite extensively, with an occasional question by Landis providing new stimulus for more monologue.

Bob Tucker, on the other hand, intervened very seldom. His questions were treated by Wilson in an off-handed, frequently almost superficial way, so that Bob seemed, at least to me, excluded from the real substance of the discussion. After about forty-five minutes, during which time Wilson had covered most of a large blackboard with his quick drawings of organization charts and graphs, he paused for a moment before completing the meeting. He asked me if I had any observations or questions. My response was to ask him a question in return, "Are you getting what you want out of this meeting?" Wilson stopped for a moment and seemed a bit puzzled, and then indicated that yes, he did think he was getting what he wanted, but he was curious about my question.

I pointed out that in my view most of the meeting had involved his telling the other members of the group what he planned to do, and that he had neither asked for nor received very much input from other people there, especially Tucker. Wilson turned to Tucker and asked him if he had anything more to say. Tucker replied that he did not. After a momentary glance at me again Wilson ended the meeting. He then asked if I had a few moments, and said he would like to talk to me a bit more about possible future arrangements.

COMMENT

What we have here is a good example of how *not* to begin an initial contact with a client. As I realized only some time later, after I had an opportunity to stand back from the situation a bit, my question to Wilson in the midst of the meeting, "Are you getting what you want?" was not really a question, but probably more of an indirect criticism. I had been sitting in the midst of the active discussion for about an hour and a half saying very little. What I was not fully aware of was that in this silent role a good deal of pressure had been building up within me. And, I suspect, some resentment toward Wilson's monopolization of the air time.

When I asked my question, it had come at Wilson unexpectedly and without any preparation or context. Wilson would have been very unusual if he had not had some suspicious reaction to it. By the same token, Wilson's later question of Tucker came without adequate preparation and, under the circumstances, Tucker was not likely to provide much response either.

In the framework of our guidelines for a good consulting process, I had done poorly with respect to the first two: contact and contract. Prior to this organization meeting, Wilson and I had not really made very good contact, and we had no contract at all with respect to what he wanted or expected from me. By hindsight, it would have been much better to have had an adequate period of time for our first meeting. We would then have had an opportunity to get to know each other better and to discuss our mutual expectations.

SECOND MEETING WITH WILSON

After the first meeting, Wilson walked out into the parking lot with me and as we walked it was apparent to both of us that we were each a little uncomfortable. I suggested that we get together for a follow-up meeting of just the two of us as soon as possible and he agreed.

Very quickly in this second meeting we got into better contact with one another. I told Wilson that I thought it would be a good idea for us to get to know one another better and to share as frankly as we could both what we wanted to get from one another and our concerns in working together. Wilson agreed and then, in a very straightforward manner, informed me of his primary concerns. One of these was whether in the forthcoming team-building meeting I might be inclined to encourage the project team in an "attack on the project manager." (I suspect some of this concern grew out of my intervention in the previous meeting, which he may have felt put him in an awkward position.)

His second concern was whether I was working on this project for "my own ego satisfaction, and to look good to people in the higher levels of the organization." Third, he wondered whether information that was discussed among the team might be passed on through me to higher-level people in the company, to the detriment of both Wilson and the project.

I indicated my appreciation of the frankness of his questions and said that I would answer them as best I could. First, I assured him that it would not be my intent to encourage an attack on him. At the same time, based on my previous experiences with team-building meetings, I believed that it was likely that the project team would need to deal with the project manager at an early stage in the proceedings, just as most groups I had worked with usually focused on the group leader early. I said that I believed the possibility of straightforward working relationships among team members usually had to be tested first with the highest-level authority figure in the group.

With respect to his second question, I replied affirmatively. Yes, I was in this for ego satisfaction and I did want to look good to my boss and others. What I hoped, as a matter of fact, was that the consultation on this project might provide part of a "model of the consultation process" that could be used in other programs as well. I also said to Wilson that I did not think that this would in any way be detrimental to the project or our work together. In fact, it probably ought to help, if anything. Wilson's reaction to my statement was very positive. In fact, he laughed and said, "That makes two of us. I'd like to look good too!"

With respect to the third question, I told him quite clearly what my views were on the confidentiality of information, namely, that I certainly would not pass on any information I believed was sensitive. Further, I said I would like him to make it clear to me any time we got into a subject area he wanted treated as confidential, even if it was not obviously sensitive. Wilson indicated that it might be useful to the project if some information were passed on to higher levels and sources other than project personnel. I also indicated to him after his comment that I would probably be unwilling to do any subtle "planting of information" among other people in the company, unless I was able to make that very explicit to them as well. At the end of this phase of our meeting, Wilson was quite satisfied with the responses I had given him, and said he especially enjoyed what I had said about intending to get ego satisfaction from the work. He was for that.

When Wilson had concluded his initiatives in the discussion, I informed him of what I wanted. In addition to administrative details and some arrangements with respect to timing and access to him, I said that what I most wanted was the kind of relationship with him that we had achieved in this meeting. By the end of the meeting, we both acknowledged that we had made real contact with one another and that we enjoyed each other. Wilson commented that in this brief period he felt he had gotten to know me better than other consultants with whom he had worked over longer periods.

COMMENT

This was probably our key meeting. Our frank exchanges, especially around the subject of ego satisfaction, really seemed to solidify our relationship quickly and we have since built on that relationship in our work together.

I have experienced similar "good contacts" in a number of other consulting engagements. In the Authentic-Management approach, it is very important to build a base of genuine person-to-person contact between yourself and the client. Certainly, this is not always easy nor are all managers equally willing to speak their minds. Nevertheless, most I have met are willing to step out of their role at least somewhat if the consultant is willing to step out of his or hers. In many other cases I have seen, the relationship established right from the beginning seems mostly to be a relationship between roles rather than between people—i.e., the role of manager interacting with the role of consultant. In these cases, what goes on is mostly a searching on the part of both parties to find "the right thing to say" to each other and "the right way to respond."

Finally, an obvious observation: It is important for the consultant to arrange for a client-consultant meeting to take place in an unhurried and relatively informal setting, so that they can begin to get to know one another as people. This should be done at the earliest possible opportunity. If the client is consistently "too busy," beware.

WILSON'S STAFF MEETING

Wilson and I had decided at the previous meeting that he would introduce me to his management team at their next regularly scheduled staff meeting. After a brief introduction, Wilson asked if there was anything I desired to say or do before the meeting went on. I replied that I would like to sit in on the meeting and intervene when I had a question, or when I thought I had a suggestion that might be useful. I also indicated both to Wilson and to the group that I would not feel in any way offended if, at the time of my intervention, they decided they had more urgent business than to respond to me. They could feel free to postpone or even decline to respond to my questions or suggestions.

My principal intervention in this meeting came after a rather extensive discussion by about four members of the team. I had observed that the subject matter of the discussion seemed to apply to almost all of the group, yet only these relatively few had said very much. At an appropriate pause, I made this observation and suggested that we go "around the table," with each person in the group making a brief simple statement about "where he or she was at this moment with respect to this subject" (see "Focusing on the Present," page 136). The group responded to this suggestion and, as they did, several additional very relevant points and suggestions came out. By and large the group and Wilson seemed pleased with the result.

COMMENT

The staff meeting was a good place for me to come in contact with the group for the first time. For one thing, it gave me an opportunity to see them in action in one of their typical situations; for another, it allowed them to see me and get to know me and my style a bit, under relatively safe conditions where my presence was only an incidental part of their business. The interventions I made were relatively simple and brief at this point, and we had at least some opportunity to engage with one another in a light and informal way.

INDIVIDUAL INTERVIEWS

Arrangements were made and announced to the group: I was to spend between a half hour and an hour interviewing each management-team member separately over a period of several days. There were about twenty members of the group, most of these managers of major subfunctions of the project, who in turn had organizations reporting to them. All management-team members had been informed by Wilson, explicitly and in detail, about the consulting process. He also assured them in my presence that if they had anything to discuss which they did not want reported to him or to be made a public part of the upcoming team-building meeting, they had a right to indicate this to me, and I would respect their desires. In my discussions with each I confirmed their right to privacy, while at the same time encouraging them to make their views and questions known.

In cases where I detected hesitancy to bring out some concern, I worked with the individual to explore his "catastrophic anticipation," that is, I asked him, "What would be the worst thing that could happen to you if you did talk about this information in the team-building meeting?" (see "Hopes and Concerns" exercise, page 139). In just about all cases, when we changed focus from vague dangers to more specific concerns, the individual's fears diminished and he became willing to share his point of view with the total group. At no time, however, did I exert any pressure to force this to happen. Basically, I used two major questions as points of departure for the interviews: "What do you see as the major problems or needs of this project?" and "What do you see as the major strengths and possibilities of this project?" In both cases, the broad question was followed up with more specific questions focusing on the individual and his own organization.

COMMENT

My purpose in the interviewing sessions was at least as much to get to know the people and to have them get to know me as it was to gather data. Over several years my inclination has changed. I am now placing less emphasis on the "cold" data that one can gather through individual premeeting interviews such as these, and I am more inclined toward using "hot data" which can be generated in the meeting itself through the interchanges of the people present, either individually or in subgroups.

The old argument that people will be more willing to talk in private meetings with the consultant than they will among the total group is applicable at times, but it also has a number of drawbacks. In the Authentic-Management approach we encourage people to take responsibility for themselves, and when information is reported in private and then brought out *by the consultant* without identifying the source, this is not occurring. In that case, the consultant rather than the originator is taking responsibility. I can, in fact, remember some embarrassing moments when, after posting on newsprint in front of the room comments extracted from interviews of people gathered in the room, I stood by for several minutes with no member of the group claiming authorship of any of the items on the list. In some cases, there was even a total denial of the items.

In cases where the consultant pushes participants into engagement on subjects gathered in private interviews, I have frequently seen a good deal of resistance and reluctance on the part of the participants. I have also heard, subsequent to the team-building sessions, a number of people complain that the sessions were destructive and that they had been forced into confrontations with one another.

By using techniques such as the "Hopes and Concerns" list (see page 139) or other approaches that call for people to make explicit in the here and now what they want to work on, what they want to get out of it, and what they want to leave alone for now, we can help them to move a step at a time at their own pace and to take responsibility for their own actions. They can also use this mode among themselves in their day-to-day work with one another, when no consultant is available.

PRE-TEAM-BUILDING WORK

In discussing the planned team-building meeting of the Herald team, Wilson talked to me about his relations with each of his subordinates and his perceptions of them in their jobs. He had particular concerns with respect to three people. For each of these, though for different reasons, he had questions about whether or not they could be effectively utilized in their present positions. The three were Harold Lawson, the previous project head; John Lang, one of his key sub-managers; and Chuck Renfro, another important subordinate. After considerable discussion of each of these people, we determined that prior meetings should be held with Lawson and Lang. These are described below.

COMMENT

A very important point here: we did not have to "save" everything for the team-building session. It was apparent that (a) the situations with Lawson and Lang were of such seriousness and probable difficulty that the presence of the entire team might well tend to be an inhibiting influence for both Wilson and either one of the others; and (b) the amount of time that we would need to spend on each of these cases would mean that they alone would take a significant portion of our scheduled two days, possibly precluding sufficient time for some other important items on our agenda.

I have known some managers and nonmanagers as well who somehow seem to save up their complaints about the system and each other for team-building meetings. Perhaps more in the past than today, organization-development orthodoxy recommended regular team-building meetings—on the order, perhaps, of one every three to six months, with the idea that this is good mental hygiene for the team. Our position in Authentic Management is that waiting for the group session is not the best way of dealing with important difficulties. We believe this is as true for management groups as it is for therapy groups. A better way is to deal with what you need to deal with when you need to deal with it, and in the environment that is most natural for it.

WILSON/LAWSON (IN ABSENTIA)

Harold Lawson had for some time been perceived as a problem member of the team by Wilson, and apparently by a number of others as well.

Lawson was acknowledged as a brilliant and creative engineer who had almost single-handedly developed the initial conception of the Herald design. In the course of the first phase of the competition, however, NASA had decided in favor of the design of one of the company's competitors. Yet, at the same time, NASA had been so intrigued by the conception and quality of the proposal team's submission that they had chosen it as one of the two final competitors in the second phase of the design bidding.

Thus, there were rather mixed and inconsistent feelings about Lawson and his design among the people of the program. Lawson, by nature and background primarily an independent, lone-wolf sort of person, had not been picked to head the second phase of the competition. Dick Wilson had been brought in from another program instead. As best we could tell at this time, Lawson was not terribly disappointed in this move, since he did not expect the managership himself and possibly would not have wanted it even if it had been offered to him. Yet, at the same time, Lawson, who was a very strong willed as well as competent individual, cast a dominating shadow on the proposal team. His technical knowledge and intelligence were such that it was very difficult for anyone, including Wilson, to challenge him on any aspect of the design. (It later came out during the team-building session that almost everyone on the team felt it took the *whole team* to challenge Lawson on any technical position he held.)

Wilson, as we began to speak, had a very real question regarding Lawson—specifically, whether he really wanted Harold to remain on the team or not. Wilson's primary concern was that Lawson might be so locked into his original design (which he still believed in strongly) that it would be difficult for him to give it up and focus on the alternate design the customer had decided on. In any event, Wilson was also worried that Lawson's dominance in the design group would be so strong that few would be willing to challenge him or press their own views in determining how the new design should be developed. On the other hand, Wilson was very reluctant to give up Lawson's great competence and also felt it would be unfair to ask him to leave after all he had contributed to the program so far.

Wilson had originally asked me to sit in with him in his planned confrontation discussion with Lawson. However, since I was going to be out of town, I suggested that he and I get together before his scheduled meeting with Lawson and work a little to explore some possible ways in which he might approach it. After a short while, it became apparent that Dick had not made up his mind on the subject of whether to keep Lawson or not, and was having difficulty doing so.

After some introductory comments on my part, I asked Dick if he would be willing to play out an imaginary dialogue with Lawson, taking both parts himself. (See "Polarization" exercise, page 82). Dick has an adventurous spirit and, after some hesitancy (and, as he informed me later, some suspicion about my sanity), he entered into the exercise with spirit. In the course of this imaginary dialogue what emerged was that Wilson, although not fully aware of it, had in some back part of his mind been planning program approaches that would take advantage of Lawson's special abilities. As he went further, Dick seemed to get more and more clearly in touch with the fact that he really did want Lawson to continue on the project. And in the same process he recognized that the issue had now changed to *how to keep Lawson, and still prevent his excessively dominating the project's design process.*

By the end of our session, Wilson was pretty clear on the messages he wanted to convey to Lawson. First, he did want Lawson to continue working with the project; second, his own personal concerns were that Harold would overwhelm other members of the design team unless adequate safeguards were set up; and third, he had some ideas about how these safeguards might occur and he also wanted to hear Lawson's reactions and ideas.

At the conclusion of this closed-door session, which had taken about forty-five minutes, Wilson was very pleased with his new clarity and even admitted that my suggestion of the dialogue had not been as crazy as he first thought. In fact, he was already speculating about using it again to explore some other issues. As a final word, I cautioned Dick not to expect, or even look for, a replica of the imaginary dialogue he had just completed when he really spoke to Lawson. I suggested rather that he treat the encounter in an entirely fresh way.

WILSON/LANG

John Lang was another problem case of Wilson's, in some respects even more worrisome than Lawson. If Lawson had been overly influential, Lang was uninfluenceable. Lang was responsible for an extremely important, though very specialized, aspect of the project. The specialty was not at all familiar to most of the other members of the team and yet they were affected significantly by what Lang and his organization did. Dick also had some question about whether he could effectively communicate with Lang and so especially wanted me to sit in on their meeting.

In the early stages of the meeting I made clear what I saw as my function in the session: I was to assist where I could in sharpening up the communications between the two of them, commenting on what I saw as major points of issue between them and suggesting what some alternatives might be. I also asked Lang how he felt about my being there. His response was fairly neutral. I further asked Wilson to state as clearly and directly as possible what his reason for calling the meeting was.

As the meeting progressed, it soon became apparent that there was indeed considerable difficulty in the communication process between Lang and Wilson. Lang tended to be guarded and noncontactful, and when questioned by Wilson about specifics, his responses gravitated to the level of generalization and abstraction. Wilson started off patiently, but became increasingly exasperated, though he still held himself in tight control. When Wilson raised a personal concern about Lang's nonresponsiveness to other members of the team, Lang translated that into an organizational generalization and dealt with it in a way that excluded his own involvement, thus preventing the issue from really being addressed. Though I attempted a few times to help Lang focus on specifics, I was mostly unsuccessful.

What ultimately emerged later in the meeting (as a matter of fact, made clearest by Wilson himself) was that Dick's style of interacting on project business was to be personal and direct; Lang, on the other hand, almost totally avoided that kind of contact. With some encouragement on my part, Dick spoke explicitly of his view of the differences between them and Lang acknowledged the observations to be true in his view as well. He seemed to be somewhat touched by Wilson's attempt to reach him and in a small way indicated that he understood and perhaps even sympathized with Wilson's desire. He also made it clear, however, that he was not willing or able to respond at this level, at least not at this time. I, in turn, emphasized this point of their difference to Wilson, as well as the fact that "right now that's where you both are with each other." I further noted that I considered neither of their attitudes either right or wrong per se, though the difference between them was a source of difficulty in their communications.

My primary emphasis in working with Wilson and Lang at this meeting was to establish some clarity with respect to their working relations with each other, particularly to help Dick determine whether he thought he could get through to Lang sufficiently to make for a viable working relationship. While Wilson to support his case was tempted to refer from time to time to the problems that *others in the group* were having with Lang, I encouraged him to stay with the things that were most relevant *for him* and pointed out that others could speak for themselves in the general team-building session. Toward the end of the meeting, Lang spoke a little about his own feelings of isolation in the group, both because of the nature of his work and possibly because of his personality style as well. By the end of the meeting, without either of them having explicitly acknowledged a change, both Lang and Wilson were in much better communication with one another. Wilson felt at least somewhat encouraged by the change and both he and I indicated to Lang that there would probably be a number of people in the group who would have business with him. He smiled wryly and indicated that he would not be surprised.

THE TEAM-BUILDING SESSIONS

The following is only a brief digest of the team-building sessions. I am selecting several incidents or segments to describe, in varying detail, in order to illustrate certain key points. It was a very active two days and, accordingly, many incidents will not be covered here.

The Herald team-building sessions were conducted in two days with a single day intervening between the two. The first day included dinner and a postdinner evening session that turned out to be very fruitful. The immediate point to be made about the Herald team-building sessions is that they had a good balance of focus, including structural and organizational matters, procedural items, and interpersonal concerns. In many ways, the interpersonal items were almost indistinguishable, since they were usually an integral part of task-oriented discussions.

Prior to the meeting I had made a brief summary of important trends that had emerged in the interviews. I also made some of my own observations on the issues that I believed were most significant. Of at least equal importance, the group was asked to go through the "Hopes and Concerns" exercise (see page 139) and to share, on a voluntary basis, what he thought was the best thing that could come out of these meetings for him and what his greatest concern was about the meetings. The information derived from this exercise plus the premeeting-interview data provided the basis for building an agenda for the meeting.

COMMENT

As we discussed in more detail in the "Hopes and Concerns" exercise, both hopes and concerns can provide very important information for the consultant and the team. For example, a few people on the Herald team indicated their concern that the team-building session might be nonproductive or even disruptive. (I have been involved in sessions where such concerns were expressed even more strongly by greater numbers of people.) My first focus in this case as well as in others was to ask those who voiced these particularly frightening concerns if they would be willing to be somewhat more explicit about how the session might turn out to be nonproductive or disruptive. One man had previously been involved in a team-building session with another organization. This session had, at least in his perception, resulted in a dispute between two people who, after the meeting, "hardly spoke to one another anymore." I asked if he thought such a thing might happen in this group. After some thought, he indicated that he did not believe so, since the two other individuals had experienced very bad relationships with one another even before the meeting.

I continued to encourage those who were concerned about a possible negative impact of the meeting to be increasingly more specific and explicit about their concerns. *I did not attempt to refute the concerns or minimize them,* but rather, in a step-by-step fashion, to move from the abstract to the concrete. The effect here, as in most other cases, was that those involved worked their way through their worries and were soon able to get on with the business at hand.

In cases I have encountered in other meetings, the concerns have sometimes been more tangible and have required a more substantive response. My strong belief is that it is better to recognize and acknowledge participants' concerns even when (or perhaps *especially* when) they are serious and real. I see little good in ignoring, avoiding, or minimizing these conditions—that won't make them go away.

With respect to the meeting design, we found that the intervening day between the two days of sessions was not disruptive. Though we had set the meeting up this way because of a conflicting schedule, it may even have had a beneficial effect. In working with other groups, I have come to prefer an approach in which about half the scheduled time is spent off-site—that is, away from the plant location—and the second half on-site, in the familiar working environment of the group. (This, of course, assumes that in the second half arrangements can be made so that group members will not be interrupted by telephone calls or other distractions during the meetings.)

The benefit of beginning at an off-site location is that it allows people to get together in an informal, out-of-plant setting and usually encourages less-structured and traditional interactions. The benefit of concluding the team-building meeting "back at the ranch" is that it helps people to carry forward these newly learned interaction patterns in their familiar environment. Some of you who have never tried this approach may be as surprised as I was to discover how different and more difficult it is to maintain new patterns when the group is back in familiar rooms and around familiar desks.

DUNN/WILSON

Very early in the session, Ralph Dunn, one of the two principal members of an important suborganization of the project, informed Wilson that he had to leave early to go out of town on project business. Wilson and others in the group were somewhat disturbed at this announcement, since it meant that both Dunn and his coleader would be away at the same time. This, as I learned later, was a recurring problem. At any rate, Wilson stated that before Dunn left he wanted to deal with an issue between them. After he had done some generalizing, I asked Dick to state directly to Ralph what it was he wanted of him. Dick said, "I want you to speak up more often and more forcefully on work-related matters, rather than to defer to your colleague." In response, Ralph indicated that he had some reluctance to interrupt others, especially the more-vocal members of the group, but that he would try to do so more frequently from now on.

From his tone of voice it was not clear to me, nor did I think it was clear to Ralph, whether he really meant what he was saying or was merely trying to placate or say the right thing. Though it was relatively early in the group's history, I asked Ralph if he would be willing to try an experiment. With very little introduction (I probably should have given more) I asked if he would be willing to say, "Yes, I am willing to interrupt others more often," and, after a moment, to then say, "No, I'm not willing to interrupt others more often." After a short hesitation, Ralph tried both statements, but still did not seem clear, and so I asked him to repeat both statements two or three times more. This he did, and each time the "Yes, I am willing" became stronger and clearer. So also did Ralph's satisfaction, especially after I asked him to make the statement directly to those in the group for whom he thought it was most relevant.

Several of the other participants became involved in the exercise and indicated by their excitement and smiles that they were pleased with Ralph's more forceful expression. After a while, though, two other members of the group indicated to me their displeasure with what had happened—they believed I was "treating Ralph like a child" in asking him to repeat himself. I discussed the purpose of the exercise in greater detail at this time. I also asked one of the protesters to check with Ralph regarding his reactions. Ralph reported that he had not felt put down, although he had felt a little bit uncomfortable at first. He also reported, in conclusion, that he felt it had been a very worthwhile thing for him to do.

COMMENT

This had been an icebreaker in the use of some relatively unusual techniques. The incident had been a bit awkward for me and others and, as I mentioned, I probably should have provided more background as to the purpose of the exercise before asking Dunn to try it. In any event, it proved a useful base for subsequent requests that I made of people to do unfamiliar things. I had also emphasized at the beginning of the meeting and later, too, that as far as I was concerned, any of them had the right to decline any requests that I or others made of them. With that as an active ground rule, each member of the group felt increasingly confident that he was in charge of what he did or didn't do. There also seemed to be a decreasing reluctance to try out new things.

WILMAN/LAWSON

Dick Wilson announced at the meeting that he had selected Ed Wilman to head up the new design team for the project. It was immediately recognized by several people in the group that this could be a problem in light of Wilman's prior relationship to Lawson, his former boss. As mentioned earlier, Lawson had almost single-handedly determined the phase I design. Lawson and Wilman engaged in some discussion about the design function, but it was at a very general level. I pointed this out to Wilman and asked if he had anything more specific that he wanted to say to Lawson and whether he was willing to do that. Wilman said he wanted to do that and I asked him to speak briefly and directly to Lawson. Wilman spoke more clearly of his difficulty in influencing Lawson in the past, his awe of Lawson's technical ability, and his anxiousness with respect to whether he could operate effectively with Lawson still in the picture. He was particularly concerned about whether he would be seen as the real leader of the group by those who now would report to him.

At the same time, he also made the point with real sincerity that he had tremendous respect and even affection for Lawson. Lawson acknowledged Wilman's points, but also pointed out that there was little he could do to establish Wilman's position with his subordinates. At this point, I asked Wilman what *he* intended to do about this situation. After some brief discussion, he recognized and acknowledged that he had to take responsibility for himself and actively take charge of the spacecraft design. He also realized that he could and would do what was necessary, now as a coequal of Lawson's, to get his attention and influence him as required.

Soon afterward, following a thorough exploration and discussion, Dick Wilson decided to establish a special design review group composed of himself, a senior company executive, and Harold Lawson. Lawson also made it clear that he was indeed willing to take on this new role and to relinquish any direct design responsibility. Both Wilson and Lawson made the point (to which Wilman agreed) that Wilman would need to take a strong, affirmative stand to "prove to the troops" that he was indeed the boss of design. (Even as the meeting progressed Wilman began to do just that.)

RENFRO/WILMAN

Chuck Renfro had been very quiet in the staff meeting that I had previously attended and in the current team-building session as well. Initially he said little, even in response to direct questions from me and others. After some questioning about whether or not he was willing to participate, Renfro indicated he was. What emerged as he spoke was that for some time he had been feeling that he got insufficient direction for and definition of his assigned tasks, responsibilities, and objectives from Wilman, his acting manager. Wilman, on the other hand, countered that he did not feel Renfro exercised sufficient initiative in getting his job done (though he had never voiced this to Renfro before). After some work with them both, Wilman went on to make his expectations clear: he wanted Renfro to take charge of defining his own job and in getting those things done on the job that needed to be done, without close supervision. Wilman pointed out that it was essential that he have this kind of working arrangement, especially in his new assignment. Renfro, however, seemed to be having a difficult time really understanding Wilman's point of view. He continually construed Wilman's comments as criticism of himself, and either defended his position or seemed to retreat into making no response at all.

I asked Renfro if he would be willing to conduct a dialogue (similar to the format Wilson had used in the premeeting session I had with him) in which he took the parts both of himself and Wilman. He consented to do this and within a relatively short time became quite clear on Wilman's message, for he began to hear it coming from his own lips. Renfro also began to realize that he was not clear at this time on whether or not he could handle this assignment in its more independent context. Finally Renfro and Wilman agreed that Renfro would try it out for the next month or two; then, the two of them would get together to determine whether Renfro would stay on the job or move to another less-difficult one. Both were satisfied with the arrangement and Renfro indicated that he now felt considerably relieved, since he had spent the last few months "sweating about it."

WILMAN/OTHERS

Almost immediately after Wilman's interaction with Renfro came his encounters with a number of other team members who were to be working in his organization under the new structure. These were to be temporary assignments for an established (though lengthy) period of time to perform particular aspects of the design process. Wilman had serious doubts about their commitment and willingness to work for him. He also questioned the desire and initiative of each to define those parts of the (overall design) job he wanted to do and felt he had the skills to do. The other team members, on their parts, had misgivings about whether Wilman indeed wanted them in his group and whether he would be willing to be clear about what he wanted of them. Once more I asked those involved to state what they wanted of each other, and they did so. When the exchanges had concluded, all were clear that Wilman indeed wanted and expected them to play a significant part in defining their own assignments. They, in turn, became enthusiastic about joining him and spontaneously formed themselves into a subgroup with the task of defining individual roles and schedules, to be reported back to Wilman and the total group at a later meeting.

COMMENT

This again was an example of recognition of the blockages in the system (both sides wondering what the other was thinking, and whether they were being accepted or rejected). After recognition, individuals were encouraged to become explicit about what they wanted of each other and, finally, were mobilized for action. In a subsequent meeting, I learned that the contemplated subgroup had been formed and had taken action quite successfully.

LAWSON, LANG/OTHERS

While Lawson and Lang differed quite a bit in some of their individual characteristics, they had in common the fact that they were perceived by most members of the group as quite difficult to influence. By the time this subject of the team-building meeting arose, the group had had a fair amount of exposure to the Authentic-Management approach and the effectiveness of "asking for what you want." (Almost all were enthusiastic about the progress the group was making.)

In the course of their discussions with Lawson and Lang, several group members indicated that what they wanted was for Lawson especially to be less insistent in the technical positions he took and less "overwhelming" with his reasons in support of his positions. Lawson considered this request for a while and then replied that he thought he would have a hard time changing his personal style after all these years. I supported him to a certain extent in this position by indicating that even if he did make "a New Year's resolution" to change his style it would be awfully difficult to maintain over any sustained period of time. I suggested that the requesters consider an alternate question, namely, "What are *you* all going to do to get Lawson to listen to you?"

One of the group members responded quickly, "I guess I'll have to yell at him." It was said jokingly, but it was picked up by another member who called out, "Maybe I'll hold him while you yell at him." Soon the entire group was in jovial good humor and, at the same time, recognized without resentment that at times maybe "all of us will have to combine to take Lawson on." This was in marked contrast to placing a burden of guilt on Lawson for being unreachable. And, with a grin, Lawson responded that he would appreciate it if they *did yell* just about as loud as they needed to in order to get their points across. He also volunteered that he would try to remember to be cooperative as well, especially if they reminded him when the situation arose. At the conclusion of their exchange, both sides seemed well satisfied.

In the case of the group's engagement with Lang, the resolution was less clear. Although he indicated to the group that he would be willing to have the same sort of treatment as Lawson, he did not seem to have the same degree of involvement in his statements that Lawson did. Wilson, based on his prior discussion with Lang, helped both Lang and the others to focus on Lang's feelings of isolation from the group and his feeling that they lacked interest in his part of the project. In the following discussion, it became apparent that as a way of coping Lang had built a rather strong protective style around himself and what he thought was right technically. He reported that he had very little expectation of others' interest in his area, and his own personal style seemed to help produce a self-fulfilling prophesy. Lang had occasionally asked team members to attend special briefings that he gave but had gotten little response from them. A number of the team members who had received the invitations indicated that they felt the invitations had been vague and halfhearted. They asked Lang if he would make them more explicit the next time. Lang agreed to do this.

It was not clear to me at the time whether or not any significant improvement had occurred in this set of working relationships. I learned later, over a period of several years, that it had been a beginning, and while progress with Lang was relatively slow, it did occur to a significant extent.

THE DEPRESSION

The events described in this segment of the case occurred at the end of the first day of the team-building sessions. I have saved it for last, probably because, at least in retrospect, I enjoyed it most.

As mentioned earlier, the work of the Herald team was to prepare a proposal for submission to NASA in an effort to win the contract for building a major space satellite. The team was in competition with another aerospace company. What I had not mentioned before is that almost unanimously the team members believed that they had very little chance of winning.

We had worked together in the team-development session all day and into the early evening. Intermittently, as other matters were addressed, people would make points about the competing company's advantages: they had a more acceptable initial design, they had more advantageous political connections in Washington, they probably had lower costs, etc., etc. Each time one of these points had been made during the day, however, either Wilson, the project manager, or Landis, the marketing director, would quickly step in and counter the speaker. Their point, of course, was that the group needed to maintain a positive attitude and a sense of confidence if we were to have any chance at all.

By dinner time, however, it seemed clear to me that team-member attitudes were *not* positive, nor was much confidence evident—and I believed that both those facts needed to be recognized as reality and dealt with. With the consent of Wilson, we decided to try something different. After acknowledging the low state of confidence in the group, at least with respect to our chances of winning the proposal, I asked that each person in the group state his reasons in turn for thinking that we would almost certainly lose. At first the marketing director reacted with horror to this suggestion, but with Wilson's reassurance, he finally grew quiet. (Later on he also gave several reasons of his own for why he, too, thought we would lose.)

As we started the circle of team members, the first speaker gave two or three reasons, speaking in a very heavy, almost despondent tone. The same thing happened with the second, third, fourth, and fifth speaker. By the time we had gone about halfway around the circle, just about all the reasons for losing had been mentioned at least two or three times and speakers were beginning to sound redundant. Another curious thing was also happening: people's voices began to reflect less depression than they had in the early stages of the exercise, until by the time we were about three-quarters around the circle, people were actually clowning a bit and laughing freely. When we had finished (and even Wilson and Landis participated), unaccountably—and paradoxically—the mood and tone within the room had entirely changed. The group's energy had dramatically increased; people were *done* with the subject of losing and were ready to begin on how to win.

COMMENT

As I learned weeks later, that evening marked the last time there was any substantial talk about losing the program, not because either Wilson or the marketing manager prohibited it, but because the people in the group had *finished* with the business of losing.

There are a couple of nice things to report about this story. First, we won! Secondly, Wilson, a very bright guy with a sense of humor as well as competence, was taken with the idea of recognizing and dealing with reality. Sometime later in the course of the project, after a long period of great problems and extensive overtime, he had a large newsprint sign posted in the project area. It said, "Today is September 12, the official low point of this project." A day or two afterward, an unidentified member of the team added his own postscript with a felt-tip pen, "No wonder I feel so lousy."

Overall Wilson and the other members of the group assessed the two days as being very worthwhile from the standpoint of the project. In addition to the incidents we covered here, the group also did a considerable amount of work in actual organization, the setting of some basic though informal "policies," and in developing some preliminary schedules. In subsequent meetings I had with the team, mostly during staff meetings, I found myself well accepted, feeling and being encouraged to feel part of the team. Harry Francis, one of the people who had indicated the strongest concern about the disruptive possibilities in the team-building session, told me at the end that he had been involved in three previous team-building sessions in other organizations and that this one had been the most useful and constructive of all.

Of course, it isn't likely that I would have chosen this case if it hadn't been "a winner." At the same time, though, one of the messages I would like to get through—especially to the readers who are consultants—is that it was a far-from-perfect job of consultation. I made mistakes (others besides the ones noted here), yet overall the whole thing worked—partly because people, including me, did what was natural for them to do, including making mistakes.

Sympathy

My friend, it may pain you to hear
And probably pain me even more
    to say, but
You give me nothing very good
    when you give me your sympathy

Love and gentleness are other
    matters
But even those are best for us both,
    giver and receiver
If they are firmly handed
    and firmly held between us
Soft and yielding pity will not
    support my sorrow or me

When all is truly said
Only I can support myself
And only you support yourself
Not in isolation
We may touch and hold each other
But we ought not suffer for
    each other

For that only confuses my grief
    or yours
And keeps it from full feeling
    and clean completion
And if it is not full felt
    and cleanly completed
Mourning never ends

No. Suffer not for me and ask
    me not to suffer for you
Let us not cloud or dilute sorrow
Do not give me sympathy
Rather, in my time of need
    grant me better than that
Your hand and heart to hold to while
    I feel my own pain
And your smile and joy with me
    when I am done with it.

The Consulting Process

Notes to the Consultant

To grow: Burn your own cover. Bust your own games.

A "G" AND SIX "C'S"

This section of the book is particularly oriented toward the organization consultant. We intend to cover, in a relatively compressed format, a number of aspects of the consulting relationship and process. We begin with what we believe to be seven basic elements of particular importance. These are:

- Grounding
- Contact
- Contract
- Clarifying
- Concreteness
- Checking
- Closure

GROUNDING

The concept of "grounding" is a key one in the consulting relationship. Being grounded allows a consultant to be solid, clear, and available when first making contact with a client and during their work together. By contrast, when a consultant is not grounded, he or she is often unsure, hesitant, confused, and therefore not fully available to the client. We think it worthwhile to establish a fairly regular habit of ensuring your own grounding prior to meeting your clients. Generally this requires that you:

1. Stop for a moment.

2. Get a sense of your boundaries—"Here I am, and these are my limits." (See the chapter "Self-Boundaries and Grounding.")

3. Check and acknowledge your awareness. What are you most aware of now—thinking, worrying, dry throat, constricted breathing, feeling rushed, nervous, etc.?

4. Intensify your feelings a bit and then, when you are ready, let them go.

5. Breathe fully and feel your solidity. Find your calm center.

6. If you are still up-tight after these steps, identify to yourself what you are afraid of—what is the worst thing that might happen in the engagement you are about to have? Say it out loud and hear yourself.

Other techniques for grounding are available as well. For example, get in touch with what is going on inside your boundaries. Begin by simply shifting the focus of your attention to your skin surface, slowly from head to foot, becoming aware of the sensations you receive (e.g., warmth or cold, tight or loose clothing, etc.). Then, focus your attention on what you are experiencing internally: tension in the legs, shoulders, jaw muscles, etc. After completing this survey, pay attention to what you are literally seeing, hearing, smelling, etc., to come in contact with the space around you and with the more general environment.

The more you practice grounding, the faster and easier it becomes. Eventually you can "get grounded" instantly without following the steps.

CONTACT WITH THE CLIENT

The quality of work in a consulting relationship is almost invariably related to the quality of contact between the client and the consultant. Good contact between client and consultant is a mutual experience; it involves each person focusing attention on the other, so that each sees, hears, and experiences the other as a person rather than as a mechanism. Two things about contact should be emphasized:

1. Make contact with your client before beginning to work on his or her problem.

2. Regularly check and reestablish contact from time to time throughout your engagement.

To further clarify the consultant/client contact process, let's look in a somewhat more-detailed way at suggestions and observations we have found relevant.

Learn to slow down and resist the common tendency many of us have to plunge ahead and "get down to business." Assuming that you've made contact with yourself (grounding), make contact with your client. Take a moment to look at the client and *really see him or her*—and that, of course, does not mean staring. Allow the client a moment to see you as well.

It is often helpful to share early in your meeting whatever it is that's going on with you. That doesn't mean that you have to be heavy or ominous about it, you may merely say something like, "I ran into a traffic jam on the way over here and I'm still a bit tense from that. I'd like to sit here for a few seconds and unwind." Or, "I'm a little anxious about our meeting today. This is the first time I've consulted with your company, and I'm pretty excited about it, too." What you say does not have to be profound or even terribly sensible. It is, however, a way of breaking the ice and bringing your interaction into the present. It also demonstrates your willingness to reveal yourself some and often encourages a similar movement from your client.

Once you have made your statement of where you are now, the client will generally pick up on it, often gratefully. The honesty of this initial exchange can often be carried forward into the further discussion, and that, of course, can enhance the effectiveness of your consultation significantly. We want to emphasize, however, that we're not proposing this approach as a manipulative device. Share only what you feel willing and comfortable to share rather than forcing yourself (or the client).

Some time after this initial exchange, you can further enhance the authenticity in your relationship by telling the client something more about you, what you do, and how you do it. We have found that this is helpful in giving the client a better idea of what to expect and it also provides a chance to sit back and relax a little before getting into the problem. The client is given encouragement and an initial framework to share some information about who he or she is and his or her style of managing, if the client chooses to do so. Again, you are working on building authenticity into your relationship. Following are some descriptive statements the authors have used with clients in their early contacts. We strongly suggest that you use only those that are real *for you*, phrased in your own words. You will probably have others to add as well.

- I view the consulting process as one where you and I, the client and consultant, are *jointly engaged* in an effort to identify and deal with some problems.

- I don't approach this situation with a catalog of ready-made solutions. Based on my past experiences, I have found that I seldom know "the answers" or what is best for you and your organization. What I can do, I believe, is help *you* to find the answers that you need.

- What I would like to do as we go along is to share with you my reactions to what you are saying, and sometimes I'll probably ask you some hard questions. You may not always like what I say or what I ask, but to the extent that I can, I will be straightforward with you.

These or other comments of a comparable nature may be made as the engagement goes along. You don't need to crowd all of them into the first ten minutes. Finally, in this initial phase of the conversation you can also talk about your own strengths and weaknesses—what you do well and what you don't do so well. Again, this candor usually increases rather than diminishes the client's respect for you and frequently he or she will reciprocate in feeling freer to talk about personal weaknesses or problems.

In summary, throughout the initial phase and subsequent phases of the engagement, we believe it is important to determine whether you and your client are in contact. Are you really seeing each other? Are you engaged as real people or are you one role (consultant) talking to another role (client)? If, after you have spent considerable time with your client, you find that your contact is not satisfactory, you are at a critical choice point. You may decide that you and your client are not ready to engage and the probability that good work will occur is low. If that is the case, you have several options:

- You may consciously decide to ignore the lack of contact and to pursue your business with the client as best you can.

- You may choose to interrupt the process and inform your client of your perceptions. In doing that you may want to ask if there is something about your own approach or style that is interfering with the connection between the two of you.

- You may tell the client that you are not optimistic about going further and then engage him or her in a discussion about what to do next. If the client is not contactful or straight in dealing with you now, chances are he or she will not be later on.

- You can hope that the contact may improve in the problem-exploration phase, later on. You can hope, too, that other organization members you will be dealing with later in your consultation will be more contactful, and that time and patience will ultimately pay off. The significant point to be made at this juncture, however, is that the decision by you the consultant is a conscious one about whether to proceed or not.

Some additional things can be noted about the power relationship between client and consultant. We have talked about building a genuine relationship between client and consultant, as person to person. Before that gets built, however (and sometimes it never does), there are very frequently some power-role dynamics that are not entirely obvious. These include:

- Even if the client has brought you in with the best of intentions and the purest of motives, he or she may be drawn into a kind of competitive relationship with you, frequently without being conscious of it. Remember, most of us have been conditioned to want to look good, yet the manager is about to talk to you about a problem he or she has. Therefore, the manager must admit, at some level of awareness, that *he or she* has not been able to handle the problem alone. Thus, in talking to you about it, the manager may feel "one down." If you sense this kind of competition or resistance and it doesn't seem to be passing, you will probably have to deal with it, perhaps by sharing your perception and with it your own reactions.

- If you are an outside consultant, especially an academic, the above is especially true. In addition, some clients seem to feel a kind of compulsion to impress you with theoretical knowledge, particularly if you talk to them in "technical" language. Incidentally, what may happen afterward (I've heard it a number of times) is that the manager will tell other insiders how hard it is to understand academics and how impractical they seem to be.

- Make it a first priority of yours to move as soon as possible to a relationship with the client in which that uptight look has left his or her face and you are not straining forward on the edge of your chair.

- Take charge. That doesn't mean you have to dominate the meeting, but it does mean you should have a very good idea of what the process of this consultation is and that you can explain it fairly lucidly to the client. Let your client know what you are trying to do. You are trying to work *with* the client not *on* him or her, and you would like to do it with cooperation rather than resistance.

CONTRACT

In the contract phase both the consultant and the client jointly explore and negotiate what each wants to get from the relationship. Two dimensions are involved here: the current meeting between the consultant and client and the longer-range objectives for organization improvement. The consultant's responsibilities are to help the client clarify the problem, where *he or she is* in relation to the problem and, most importantly, *what the client wants for himself or herself.*

If the consultant and client have established good contact, the contract phase will usually be fairly informal and freewheeling. An indication of poor contact, in fact, is when the client still appears distant and hesitant in discussing his or her situation.

One good approach for negotiating the contract is similar to the "Hopes and Concerns" exercise (see page 139). This technique can be used both to negotiate the contract for this meeting and for the longer term as well. We suggest that you start with what the client wants from this meeting and in the initial stages of your engagement place most of your emphasis here. As we will discuss later, the more the client becomes realistically focused and actually in touch with what he or she wants, the more likely the client is to specify meaningful requirements for the overall job. On many occasions we have intentionally postponed the definition of a long-range contract until late in the first meeting, or even into the second meeting. By then the client is frequently much better able to be specific and explicit.

Some items that are particularly useful in developing the contract are as follows:

- Ask the client, "What is the best thing that could happen *for you personally* as a result of this meeting?" and "What is the worst thing that could happen for you personally as a result of this meeting?" You should emphasize that the client answer these questions from a self-oriented position at this point rather than thinking of the good of the company, or subordinates, boss, co-workers, etc. Suggest to the client that he or she write down a few personal notes; allow a few moments for this. You as the consultant may also want to answer these questions for yourself and make your own notes.

- Have the client share his or her list with you (and you may share yours with the client). You may need to work together a bit to clarify and make more explicit the information the client has noted.

- Pay particular attention to the client's worst expectations. This often provides valuable additional information and focuses on concerns that need to be dealt with rather than ignored. Once more, in the Authentic-Management approach, you are dealing and helping the client to deal with what *is*, rather than restricting yourselves to "organization talk."

This process, or some modification of it, may be repeated later when contracting for the longer-term objectives as well.

There are several things to be alert to in the client's expectations. Most clients are to some extent locked into thinking about what they *ought to* want as opposed to what they really *do* want. Help the client become aware of this and of the difference between what he or she should want and what he or she does want. Help the client recognize the legitimacy of being concerned about one's self, often a difficult realization for managers. Again, make it easy for the client to say that he or she wants to look good, get promoted, impress the boss, or whatever. You will usually find that your client's energy as well as your own is most available in these practical, self-oriented desires. And, strangely enough, when these personal energies are well focused, they usually benefit not only the individual, but the organization and others as well.

A second potential difficulty is the client's use of abstractions and generalizations when expressing wants. We talk further about this in the next section of this chapter, "Concreteness"; for now it is sufficient to say that the consultant should work to help the client express his or her wants specifically. For example, when the client expresses a desire to improve communications in the organization, the consultant should help the client to identify *who* needs to communicate better, about *what*, to *whom*, and for what *purpose*. As a consultant, you should be particularly alert to go beyond popular phrases such as, "communications problems," "lack of cooperation," etc. The questions—who, what, when, where, and how—will help in this area.

Third, it is important in the contract phase to be clear about who ought to be involved in each element of the negotiations. For example, a certain manager may want you, as a consultant, to work on the resolution of conflict between two subordinate managers that report to her. In a case like this, it is generally advisable to meet first with the people involved in order to determine whether their perception of the problem is the same as the client's. We have found that when we explain this to the client, he or she usually agrees with the approach and willingly encourages such a meeting.

Fourth, keep in mind that the client's presenting problem is not necessarily the actual problem. For example, a manager may request a team-building session or an analysis of his organization system as a means of building more effective cooperation and operations among his staff. Later, you may discover that the real issue is more specific—i.e., the client may be partially intimidated by one of his more-aggressive and independent subordinates and hopes that, as a result of the team-building meeting, the subordinate will become more manageable. Many of us frequently are inclined to generalize our difficulties and thereby distance ourselves somewhat from the discomfort we experience from them. When contemplating working with groups in team-building sessions, intergroup exercises, or other formats, the consultant should always consider whether prior individual meetings or one-on-one meetings might not be more effective and a better use of time. (The Herald case provides an example of two such meetings prior to the actual team-building session.)

CONCRETENESS

Concreteness is largely a matter of coming down the ladder from the abstract and general to the specific and concrete. One of the most-effective techniques we know to help your client move toward increased specificity is to use the specific question words: who, what, where, when, and how. The following dialogue may serve as an example.

CLIENT: The problem is that there is a lack of coordination among my staff groups, in fact there is some antagonism between the groups. As a result, the services they perform for the line managers have suffered and I've been getting several critical reports from the managers.

CONSULTANT: Specifically, who is it that is failing to coordinate with someone else?

CLIENT: Well, it's primarily Lou, the supervisor of Methods and Standards. He ought to coordinate more with Sharon, the supervisor of Technical Training Operations. If those two would get together, that would solve most of the problem.

CONSULTANT: What would help solve the rest of the problem?

CLIENT: Well, they each need to get together with me more often and help keep me better up-to-date on what they are doing.

CONSULTANT: So the problem seems to primarily involve you and Lou and Sharon, is that right?

CLIENT: Right.

CONSULTANT: Before we actually involve Lou or Sharon in this discussion, if we do, I would like to get the problem defined more specifically.

CLIENT: All right.

CONSULTANT: First, concerning Lou, specifically what is unsatisfactory about what he does? I'll take some notes as you talk.

CLIENT: *(Here the client gives several items of unsatisfactory performance).*

CONSULTANT: *(Consultant asks, where necessary, for each item: to whom is this unsatisfactory, how, or in what ways, when, where, etc., until he has a concrete list. He then continues the same process for Sharon. Continuing the example, let's go on with the dialogue around one of these unsatisfactory items.)*

CLIENT: One of the unsatisfactory things that Lou does is that he seems to have more loyalty to the line managers than to our central staff.

CONSULTANT: Describe more specifically what you mean by that.

CLIENT: He continually goes out of his way to satisfy their requests. He'll send out special reports without checking with anyone. Sometimes they are contrary to our policies. He's spoiling them to the point that they expect special treatment more than we have time to give and then they complain about not getting it.

CONSULTANT: With whom does he not check and about what?

CLIENT: He doesn't check with Sharon to see if they are in line with our training policies and he doesn't check with me to get my reaction. I don't know anything about his report until a manager calls me with a question about it, and then I look as though I don't know what's going on.

CONSULTANT: How long has this been happening and how often does it happen?

CLIENT: It has been going on for about eight months or so, at least once a month.

CONSULTANT: What have you done about it?

CLIENT: Well, I talked with him a few months ago and he got a little upset and said he shouldn't have to check out everything he does with me or Sharon. But he did say he would check with her and with me more often. Since then he has improved only slightly. So last month I sent him a very critical note attached to a report he had sent out that I had not seen until I got a copy from one of the supervisors.

CONSULTANT: What are you going to do now? (We have found this question to be a very useful one many times. Frequently the client knows what needs to be done, it's only a matter of helping him get to it.)

CLIENT: I guess I have to talk to him again and this time be firmer.

CONSULTANT: Is that satisfactory?

CLIENT: Yes, I think so. I should have been firmer a long time ago.

The above dialogue is, of course, intended to illustrate the process of getting concrete, rather than an ideal solution to any problem. At some point from here on the consultant needs to check with the client about what he needs to do next, and to review any options that he, the consultant, sees. If there still is (and we might suspect that there well may be) some reluctance on the part of the client to confront Lou, the consultant might work further with the client to help him find what his concerns are about, and how he is stopping himself from dealing with Lou. Further possible steps might be to arrange a meeting between the client, Lou, and Sharon, with a focus on what each of them wants from the others.

Managers, consultants, and most other people as well frequently communicate their ideas, positions, experiences, and wants in such an abstract and general way that it is often not clear to others exactly what it is they are saying or what it is they want. Not surprisingly, the speaker is often unclear in his or her own mind as well. In the previous dialogue, for example, the client notes, "One of the unsatisfactory things that Lou does is that he seems to have more loyalty to the line managers than to our central staff," a conclusion drawn from the fact that Lou sends out special reports without checking with Sharon about the training policy or with the manager about staff policy. What the client wants is for Lou to first check with Sharon and himself.

We suspect that 70 percent or more of the problems a consultant encounters involve helping the client become more clear on what it is he or she wants *for himself or herself,* either from himself or herself or from others. The key to determining a client's wants is concreteness.

At some relatively early point you ought to have a fairly clear picture about certain things:

- What is your client's complaint?

- What does the client want to see changed, even if he or she doesn't yet know how to do it?

- Is the client willing to *do* anything? If so, what? What is he or she unwilling to do?

- Does the client still hold any hope of resolving the problem?

- If the client is afraid of something or someone, who or what is it?

- Is the client afraid of what those higher in the organization might think or do, or of using power on those below (see "The Myth of Omnipotence")?

- Is the client afraid of trying something that might not work?

- What is the core of the issue and the point at which the client is stuck? (It may take a while for this to emerge clearly, but most frequently management issues come down to: Shall I do this or that? Shall I do something or nothing?) If the client isn't making the decision, how is he or she stopping from doing so?

■ Is the client willing to see himself or herself as part of the problem rather than putting it all "out there with them."

One idea that is usually helpful in working toward greater specificity is to think and talk—and help the client to think and talk—in short, simple, and direct terms: I like this, I don't like that, I want this, I don't want that, etc.

A technique useful in helping you as a consultant keep in touch with the concrete and specific is to get into the habit of maintaining a mental image of what the client is describing. Try to see it as a kind of movie in front of your eyes. For example, if your client is describing a conflict incident that took place during a staff meeting, picture the event in your mind's eye as if it were happening. See who says what to whom and how it is said; who responded and what he said and how; and then what happened next, and so on.

Typically, there are significant gaps or holes in a client's description, especially of a problem that concerns him or her. We all have a tendency, at least to some degree, to relate an incident in a way that shows us as the "good guy," or the "helpless victim," or the "righteous one," etc. Thus, we have a tendency to omit, add, or in some way alter our description. Often these holes or fuzzy parts in a client's report are where the real potential pay-off is. Again, the objective is to see and help the client to see the full picture—which means helping him or her to fill in the gaps.

CLARITY

Clarity is, of course, important throughout your consulting engagement. In terms of the contract, be sure you understand what the client wants with respect to the problem and what he or she wants from you personally. Further, the client needs to know what kinds of help to expect from you and what kind if any he or she should not expect.

Later, as the consulting process proceeds, be explicit about what you are doing at each step along the way. In general, it is better to finish one thing before starting something else. It is particularly useful for the consultant to be explicit in outlining the options available to the client at each step and to help the client make clear choices. From your standpoint as consultant, you need a clear answer from the client about what he or she will or will not do next.

If *concreteness* is the specificity of the client's situation and all its relevant elements, then *clarity* is the consultant's own sense of "in-touchness" with the direction and progress of the consulting event. In the process, this clarity may include your intellectual understanding of what is going on (if you are working at the moment from an intellectual base—rational and logical); or, it may encompass an intuitive grasp of what is going on (if you are working at the moment from a more spontaneous and impressionistic base).

We are not saying, by the way, that you ought to be in either one or the other of the above modes to the exclusion of its opposite. There are certainly times when one will be more relevant and useful than the other and vice versa. Interestingly enough, we are *not* advocating that you *always* have a clarity in your engagement. Frequently we find ourselves working with a client for anywhere from a few to perhaps fifteen minutes without being very clear at all about exactly what is going on. We may be just getting a feel for what is happening by letting the information wash over us, or we may be letting the client ramble on because of some hunch we have about where he's going. Or, we may not yet feel comfortable enough with him to interrupt. However, *at some point in time*, we are going to need to stop the action for a moment and make sure we get an adequate perspective on what is really of primary concern.

There are several fairly easy approaches to establishing clarity. As in many aspects of Authentic Management, what seems most useful is the most obvious. You may simply stop for a moment and say, "I seem to be slightly confused. I don't know what the point you're making is and I'd like to get clear on that before we continue." It is perfectly legitimate to be confused and lost and to say so to the client. As far as we know, we have never lost a client's respect or confidence yet by letting him know we did not understand what he was saying or the point he was trying to make. If you are confused it is usually because you have lost track by allowing your attention to be diverted, perhaps by being in your head, thinking or theorizing, or else because the client is just not communicating clearly. In either event, the only way to get back on track is to stop and share with the client where you are. If the client is being unclear to you, chances are he is not being clear to himself either. If this is so, you can work together to get a better focus, and this, of course, can help you both. Saying to a client that you are unclear about what is happening often provides a break that allows the client to bring you up-to-date by providing more specific information, or helps him to be aware that he is unclear as well.

Another way to encourage clarity is to say to the client (actually you're saying it as much to yourself), "Let's stop for a minute and let me think out loud about what it is I believe I have heard you say so far and what my impressions of it are." Then you can take it from there, going as far as you are willing to go.

Clarification is, for us, one of the more satisfying parts of consulting. It is the reinforcement for contact, going more deeply and directly to more and more honest levels of communication. Clarity comes from being thoroughly involved in what is going on in the now.

CHECKING

Most simply, checking is the mechanism for obtaining clarity, both for yourself and the client. Checking involves stopping the action temporarily at various points in the process in order to take a reading with the client about: where you both are, how you both are doing with respect to your joint effort and with respect to each other, and finally to assess what needs to be done next. Checking is important for several reasons. It gives you an opportunity to deal with any problems or concerns that may be interfering with the work you and your client are engaged in together. It is an opportunity to stop and explore different perspectives on where you are now compared to where you began and where you need to go. And, it is an opportunity to just sit back for a moment and appreciate your progress (compare to the rhythm of contact and withdrawal, see page 125).

The analogy that comes to mind in talking about checking is two mountain climbers climbing a mountain. Neither climber can make it to the top without the other, so they must work together at each step along the way. At some points the climbers may stop and check one another: "I need to rest for a while, how about you?" or, "I think we need to take the left approach rather than the right for the next part of our climb, do you agree?" When problems arise or are imagined to exist, the climbers will stop and deal with them. They will pause to determine the best route to take next, or to backtrack if they have gone the wrong way. And they will stop occasionally to appreciate how far they've come and to see the view. Finally, they will look ahead to see if they can continue further in the time they have left or whether, in fact, they even want to go further. In time, with practice, checking should become a natural and matter-of-fact part of your consulting skills.

The consultant can stop and check where he or she and the client are at several points in the process. Again, there are no set rules, but the following guidelines or clues may be helpful.

- Check when you are not clear about where your client is, especially when you suspect something is going on with him or her. Abrupt changes in "feeling tone" and long pauses are strong clues that something is happening with your client. For example, a client may be talking about his problem and all of a sudden his face changes, or he lets out a long sigh, or his body posture or voice change significantly, or he becomes quiet for a long period and seems to be thinking about something else.

- If the above happens, you can do several things, depending on which seems most appropriate. You can:

  Do nothing.

  Share your observation, e.g., "I am aware that your face just changed as you were talking about _____. Did you notice it?"

  Ask the client what is going on, e.g., "What just happened?" Or, "I'm imagining something is going on with you now. Are you willing to share that?"

  Or, you can be more explicit, "I'm imagining that you're feeling angry (or sad or upset) now. How are you feeling?" Or, "You seem to be thinking. What are you thinking about?"

- These interventions are, of course, just a starting point and it is difficult to give specific advice on what to do next, since that depends on your client's response and the relationship you have established. The client's response may open up a whole new area for possible exploration. You both need then to decide whether you're willing to work on this new area—now, later, or not at all. On the other hand, the client may deny that anything significant is happening. As the consultant, you can accept this response and let the matter go, not believe the response and still let it go, or not accept it and tell the client so. Whichever you choose, you need to stay clear about where *you* are and what is going on with you.

- Check when something is going on with you that you want to share. For example, you may be feeling frustrated, confused, angry, etc. Share where you are first, then check where your client is. Be explicit about what you are doing: "I'd like to stop for a moment. I'm aware that as you are talking I'm beginning to feel sidetracked. I'd like to get back to what we were talking about earlier. How do you feel about that?"

- You can use checking to reestablish contact after a break in the action. For example, if you and your client, after taking a short break, are trying to get back to where you left off, one good way to do it is to each share where you are now, again with the consultant taking the initiative.

Checking is a useful technique for assessing how you and your client are doing—that is, how you feel about working together, the process you are currently using, whether or not you are on the right track, etc. Of course, it is not necessary to check out all of these areas in every consulting engagement. We do recommend, however, that if you do not explicitly check out these aspects of your relationship, you should at least have a pretty good idea about how they are going.

In the checking process, make it easy for your client to be critical and to share his or her real concerns and any objections to what has been happening between you. As we have stressed before, a good rule of thumb is for the consultant to set the example by stating first where he or she is. You will probably make it easier if you ask the client explicitly and directly for the information that you want, first explaining your reasons for asking.

When you are making a request or suggesting that your client do something, it is a good idea to check and see whether or not he or she is willing to comply. This checking gives the client the responsibility for deciding his or her own action or inaction and underscores the client's right to say no. Checking such as this also helps keep the process on track in a clear and focused way.

Many of your interventions naturally will be questions, requests, or suggestions and it is perfectly legitimate for a client to choose not to do what you have requested. Problems arise, however, when the client's refusal to comply is not explicit, which is frequently the case. What may happen instead in these instances is that the client changes the subject or gives you several excuses for not complying. At this point, some consultants fail to encourage the client to take responsibility for his or her decision and both parties simply slip away from the subject without acknowledging that they are doing so. Generally, when you make a specific, direct request of your client, you deserve a specific and direct response. When this does not occur, the interaction is typically diluted and obscured. If you look closely, you will frequently find that this kind of avoidance may also be a source of the problem the client has called you in to consult about.

CLOSURE

Good closure is a relatively simple and yet quite important part of each consulting engagement. If in your consulting interaction you have observed most of the guidelines we have discussed so far, then closure will tend to be a natural part of the process flow. Still, several items ought to be checked out specifically:

- Check performance against the original contract.
- Identify unfinished items.

- Identify what needs to be done next,
  if anything, and when.

In referring back to your original contract with the client, it will be useful to discuss how each of you feel with respect to the client's best expectations and worst concerns. You may also want to review your own with the client. Take a few moments to get in touch together with what you have accomplished; what changes have occurred, if any; the way in which the client views his or her issues; and what you see as the major opportunities and obstacles in the near future.

It will also be useful to identify and write down any pending or unfinished items either of you are aware of. Both of you should have a fairly clear idea of the next steps to be taken, both by the client and by yourself. With respect to the major thrust of action in the future, we believe that whenever possible the client should be encouraged to take primary responsibility for follow-on. At the same time, if it is agreeable to you both, you may serve the client by reminding him or her and assisting as appropriate. You should be somewhat cautious, though, to assure that any action program that grows out of your initial consulting remains *the client's program* rather than yours.

Addendum: Thirty-Three More Suggestions

1. Pay attention to the first things the client says. There's an old saying in therapy that the clue to a patient's neurosis can be found in the first words he says to the therapist. In an organization-consulting context, this is probably a gross exaggeration, but usually a great deal of information can be gleaned in the first several minutes of conversation. What you ought to be especially alert to is whether the client really wants to work on the problem or not. Did the client call you in because he or she wants you, or because it's the "right thing to do," or because someone above has put the pressure on, or because he or she just wants someone to confirm his or her own point of view? Good consulting work can be done in any of the preceding contexts, but the place at which you start will differ significantly depending on where the client really is. So check it out.

2. Watch out for overly long answers from the client, especially those that seem to wander off the subject. A good consultant ought to know how to interrupt, politely but firmly, to help both consultant and client stay on track.

3. Pay attention to whether your client suffers from that common malaise, *the unwillingness to say no*. Elsewhere we have covered this in detail, but it's worth mentioning again here. Managers, as well as others, get themselves into terrible difficulties because they somehow don't feel it's legitimate for them to say no (as often to those below them as to those above them in the organization hierarchy).

4. Be especially alert to silences and gaps in the conversation with the client. When your client stops talking and sits gazing off into space, it's very probable that a lot of thinking is going on. If you are going to be a real party to the business of working with him or her on the problem, you ought to know what he or she is thinking about. *And it's really quite legitimate to ask.* Watch out for the person who is only willing to do the real work inside his or her own head. We have been involved in or observed situations many times in which the most-important subject matter was being dealt with silently, and only after the client was asked to share it out loud could a new approach to the problem be worked out.

5.   Whenever possible, encourage your client to tell you what his or her problem is *before* giving you a load of background information. Sitting, watching, and listening as the client draws and talks about the company organization chart, its products, and its last twenty-five years of history can be boring and is seldom very useful unless these things have some relevance to the problem at hand, and you have some idea of what that problem is.

6.   Be alert for problems that aren't really problems. In our consulting, we have frequently found it very useful to ask simple questions such as, "What are you doing about that?" "What's wrong with what you're doing now?" "What are you going to do?" "Is that satisfactory?" etc. Sometimes the client is already doing exactly what he or she needs to do, but just isn't terribly comfortable about it. But then there are a lot of things we do in life that we're not terribly comfortable with.

7.   Don't make hard and fast rules about things. Giving advice is seldom useful, but if you have a piece of advice that seems to you to be relevant, give it and get it over with. If the client takes it, that's fine; if not, at least you'll be able to let it go and turn your attention to other things.

8.   Get out of the habit of giving the answer in your question. Rather than ask, "Have you done A, B, and C?" ask, "What have you done?"

9.   Be alert to imagery and figures of speech, for frequently this is where the energy is, rather than in the stiff organization jargon. When the client says, "I feel like I have an albatross around my neck," or, "I feel like I'm sitting on a fence," play around with the images for a while: Who does the albatross look like? What's on each side of the fence?

10. Consulting isn't always a matter of helping the client to make big decisions or solve big problems. You can help your client learn to make small choices and, sometimes, to live with ambiguity and discomfort.

11. Remember, it's the client's problem, not yours. If you find yourself working terribly hard and the client doesn't seem to be, it's time to take a look at what's going on.

12. Remember: Any problem that exists is there for some reason—it serves some purpose. In Authentic Management our emphasis is on problem contact rather than problem solving. Resist the temptation to rush into finding solutions. A couple of worthwhile avenues to explore at times are: What would you do if you didn't have this problem? What's in it for you to keep this problem?

13. Don't overdo asking questions. Be especially alert to your own leading questions and check for yourself to find out whether you're sometimes asking questions when what you're *really* trying to do is make a point or offer an hypothesis.

14. Practice becoming aware of where the energy is and where the deadness is. Sometimes what is being said isn't nearly as important as the amount of enthusiasm, excitement, or involvement being demonstrated, if you will only tune into it. Recognize and help your client to recognize the legitimacy of dealing with "feeling tone" as well as subject matter.

15. Find out what your client wants. Don't be a solution (e.g., team building) in search of a problem.

16. Who are your clients besides the person who called you in? Are there people who want you there and some who don't? What are you going to do about it?

17. Be the first to level—set the pattern. Tell about your style and MO, what you do well and what you don't. Talk plain, not BS (Behavioral Science). Make contact. If you can't or the client won't, beware.

18. Don't rush immediately into identifying "the problem"—even if it seems obvious. Let the information wash over you for a while and see what sticks.

19. Don't lead or get led off into "systems" work too early. First make sure you see *people* and you get seen as a *person*. It's not that systems aren't real, but if people aren't talking to people first, there is no reality, only avoidance by abstractions.

20. Think of what's going on *now* as a stream running its course. Where is it blocked and how? Is it going where it needs to go? Have things changed so that it really needs major redirection? Don't make the job any bigger than necessary. Sometimes it's just a matter of cleaning the present channels. Every once in a while you may need some real dynamite work to blast out a whole new channel.

21. Be, and help the client to be, as clear and specific as possible in operational language—e.g., it's not that "we have a personnel problem at the department manager level," it's that "Joe Doaks, the department manager, isn't doing his job well enough to suit me because he seldom meets his schedules."

22. Start with the easiest, most-promising problem areas first, *not* the toughest. Get to know the clients, their organization, and how they work. Let them get to know you too—including your idiosyncrasies. Build gradually from the easy problems to the more difficult ones.

23. A tough one for some people: Try to see the light, even the funny side of things—even heavy things. Build a climate between you and others that permits experimentation. Try saying the unsayable, e.g., "Joe is a pain in the ass." Consider the unconsiderable, e.g., "We ought to change the whole damn distribution system." On this item we aren't advising you to push yourself very hard. Go forward at your own pace.

24. *Play around* more and encourage the client to as well. Out of loose, unlikely speculation may come some new, real possibilities. You and they can find out that it's fun to be irresponsible from time to time, at least with words. Remember, "Sticks and stones can break my bones but words will never harm me."

25. Get to know the impulse and its paradox. If you are less afraid of it, it may work for you in surprising new ways. Anyway, it's no worse for people to know they are at loggerheads and acknowledge it, than to know it and pretend it isn't so.

26. Be willing to scrap ideas, plans, and other things that don't work; don't hang on to protect your image. Chances are people already know you've blown it anyway. If you set the model as an image protector, they will probably follow your lead and protect their images too. That's what happens in a lot of organizations. Conversely, if you own up to it when you've goofed, and can say so without making a big thing of it, that can set an example too. (In work the authors have done together one of the things we are frequently complimented on is our willingness to be confused, disagree, or even argue with one another right in front of our clients.) When it comes down to it, you, we, and everybody are only people—and that ain't really too bad.

27. Organize your efforts for ongoing work, even when you're not there. When you can, connect with an inside person in the organization or even a small task group. You may know OD but they know their particular organization. Find people who are interested, willing to work, and are well respected. If you can't find them, beware, your efforts may not be of much use.

28. Don't get locked into the original goals. Check periodically to see if they are still right. Circumstances or people may be changing and perhaps the goals should, too.

29. Sometimes help your client to consider giving up. In the tradition of the red-blooded, American hero epic that probably sounds outrageous, but it really is tremendously useful to have access to your ability to surrender— to say there's nothing more I can do about this particular issue and to accept your lot. A number of good things can come from the ability to give up. For one thing, the client can stop wasting energy, emotional as well as intellectual, in fruitless internal struggles; for another, a clear surrender is like a clear ending, and it very frequently provides a surprising basis for a new thrust of productive energy in another direction.

30. Generally (though there are some exceptions) advice isn't very helpful. People usually have the best answers to their own questions within themselves, and the most useful thing you can do is to help them tune in on their own resources. (By the way, that doesn't mean indirectly leading them to where you think they ought to go.)

31. Watch out for the "yeah-but" game. That's when the other guy seems to be asking you for advice, but always responds with, "Yeah, but I tried that last month and it didn't work," or "Yeah, but my boss is too hard-nosed for that to work," etc. When that happens, stop the action and check again to see what the other person really wants of you. It may be he or she just wants somebody to complain to (and there's nothing wrong with that as long as you're both clear about it).

32. Another tough one for some people: Remember, your first priority as a consultant, counselor, friend, or just plain human being is to *take care of yourself*. The myth of the selfless helper just isn't serviceable. If you are sitting there confused, frustrated, angry, scared, or whatever and holding it in for the sake of the other person, you are not likely to be much use to him or her and you are probably going to go away with a headache or stomach ache. What's more, the client will probably pick up your negative "vibes" and reflect them, which increases the tension for you both.

33. Always stay alert to the fact that the functions of counselor and counselee can be fluid. When it comes right down to it, you and the other person are not roles but people and, at best, you both may learn from each other.

Conclusion

Alternatives to Theorizing

Everyone isn't always looking at you. You are only the center
of your own universe.

One of our main objectives in this book has been to convey a simple, but
powerful, idea: *The truth can be trusted*. While we have talked about a
number of concepts and theories and outlined even more techniques and
methods, our real emphasis has been on encouraging you, the reader, to
expand your range of perception. Quite simply, we want you to become
more aware of what *is* happening both inside and outside of you and then
to deal with what is rather than what ought to be (according to your and
other people's theories about things).

This, of course, is not easy. When our senses—eyes, ears, internal
feelings of tension—tell us that we are in the presence of strong emotion
(our own or others') and that the situation is unpredictable and potentially
turbulent, we are likely to be uncomfortable, possibly *very* uncomfortable.
And if, at the same time, our thinking minds pull from their storage bins
a familiar theory or model that seems rational and cool, and a way out of
our discomfort, most of us will grasp for it as quickly as we would a life
preserver. Even when the situation is not so much an emotional one, but
rather only an unfamiliar and therefore an ambiguous one, most of us
have conditioned ourselves to grab for our theory life preservers as quickly
as we are able.

We who have been raised in Western cultural and educational traditions have learned to depend on rationality, logic, and theorizing in our
dealings with people and situations. As a result of this bias, we have
developed magnificent processes for handling complex data in orderly ways.
However, in our exclusive devotion to the logical, rational, and theoretical,
we have cut ourselves off from a great deal by blocking out much of our
access to intuition, inspiration and other noncognitive resources in our
lives. Even when we do recognize emotions as legitimate aspects of orga-

nization behavior, many of us treat our feelings and those of others only as data to be factored into our theories. And often, when we have avoided the uncomfortable and unfamiliar by taking refuge in our mind-formed theories and models, we have missed seeing and dealing with what is real.

The case we are making here is that much can be gained by learning how to let go of your cognitive, intellectual processes from time to time and to experience with senses other than the cerebral cortex what is happening both within and outside of yourself. In a number of Eastern religions and philosophies (e.g., Zen, Tao) and in some recent Western experimentation, we may learn that more is going on within each of us than can be grasped with our thinking minds alone. Other parts of our bodies and other ways of perceiving can and do produce marvelous clues to what life is about and the variety of ways there are for being in the world.

This may all seem rather esoteric and, at first glance, more relevant to religious or spiritual realms than to organization affairs. But we believe, and have found in working within organizations, that the opening up of these "new" paths of perception has great applicability and potential for increasing the energy and capacity for thought and action of managers and others.

Most of us are often limited or even trapped by the ways we perceive events and phenomena; we tend to be theorizers, whether explicitly or unconsciously. A good deal has already been written in the behavioral-science literature about the effects of our filtered thinking in distorting or even excluding perception. People typically have theories about almost everything that goes on from one moment to another in their lives. The theories may be structured and formal or merely loose collections of assumptions hardly registered in the awareness. They may focus on grand issues—e.g., the pattern of United States foreign policy; or on the most mundane moments of day-to-day life—e.g., women ought to precede men when leaving the elevator.

Within our accustomed frameworks, there are, of course, a number of advantages to having a theory. Perhaps most important, it feels safer—it helps make the world more predictable and helps us feel more in charge of things. But the very act of mobilizing our theories in order to understand and control what is *going to happen* detaches us from the event itself. In the act of theorizing, we leave only a limited part of our awareness and energy available to deal with *what is* happening.

There may be, at present, an overemphasis by organization and management theorists on systems approaches to organization dynamics. Systems thinking has become one of the fashionable ways for analyzing and treating management problems. These concepts are valid and we certainly recognize the interrelatedness of organization parts, environment, etc. However, the systems way of looking at things has oftentimes become synonymous with making big abstractions—converting here-and-now people or process troubles into important-sounding but distant generalities. It is possible to climb the abstraction ladder to so high a level that we are totally out of touch with what is going on and what needs to be done about it.

In a recent conversation with one of our colleagues who was engaged in consulting with the commanding officer of a military unit, he complained of the fantastic complexity of the United States Army as a system. Changing the philosophy, policies, and procedures of this system would require intervention, as he saw it, at the Pentagon level and would take years. However, in our discussion, when we changed focus to concentrate on *what* really needed to be done and *who* needed to do it (not to change the whole Army but only the unit he was consulting with), the problem became decidedly more manageable.

Our theories are frequently distorting screens that stand between events and our experience of them. The distortions can occur at different points with different consequences. First, you may theorize before an event, that is, in preparation for it. If you do this, you most often wind up with a framework that you subsequently attempt to confirm in the ensuing transactions. What often happens, of course, is that you discount, distort, or ignore any aspect of that event that doesn't fit into your preestablished theoretical framework. Under these circumstances, information that does not fit the theoretical model, but is compelling enough to demand inclusion, will tend to threaten or even destroy the theoretical model, leaving the theorizer in confusion and frequently grasping desperately for a replacement model.

We know of one instance where a highly capable pair of consultants, specialists in one of the systems approaches to organization development, worked with a group of aerospace-engineering managers for several days, guiding them through a preplanned process to focus on the needs of the organization. Yet, from the standpoints of both the consultants and the participants, the work was largely frustrating and unproductive. We observed the process, and the reasons for the failure were not difficult to see. The consultants *had a theory* about working with management groups, a theory that had grown out of experiences with managers in far less-sophisticated organizations. Those aerospace managers had long years of familiarity with systems work and had already incorporated into their planning approach most of what the consultants had to teach. The managers did have a number of problems, but they weren't systems problems. At the same time, the managers had a theory about working with organization consultants—which was to follow their instructions and trust that the consultants knew best. Despite several false starts and their accompanying confusion, however, neither the consultants nor the managers were able or willing to let go of their theoretical assumptions, and so the effort failed.

When theory lock-in occurs in the midst of an event, a slightly different, though related, pattern develops. We are reminded of a Christmas job with the Post Office that one of the authors had during his college days. The task was to sort mail into pigeonholes according to the city for which it was destined. Similarly, many people seem compelled to try to slot incoming information into one or another of several possible hypotheses, until finally the weight of data for one pigeonhole qualifies it to be the winner. From that point, the slotter may once more begin to select subsequent information to conform with his or her predominant theory.

We suspect that a number of readers may now be ready to ask: Are you really advocating abandoning all theories and all theorizing? Our answer, of course, is no, we're not.

From Buddhist literature comes the expression: A wise man will use a raft to cross a river, but once on the other shore, he leaves the raft behind. So with theories, *learn them and then let them go.* Allow yourself to develop a sufficient trust of your own internal processes to enable you to enter fully into what is going on, knowing that when the theory you learned is relevant to the situation, it (or appropriate parts of it) will reoccur to you.

Theorizing can be useful at the conclusion of an event. It may prove quite meaningful to look back over a series of occurrences in which you were fully involved and to generate some tentative hypotheses about the behavior and organizational interactions of both yourself and others in the engagement. But even here the theorization should be light and resilient rather than profound and restrictive. The theory ought not become a matrix into which you must fit subsequent life experiences.

In this "humanistic" age of organizations, many have been deploring the dehumanization of people in favor of machines. We have lamented the depersonalization of people for the purpose of optimizing computer programs, and we assert that to do so is counter to the principles on which our society was founded. We need to recognize as well that in our quest for orderliness and predictability, many of us frequently play these "fitting games," and when we do, we too dehumanize the human participants, including ourselves. We would do well to learn to live with more ambiguity and with the excitement that comes from our own involvements as real live people (rather than as specialized two-legged machines) in engagement with other real live people.

An incident in a training workshop we recently conducted for consultants and their clients illustrates the difference between machinelike versus human engagement. As one of the trainee-consultants in the group worked with his client, he asked question after question and received response after response. Despite his intensive questioning, though, nothing seemed to happen—no greater clarity emerged and seemingly promising avenues dead-ended in blind alleys. Eventually, most of us who watched the work were experiencing strong feelings of boredom and frustration. Yet both the trainee-consultant and his client sat expressionless in their accustomed roles, betraying none of their own feelings. Finally, the trainee-consultant asked his client, "How do you feel?" and at that point his instructor interrupted and asked him, "How do *you* feel?" The consultant turned and said, "I feel frustrated and helpless." His instructor replied, "Tell that to your client." This he did, and at that moment his client's face broke into a broad, relieved smile and he said, "So do I. We're just not getting anywhere." From that point both people let go of their specialized roles and began to really talk to one another as people. With this new basis of communication they were able to work together to identify what the real problem was and what needed to be done about it.

Another helpful borrowing from Eastern philosophy is the principle of "now-ness"—what we need to do we will do without having to plan it out. Our total organisms—rather than just our intellectual minds—know what we require. In many training workshops and consultations we have been repeatedly excited and delighted as managers, specialists, and organization-development practitioners experience what it's like to momentarily give up trying to control and predict where a particular counselor-counselee ought to go. When the course of the interaction is given free rein, more often than not a new and surprising clarification emerges, often from a quite unexpected source and at a most unexpected time.*

In summary, what we are suggesting in Authentic Management is that all of us can expand our range of ways for dealing with people and problems. To do so, we need to learn to suspend occasionally our logical-rational controls. We need to learn to float for a while with what is happening, to involve ourselves fully, to forget who we are "supposed to be," what our appropriate roles are, what our relationships ought to be, what

---

* As this particular section was being written, one of the authors was interrupted by a scheduled counseling meeting with a forty-five-year-old high-level project manager who had experienced a great deal of difficulty on his most recent assignment. Many things had gone wrong and he had catalogued them with the intention of presenting a documented briefing to his superiors. He had come to me ostensibly to try out some of his ideas on how to make his case most effectively. As we talked, I shared with him (with a bit of trepidation on my part) my impressions that he really didn't seem very interested in project management. My comment was impulsive and clearly not well founded in "the data," and I made that clear when I spoke. His reaction was surprising. He sighed heavily, then smiled a little and said, "Yeah, I'm really tired of this work. I'd like to get away for a while." This brief exchange was a turning point in our discussion and from that moment we turned our efforts into much more relevant channels.

kind of behavior is supposed to be "helpful" and "constructive" and what kind is supposed to be "improper" and "selfish." We need to allow ourselves the possibility that there are some things we don't know in our intellects, but may know in our total selves and not yet be aware of. And the way to find out is not to strive and grope, but rather to let go and allow. We have the opportunity to discover—to be surprised and delighted or, perhaps, shocked and disappointed by our discoveries. That, after all, is the nature of truth. Very often our theories are barriers blockading our own penetration into ourselves, penetration that might indeed reveal our confusion, sadness, anxiety, anger, and so on. But more important, it would also reveal to us our own real selves, and our potential for energy, excitement, joy, and creativity.

The Cloak of Omnipotence:
A Parable

In the forest about a mile or so from Organizationville, there once lived a lion whose name was Lionel. From the time he was a cub, Lionel had been an outstanding lion. He was strong and quick and intelligent and very well liked by his fellow lions as well as the other animals in the forest.

Lionel's parents were very proud of him and often remarked to each other, "Lionel is a natural leader. He will go far when he grows up and will do important things."

Lionel played and studied hard at Lion elementary school. He was happy and free. Being around him was very pleasant for others. Even when all the young animals played touch football and Lionel would block them quite hard, they would all laugh and get up and play some more. The other animals knew that Lionel was kind and had a good heart, so none feared him despite his great strength.

One day as they were playing, Lionel's mother happened by the playground just as Lionel was making a particularly spectacular block in which he knocked down Willie Lion with his shoulder, Charlie Bear with his hind quarters, and even brushed Ronald Zebra out of the play with his tail. Lionel's teammates congratulated him, and even the animals on the other team slapped him on the shanks and said, "Well done." But Lionel's mother gasped with alarm and called Lionel to her.

"Lionel," she said in a worried tone, "I am concerned about the way you are playing with the other cubs. You must realize that you are bigger and stronger than some of the other animals, and you might hurt them if you play too hard."

"But, Mother," said Lionel, who was puzzled, "the other animals play as hard as they can, too, and sometimes they knock me down, or sometimes they dodge around me."

"Still and all," said his mother, "I am worried and I do wish you would be more careful and not play as hard. I don't know what I would say to their mothers if you hurt any of the cubs. You wouldn't want others to think of you as a bully, would you, Lionel?"

"No, Mother," said Lionel, though he wasn't quite sure what a bully was.

"That's a good cub," Lionel's mother said, smiling. "Now you can go back and play with your friends and I will get your favorite dinner at the market. Remember, always be considerate of other animals' feelings and they will like you."

"Yes, Mother," Lionel said, and he returned to the game.

As he played, Lionel tried to remember his mother's advice. He held back his strength when he blocked and he even slowed down a bit when he ran. He still played pretty well, but not as well as before, and somehow in this game and those that followed he never had quite as much fun. Still and all, life was happy for Lionel in his cubhood and he had few cares or worries.

Time passed, and one day when Lionel had grown to almost his full size, his father called him into the den for a talk.

"Son," said Lionel's father, "the time has come for us to discuss your future. You have had a happy cubhood and your mother and I are very proud of you, but now we should give serious consideration to the serious business of your higher education and career."

Lionel listened politely to his father but also felt a small twinge of sadness, for he knew he was growing up and he would miss being a cub.

"Your mother and I," continued his father, "have long thought that you were gifted with a great deal of potential, and so we feel that you should attend Animal University and perhaps major in leadership. How would you like to do that, son?"

"It sounds okay, I guess," replied Lionel, with a shuffle of his rear paws and a quick glance outdoors where Charlie Bear and Ronald Zebra were chasing each other in a rousing game of tag.

Lionel's father cleared his throat to reclaim his son's attention. "Attending Animal University and preparing yourself for leadership is an honor, Son, and it is also a heavy responsibility." Lionel's father stroked his whiskers slowly and looked very serious. "One day you will probably be responsible for leading many of your fellow animals in important activities. Animals like Charlie Bear and Ronald Zebra will turn to you for direction and advice. So it is important that you study hard and listen carefully to your professors. They will help you to prepare yourself to do the fine job of leadership that your mother and I are sure you are capable of."

"Yes, sir," said Lionel quietly, and being a well-brought-up young lion, he heeded his father's advice. Soon Lionel did indeed pack his suitcase and head for Animal U.

Animal U. was an interesting place, and by and large Lionel enjoyed his time there. He studied hard, met some pretty girl animals, learned to drink beer and sing songs with words he wouldn't have mentioned around his parents, and even tried out for the Animal U. football team. In this endeavor Lionel quickly discovered, somewhat to his surprise, that when he held back his strength in making a block, many other animals ran right over him. Some ran over him even when he didn't hold back.

As the years went by, Lionel made good progress in his studies. He learned many useful things about leadership, such as how to think about what will need to be done in the future, how to arrange where other animals should stand and how they should move in order to be most efficient, how to get someone else to do something that you want to get done but haven't time to do yourself, how to keep track of what has been done and subtract it from what was supposed to be done, and finally, how to write reports about all of these things.

When Lionel was a senior, he signed up for a special course called Animal Relations in Leadership, which was taught by a very famous professor, Dr. Sherwood Giraffe. In Dr. Giraffe's class, Lionel heard again what he had heard from his father—that leadership was a very important responsibility.

He learned too about Animal Psychology and how easily other animals' feelings could be hurt if the leader was harsh with them.

He learned that it was good for a leader to suggest and even persuade, but not good for a leader to order or demand.

He learned that a leader ought to ask other animals for their opinions before giving his or her own, because other animals were likely to be overly influenced by what the leader said.

He learned that while animals respected and admired their leaders, they also feared them because they tended to think about leaders as they had their fathers when they were cubs. So a leader had to be very careful not to use authority in a way that would injure or frighten or upset his or her followers.

He learned that a leader ought to always appear confident and not reveal to others any doubt or confusion or uncertainty, because they might lose confidence in the leader and begin to feel these unhappy feelings too.

He learned that a leader needed to think cautiously before speaking or acting, because a leader's words and deeds carry so much weight.

And he learned, too, that being a leader was supposed to be a lonely job.

These were serious lessons indeed, Lionel thought, but heeding his father's advice, he learned them well.

When spring came, Lionel graduated from Animal University and returned again to the forest about a mile from Organizationville to find a place where he might put to use the valuable training he had received. As times were good (the animal recession having ended the year before after a change of administration from Winthrop Bear to Everett Bull), he had little difficulty in finding employment. In fact, Lionel's first job was in a medium-sized meadow as a junior leadership trainee and first-line supervisor over his three old chums, Willie Lion, Charlie Bear, and Ronald Zebra (none of whom had been away to Animal U., though Ronald Zebra had taken two years of technical training in stripe painting touch-up work at a local trade school).

The reunion of Lionel and his friends was a happy one, and their work together in the meadow as leader and followers was happy and satisfying to them all, though if the truth is to be told, we must admit that Willie, Charlie, and Ronald knew far more about what had to be done and how to do it than Lionel did. But they were friendly and loving and patient and, as time went by, Lionel learned what needed to be learned and did quite well as a junior leadership trainee.

One day, however, at lunchtime, the four friends were reviewing their cubdom and decided to reenact Lionel's spectacular block in their most-remembered touch-football game. Just at that instant, Herbert Hedgehog, Lionel's own leader, and an important officer in the meadow enterprise, happened by. Mr. Hedgehog said nothing at the moment, but later that day he called Lionel aside.

"Lionel," said Mr. Hedgehog, "I should like to discuss a matter with you for a moment." Mr. Hedgehog smiled not unkindly. "Lionel, I could not help but notice, earlier this afternoon, your behavior with your subordinates: Lion, Bear, and Zebra."

"Yes, sir?" asked Lionel, who was puzzled.

"Well," said Mr. Hedgehog, as he smiled again, even more kindly, "it's not that you, as a junior leadership trainee, are actually any better than the other animals in the meadow, Lionel. Rather, let us say that your heavier responsibilities place special obligations on you."

"Obligations?" asked Lionel, even more puzzled.

"Yes, Lionel, obligations that may be hampered by too close and too familiar association with those at lower echelons in the organization."

"I'm sorry, sir," said Lionel, "but I don't understand."

"No," said Mr. Hedgehog, "I can see that you don't. Perhaps I can explain. We who are in leadership hold very powerful positions. Leadership has a heavy responsibility. The others look to us when they are unsure, so we must always act sure or they will worry and be anxious. They admire and respect us, but they also fear us, so we must be careful and considerate of them and try not to use our superior position and authority in ways that would injure them. A leader, in all respects, Lionel, must speak and act more cautiously than other animals, and," Mr. Hedgehog's face grew very serious, "too close and familiar association with those at lower echelons may distract us from our responsibilities to them. Leadership," Mr. Hedgehog sighed, "is a lonely job. Do you understand that, Lionel?"

"Yes, sir," said Lionel, and remembered Dr. Sherwood Giraffe's lectures.

"My suggestion is that you find a way to separate yourself a bit further from those in the lower echelons. I say this for your own good, Lionel," and Mr. Hedgehog smiled his most kindly smile of all. "For if you do what is required of you and meet your leadership responsibilities and obligations, I think you have a promising future."

"Thank you, sir," said Lionel. That evening he stayed awake late pondering and pondering on a way to separate himself a bit further from Willie Lion, Charlie Bear, and Ronald Zebra.

Finally, in the early morning hours, it came to him. Lionel decided to buy a cloak. And so he did.

It was a light-weight cloak of light-blue cotton that could be swung to and fro easily, so whenever Lionel felt himself getting too close to Willie, Charlie, or Ronald or them getting too close to him, he could swish it over and hide a bit of himself from them.

The cloak worked quite well and Mr. Hedgehog was especially pleased with Lionel's quick response to his suggestion. He was so pleased, in fact, that he put in a word for Lionel with one of the top leaders of the meadow. Lionel's performance had already been noted by the higher echelons and so, in a short while, Lionel was promoted. To take his place, he recommended Charlie Bear, and while there were some in the animal recruiting department who suggested a candidate be found from outside the meadow, Lionel's recommendation was finally accepted.

In his new position, Lionel's leadership responsibilities not only included Charlie Bear but four other first-line animal supervisors as well. Lionel realized he was now middle-leadership. One of the first things Lionel did on assuming his new position was to buy a new cloak. It was of medium weight and medium blue and considerably more substantial than his first one. In dealing with his new and heavier responsibilities, Lionel used his heavier cape more frequently too.

He would use it when he wanted things changed, but was unwilling to express his dissatisfaction with the way they were presently being done. For instance, if one of his first-line supervisors made a proposal to him, Lionel might say, "Very nice, very nice," then swish would go the cloak and Lionel would continue, "but don't you think we might possibly want to do that just a bit differently? Not that there's anything wrong with your idea, of course."

He would use it when he was disappointed, or impatient, or irritated with the way another animal was doing his job. "Mmmm," Lionel would mutter under his breath, but realizing that in his terribly powerful position of leadership his criticism might hurt the lower-echelon animal, he would say no more. Instead, swish would go his cloak and later he might mention his displeasure to the other animal's supervisor.

He would use it, too, when he was worried or uncertain, but did not want to reveal his feelings to others.

Or when he feared he had made a mistake.

Or when he was unsure of his point of view. In each case, swish would go Lionel's cloak.

And so the days in the meadow went by, and as Lionel was a strong and intelligent and competent lion, he was more and more frequently noticed, not only by the animal leaders above him but by others as well. And soon many spoke of Lionel as an up-and-coming animal with obvious high-echelon leadership potential. Not only did they speak of him that way, but a few could be seen emulating Lionel's style. They would talk as he did or stand as he did. And then, most strikingly of all, some would appear in the meadow wearing brand-new blue cloaks.

At first there were only a few, but gradually more and more blue-cloaked animals were to be seen, standing or pacing to and fro in the grass. In the practice of swishing their new cloaks, some were awkward at first and got themselves only partially covered, or perhaps forgot to swish at all, but others, Mr. Hedgehog especially, swished as well as Lionel or maybe even better.

And as the cloaks increased in number, other things began to change in the meadow. It was quieter and fewer animals smiled—and even fewer laughed out loud. More reports were written than ever before and memos, too. As the higher-echelon meadow leaders became more cautious for the sake of the lower-echelon animals, so did the lower-echelon animals become more cautious for their own sake. Animals whispered a good deal more than they had.

Still, work at the meadow went well enough (though there seemed to be fewer new ideas than before) and Lionel continued to rise in the ranks of the meadow organization until he did, indeed, become one of the high-echelon leaders.

When Lionel's old friends, Willie Lion, Charlie Bear, and Ronald Zebra, heard of Lionel's high promotion, they were all very pleased and decided to have a party for him. They asked Lionel who he would like them to invite but Lionel could only think of Herbert Hedgehog and a few others. "Leadership," Lionel sighed, "is a lonely job."

Nevertheless, plans for Lionel's party proceeded and Mr. Hedgehog, since he was closest to Lionel's echelon, was given responsibility for buying a suitable gift.

On the evening of the party, the animals met at a local watering hole and when Lionel appeared, his old friends were pleased to see that he was not wearing his cloak. And so the festivities proceeded in a boisterous and happy way reminiscent of their early cub days. In fact, at one point during the party, after much coaxing, Lionel was persuaded to demonstrate again his famous three-man block, and while it did not work as well as it originally had (Lionel had put on some weight since then and his tail was not quite as quick as it once was), it didn't turn out too badly either. All in all there was a good deal of laughing and carousing until the moment came for the high point of the evening, the presentation of Lionel's gift.

Herbert Hedgehog rose and cleared his throat. "Ahem," he began, "My dear colleagues and associates, we gather here today to honor our illustrious colleague, Lionel Lion. All of us here know Lionel and I'm certain that our chests swell with pride when we recall his rapid and well-deserved rise in our organization. However noteworthy as that may be, I am certain that we are even more proud of the manner in which Lionel has met the heavy challenges and responsibilities of his leadership position." Mr. Hedgehog paused and waited for applause and the other animals tapped their paws.

Then Mr. Hedgehog continued, "Yes, as those of you who have been privileged to enjoy his leadership can well attest, Lionel Lion has been an example and an inspiration in meeting the obligations of a true leader. His extreme patience and forbearance are renowned. Never in the years we have known him have we heard Lionel's voice roar in anger at a subordinate animal. Always has he been a considerate and thoughtful leader. Always, too, has he been a steadfast and certain beacon guiding others through both smooth and rocky waters. Calm, detached, and confident, he has not faltered in difficult moments when lesser animals might have given way to anxiety or passion." Mr. Hedgehog glanced around and noticed that others seemed to be getting a bit restless. Willie Lion was rubbing the back of his paw against his whiskers and Ronald Zebra shuffled his front hoofs a bit. Only Lionel himself seemed to be paying full attention, with a very serious expression on his face.

"In conclusion, dear colleagues," Hedgehog continued, "on behalf of us all, I should like to present this small token of our high esteem to a most respected leader, Lionel Lion."

Mr. Hedgehog passed a large white box tied neatly with a narrow ribbon to Lionel, who slowly opened it. Inside was a new cloak—but a cloak such as none there had ever seen before. It was of the darkest blue imaginable, and of the thickest and heaviest wool. And, unlike any other cloak Lionel had ever worn, it had a large dark-lined hood.

"Try it on, Lionel," Mr. Hedgehog urged.

Lionel swung the cloak over his back and flanks and began to pace slowly back and forth. It was a very large cloak and almost completely covered him.

"Gosh," said Ronald Zebra, "I can hardly see you at all, Lionel."

"Maybe you ought to get a smaller size, Lionel," laughed Willie Lion, "if you tried to throw a block in that, it would probably get tangled in your paws, and you know you're not as well balanced as you were when you were a cub."

Most of the other animals at the party laughed at Willie Lion's remark, but not Mr. Hedgehog, and when Lionel noticed Mr. Hedgehog wasn't laughing, he didn't laugh either. Instead, he tossed his shoulders and the heavy hood fell in place over his head and face. Lionel said something then but his voice was muffled by the hood, so none of the other animals heard what it was. With his hood and cloak covering him, Lionel was practically invisible and no one ventured to ask him to repeat his words. There was not very much laughter or fun afterward either, so the party soon came to an end, with all the animals going their separate ways.

Lionel wore his new cloak almost every day in the meadow, and he often wore the hood as well. Other animals remarked to each other how heavy and impressive it was and noted, too, how difficult it was to see Lionel anymore. Cloaks, and even cloaks with hoods, became more and more fashionable among the leadership animals in the meadow, until just about all wore them. All, that is, except Charlie Bear, who continued to prance around the meadow, usually quite cheerfully, without covering himself at all. It was this fact that caused Lionel one late afternoon to call Charlie aside for a talk.

"Charlie," said Lionel, whose hood now lay back against his large shoulders, "you and I have known each other for a long time."

"We sure have," smiled Charlie Bear.

"Yes," said Lionel, tugging a wrinkle from his cloak. "Well, there is something I have been meaning to have a word with you about."

"Yes, Lionel?"

"Well, Charlie, as you may know, I recommended you to be my replacement when you first became a supervisor." Lionel padded a few paces to his left, then to his right, then to his left again. "I thought that you had a promising future before you. Although you had not attended Animal University, my belief was that you were not just a run-of-the-mill animal, but a bear with potential." Lionel hunched his cloak up just the slightest bit around his shoulders. "I still believe that to be the case, Charles [it was the first time Charlie Bear could remember that Lionel had ever called him Charles], but I must admit I am somewhat disappointed in your progress since that time."

"I'm sorry you're not happy, Lionel," said Charlie.

"Happiness is not the point," said Lionel. "Leadership is a heavy responsibility and happiness is a luxury few of us leaders can afford. We do, after all, have our first obligation to those who look up to us for guidance and direction. And that obligation may be hampered if our relations with our subordinates are too friendly and familiar."

"Do you mean Willie Lion and Ronald Zebra?" asked Charlie Bear.

"Charles, as you well know, I have only the highest regard for Lion and Zebra. However, for their sakes as well as your own, it would be better if you could maintain a somewhat greater distance between yourself and them, as is more appropriate for those at different echelons in the meadow organization." Lionel did some more pacing, then stopped before Charlie Bear. "I would like to ask you something, Charlie."

"Okay," said Charlie Bear, who noticed Lionel was calling him Charlie again and felt a little, though not much, better.

"Why don't you ever wear a cloak? Almost all of the leadership animals do, you know." Lionel smoothed down the heavy cloth of his own cloak.

"Well," said Charlie, "mostly because I'm not cold, and besides I think a cloak would get in my way."

Lionel sighed heavily, "I'm afraid you don't understand, Charlie. Perhaps I can explain. This cloak I wear is not for my comfort. In fact there are many, many times when it is very heavy and uncomfortable, times when I wish I could take it off entirely." Lionel seemed suddenly very weary and weighed down beneath his dark-blue cloak.

"Then why do you wear it?" asked Charlie.

"I wear it," Lionel replied, "for the sake of the other animals, to protect them from my power—the power of my position as their leader. That is my obligation. Now do you understand, Charlie?"

"No," said Charlie Bear, "I don't."

Lionel frowned. "Don't you realize how frightened the other animals would be if, for example, I got angry and I didn't cover it over with my cloak?"

"Well," said Charlie, "some might be but others wouldn't. Actually, I think I get more frightened, or at least nervous, when you do cover yourself up."

"You still don't understand," said Lionel, who was beginning to feel annoyed. "Can't you imagine how upset and worried the others would be if they were able to see that I was upset and worried sometimes, if I didn't hide my feelings beneath my cloak?"

"Well, maybe they would be," said Charlie Bear, "but that doesn't seem so bad to me. There are a lot of other worries they always have to deal with when they're away from the meadow, you know. Any animal with a mate and cubs knows plenty about upsets and worries, I'll tell you." Charlie Bear chuckled.

"I can see," said Lionel, "that I'm not getting through to you, Charles." He hunched his muscles and the hood of his dark cloak began to rise above his shoulders.

"I'm sorry, Lionel," said Charlie, "but I just don't agree with you about this cloak business. In fact, if it's not comfortable for you, I can't see why you don't just take it off."

With one quick, sharp motion, Lionel turned away and flipped his hood into place. It completely covered his head and face. Not even a whisker showed. Charlie heard his voice, but it was too muffled by the hood for Charlie to make out any words. But Charlie Bear did not go away.

Instead he said, "Lionel, I can't make out what you mean. Your hood is in the way."

Lionel Lion was furious. With an even quicker and sharper motion than he had made to flip his hood down, he jerked it back up. "I said," he roared, "that I am very upset by your lack of understanding of basic leadership principles."

"Well," growled Charlie Bear, as he reared up on his hind legs to his full awesome height, "I am upset too. And I don't believe your basic leadership principles at all. You are a strong animal, Lionel, but mostly I remember that from the days we played touch-football together. Since you took to wearing cloaks, I haven't seen much of your strength. I think you're a smart lion but you hide that too. You're an animal just like the rest of us and you can make mistakes. And when you do, that doesn't make me think the meadow is going to turn brown and die all of a sudden."

"But, you don't understand the responsibilities a leader . . . ," Lionel hesitated, trying to find words. His cloak had slipped badly during Charlie's surprising speech and now it only barely covered his rump.

"I wish," growled Charlie, but with a bit less anger, "that you would stop telling me that I don't understand. And I also wish you would stop protecting me from yourself because I can protect myself if I need to. I'm not as helpless as you think I am. And when you hide under that big blue cloak of yours, I can't see who you are and I can't tell how you feel or what you want." Charlie Bear's voice grew softer and gentler. "What's worse is that when you're under that cloak, I can't be your friend."

"But Herbert Hedgehog taught me those leadership principles, Charlie," said Lionel, who was considerably less sure of the principles himself now.

"Well," said Charlie Bear, "I think they are hogwash."

"Maybe they are," said Lionel, "maybe they're Hedgehogwash, in fact." And he laughed, and Charlie Bear laughed, and in a moment the two old friends reached out and clasped each other's paws warmly.

In the days that followed in the meadow, Charlie Bear did not begin to wear a cloak. Nor did Lionel immediately discard his. Rather, he began to experiment a bit in wearing it somewhat less often. For example, when he was not satisfied with the way an animal was doing his job, sometimes Lionel would tell him so. The other animal might be surprised and a little upset at first, but if Lionel and he kept talking, they could usually work it out. A few times, the other animal even thanked Lionel for his advice.

And sometimes, especially with the leadership animals Lionel most often worked with, he would not cover over disappointment or impatience or irritation when he felt them, and Lionel discovered to his surprise that few of them were seriously hurt and some even argued back, as Charlie Bear had done, when they thought they were right. And Lionel as well as the others often found their arguments stimulating and exciting, and sometimes even funny.

After a time, Lionel wore his cloak far less, too, when he was worried or unsure of himself, or even when he feared he had made a mistake. But he discovered that the other animals did not crumble, nor did they even seem terribly shocked when he was confused or uncertain. Instead, some made suggestions that sometimes helped and others just worried along with him.

Finally, there came a time when Lionel hardly ever wore his cloak, although he kept it nearby in case of emergency—but then he knew he was using it for his own sake, not to protect others from him. And in this time, Lionel found that others gradually began to give up wearing their cloaks, too, though they did so considerably more slowly than they had taken on the habit of wearing cloaks. And some—in fact, Mr. Hedgehog—never did give up their cloaks at all.

Even so, anyone passing by the meadow in an afternoon would probably have noticed that there were more smiles among the animals and louder talking and a good deal more laughing, and all that seemed very nice.